1923

1923

Life in Football
One Hundred Years Ago

Marvin Close

First published by Pitch Publishing, 2022

Pitch Publishing
9 Donnington Park,
85 Birdham Road,
Chichester,
West Sussex,
PO20 7AJ
www.pitchpublishing.co.uk
info@pitchpublishing.co.uk

ISBN 978 1 80150 401 0

Typesetting and origination by Pitch Publishing
Printed and bound in Great Britain by TJ Books, Padstow

Contents

To Sheily, Holly, Jacob, Edward,
Matilda, Uddin, Patricia, Mark,
Rachel, Dom and Will.

Introduction

FOOTBALL WAS invented by posh rich people at English public schools. And then we, their lackeys, their servants, the unwashed working class – we stole it from them. By 1923 the theft had become complete. It had become ours, the people's game. We grew it in this country and then gloriously, spread it around the working people of the world. Esperanto was a wonderful idea, but it failed. The only truly universal language is football. And by 1923 it had become the most popular sport in the world.

A century ago in Britain 80 per cent of adult males smoked cigarettes, and that figure included a lot of footballers. The drink of choice was mild beer and the only takeaway on the block was fish and chips. There was of course no TV or internet and BBC Radio was only just celebrating its first birthday. It was the year that the football pools were invented but it was highly illegal to actually bet on football matches.

These were earlier, simpler times, where the life of a footballer was very different from today and this book explores how they lived, trained and played. What they wore, ate and drank. How they got around and travelled to matches and training. It looks in detail at the major events of the year – the building of Wembley Stadium and England's biggest club ground, Maine Road; the chaotic White Horse FA Cup Final; the death of Aston Villa's Tommy Ball, the only Football League player ever to be murdered; Scotland's continued success in the Home International tournament and the nation's sporting influence around the world; and the emergence of some of the world's greatest early superstars. It was a glory year for both Liverpool and tiny Nelson; the England team fielded three amateur players; and an economic slump was affecting football's finances. We will look too at how football was progressing in Europe and South America and how the press covered the game back in 1923, as well as the joy of collecting cigarette cards and the early programmes.

We'll explore the deep class divide that existed within football clubs. This was a time when boards were mainly made up of well-off local dignitaries, placeholders and businessmen who not only had little in common with their working-class footballers but generally regarded them as their servants – 'the help' hired to win their club success. Footballers in 1923 were little more than chattels effectively owned by their clubs. Once a player was signed, they became that club's property and could only transfer and move on with their employers' permission. This of course was many decades before football agents and a powerful footballers' union, though some players were starting to fight for the latter.

As well as writing books about football, I've created a lot of fiction for television, radio and theatre and with that you can plot and storyline because you're in complete control of the characters, the events and where the stories will go. Writing history and narrative non-fiction is a very different beast indeed. You set off with a plan, usually knowing a lot already about the broad brushstrokes and the stories you want to pursue. But the more you research, the more you realise that things ain't what you thought they were. The deeper you explore, the more you become blindsided by facts and hitherto little-known details that blow your early thoughts and prejudices out of the water. That's been very much the case with this book, which as a result has been a sheer joy to write.

During my research, I made some amazing new personal discoveries for myself. I did not realise that throughout the 1920s there was a thriving American Soccer League that matched the early NFL for attendances and interest. Or that Brazil's first football superstar, Arthur Friedenreich, was once banned from playing for his country because he was black. Or just how vicious the FA were in sabotaging women's football in the early 1920s. I hope you enjoy the journey, too.

As a writer, I've tried to double- and triple-check all facts and details herein, but I'm sure there will be the odd error along the way, so in advance, my sincerest 'mea culpa'.

1

Legacy of War

'The old men were still running the country. The politicians who had caused millions of deaths, as if they had done something wonderful.'

Ken Follett, *Fall of Giants*

MONDAY, 5 July 1915. It was a grey, rainy morning on the Somme. The night before had been quiet, opposing sides cocooned within their redoubts. In the British lines there had been the chance to brew tea, eat some rations, smoke a few fags and then gain some hours of slumber. A rare peace would soon be ruptured. An hour before daybreak, 200 men from the 9th Green Howards regiment got the order to advance. They emerged in the drizzle from their trenches to attack a German position 300 metres away. The aim, to overrun an enemy machine gun emplacement as part of a wider attack to gain ground across the Somme battlefront. It would become a familiar story throughout the offensive; soldiers thrown thoughtlessly forward into inevitable death. As the men were ordered to run across open ground towards the enemy, they were cut down in droves. The German machine gun nest was causing carnage.

Desperate decisions have to be made swiftly in battle and on the hoof, Second Lieutenant Donald Bell spotted a shallow communications trench that led across to the German lines and resolved to act. Armed with a revolver and a rucksack full of Mills bombs, he dragooned Corporal Colwill and Private Batey and their rifles to join him in navigating a perilous way on hands, knees and stomachs through the channel nearer towards the enemy machine gun nest. The trio spent 15 long minutes propelling themselves slowly, silently, quietly through the mud until they arrived cheek by jowl next to the German trenches. They sprung up from their cover and with astonishing bravery the three men attacked the well-populated German position with rifles and revolvers, fast-bowled Mills bombs, cricket-style, into the enemy base and knocked out the machine gun, killing 50 enemy soldiers. Many Allied lives were saved as a consequence.

For their gallantry, Colwill and Batey were awarded the Distinguished Conduct Medal. For his quick thinking and bravery, Second Lieutenant Bell became the only professional footballer during World War One to win Britain's highest military honour, the Victoria Cross. He would never hold it in his hands. Five days later, Bell again stormed a German machine gun post near the village of Contalmaison and this time he did not escape the bullets. Newly married on leave, he died aged 26 and was eventually buried where he fell.

Harrogate-born Bell was a superb all-round sportsman excelling at cricket and rugby. But his first love was football and while training to become a teacher at London's Westminster College he signed amateur forms to play for Crystal Palace in the Southern League. After getting a job back in Yorkshire teaching at Harrogate's Starbeck College, Bell signed professional terms with Bradford Park Avenue and in 1914 was part of the promotion-winning team that helped them into the top flight for the first time. Before Bell left for war,

Bradford Park Avenue's manager Reg Hall described him as 'our new jewel in the crown, a footballer who would see us happily into the future'.

Donald Simpson Bell had reputedly been the first professional footballer to sign up for action in World War One. At the outbreak of the conflict, there were around 5,000 players in England and Scotland's professional and top amateur leagues but few initially joined up. At the start of the war, the powers-that-be were convinced that football should continue to help keep up public morale. Leagues, cups and games continued through 1914 and into 1915, but as a generation of young men began to die across the water on mainland Europe, public opinion began to turn. Well-paid, fit young footballers were increasingly seen as privileged – some even called them cowards for not joining up. In the football hotbed of Sunderland, Lord Durham hoped that the Germans would drop bombs on Roker Park to encourage players and fans to think about where they should be. In London, the jingoist *Evening News* ceased printing its football editions. There were large protests outside football grounds and some players were sent white feathers and hate mail through the post. Pressure was put upon King George V to relinquish his role as a patron of the Football Association.

It became clear that public morale would now be best served by professional players seen to be doing their bit for the cause and 'footballers' battalions' began to be formed. Clubs agreed to suspend or temporarily cancel player contracts so that they were free to join up, and over 2,000 players enlisted as volunteers, inspiring fans from their clubs to enlist alongside them. In early 1915, the first footballers' battalion, the 17th (Service) Battalion, Middlesex Regiment, was formed and included the entire Clapton Orient (later Leyton Orient) first team. A few months later, it was followed by a second, the 23rd (Service) Battalion. In Scotland, the 16th Royal Scots included players and fans from Heart of Midlothian, Hibernian, Falkirk and Raith Rovers and became known as the Edinburgh Pals. In just six days the first Scottish footballers' battalion recruited 1,350 volunteers.

Other football battalions were formed around Great Britain, using players as the 'recruiting sergeants' to encourage fans at their local clubs to sign up. Supporters would find themselves fighting alongside a host of current and future international, including England players such as Major Frank Buckley, Captain Vivian Woodward, Lance Sergeant Jack Cock, Lance Corporal Fred Bullock, Privates Tim Coleman, Ernie Simms, Percy Humphreys and Ernest Williamson; for Wales, Acting Sergeant Fred Keenor and Private James Williams; and Ireland's Corporal Jack Doran. They shipped off to mainland Europe, footballers and fans with hope in their hearts.

Nearly 300 players would never return, killed on the battlefield or behind the lines from disease; many, many more would be injured. Nine of Bradford City's first team squad would never come home. Among them was Jimmy Speirs, the man who scored the winning goal for the Paraders in the 1911 FA Cup Final against Newcastle United. As captain of the side, it would be Speirs who would lift the new trophy, fittingly cast by Fattorini's Goldsmiths of Bradford. A unique character for his time, Speirs was a highly intelligent working-class Glaswegian who dealt in stocks and shares, oil and rubber. He moved to Bradford from the mighty Glasgow Rangers, and became the midfield playmaker, dictating games, dubbed 'the brains of the team'. He battled his way through the war, becoming a sergeant much-loved by his men, winning the Military Medal for bravery at the second battle of Arras in May 1917. Three months later he was killed during the Battle of Passchendaele aged 31, a young life robbed with a wife and three young children back home. His body would not be found until 1919.

His young team-mate Ernest Goodwin was a local lad still making his way in the game; not yet a first-team regular but a doughty and promising reserve. He arrived in this world as a home birth in a house that was later demolished to make way for one of Bradford City's new Valley Parade stands, a player literally born into the club. He volunteered in person at the West Yorkshire Barracks just half a mile up the hill from where he was born. Like many young footballers who joined up, he was sent abroad for the first time in his life, to France and the front line, where he spent precious few weeks before being blown up and killed, aged 22. Team-mates Bob Torrance, Evelyn Lintott, James Conlin, James Comrie, Harry Potter, Gerald Kirk and George Draycott would also perish in France and Belgium.

Eleven players from Hearts died; Brechin City lost five of their men in the war, while Orient lost three. Tragically, 34 players and staff from top amateur side Corinthians were killed. Name a club, they all lost men. Northampton Town's 35-year-old player-manager Fred Lessons was killed at Pas-de-Calais on 7 September 1918, just two months before the end of the war. His team-mate Walter Tull had perished a few months earlier, also at Pas-de-Calais, leading an attack during the first Battle of Bapaume. The first black officer in the British Army, he was struck by a single bullet, his body never found.

Not all died on the battlefield. Disease was rife in and around the trenches. Even before the Spanish flu pandemic began to decimate troops on both sides in 1917, the Great Conflict proved once again that there are many ways to die in the filth and squalor of war. Arsenal favourite Pat Flanagan, who played over 100 games for the Gunners before the war, died of dysentery in German East Africa in 1917.

Over 1,700 players made it home but in no way unscathed. Many who did return were severely injured, shell-shocked and perhaps the worst of all for a professional footballer, minus legs or feet, never able to play again. On the outbreak of war, Exeter City's highly regarded Billy Smith had agreed a move from the old Southern League club to join First Division Everton but then volunteered to fight. He made it through the entire conflict, but the day after Armistice had been declared he was shot in the leg by a sniper. The wound led to his limb being amputated. Exeter fans collected £40 for Smith, worth around £4,000 today, his footballing career done.

Smith's team-mate Fred Goodwin had already experienced crushing tragedy before the war began. Playing for his former club Brighton & Hove Albion against Luton Town in April 1912, he accidentally kicked Town player Sam Wightman in the stomach, which caused a severe rupture to Wightman's small intestine – he later died in hospital from peritonitis. The coroner exonerated Goodwin of any blame, deeming the fatal tackle to be unintentional, but it mentally scarred the player for the rest of his life. Goodwin also volunteered to fight, and soon afterwards he suffered serious injuries in battle and would never play football again. Everton's captain, Scottish international Jimmy Galt, was also wounded in action, and the severe shell-shock he suffered robbed him of a postwar career. Galt, Goodwin and Smith were just three of a legion of young sportsmen who had committed their lives to football and then bravely served their country and were now faced with uncertain futures, careers lost.

Many of the homecoming injured did get to play football again, but their experiences lived with them throughout their careers. Everton's 1914/15 top scorer, Bobby Parker, returned home with a constant physical reminder of war, a bullet lodged permanently in his back. Blackburn Rovers' Sam Wadsworth was wounded in action serving as a gunner in the Royal Garrison Artillery. He was invalided home not just physically injured, but deeply mentally scarred. For years after the war he would suffer from debilitating blackouts with what we would now probably classify as the effects of post-traumatic stress disorder. His immediate return from the Western Front was not a happy one. Demobbed in July 1919, he returned to Ewood Park to meet with the manager Bob Middleton to talk contracts. Throughout the four and a half years that he served on the front line, he would regularly return home on leave to be asked by Blackburn to play in friendlies and exhibition matches for them. In a series of autobiographical recordings made later in his life, Wadsworth recalled, 'They were glad of my services and I was pleased to play.'

Wadsworth had signed full-time for his hometown club in 1914 as a 19-year-old, in what was a dream come true. He had supported Rovers since he was a child and to pull on the blue and white quarters was all he had ever wanted in life. The ultimate kid in a sweetshop who ends up earning a living playing for the team he loves. But at the Ewood Park meeting with Middleton, his dream turned into a nightmare. The manager, clearly a man of few words, simply told Wadsworth, 'Sorry Sam. I have no vacancy. You may have a free transfer.'

He was devastated by the news. In his private recordings, Wadsworth later emotionally articulated his feelings at the time: 'That was all. What a blow. I had lived my life for Rovers. It had been all I had lived for, for four and a half years in the mud of Belgium and France. Not very nice treatment. I came back home broken-hearted. I was never to play again for my favourite team. I thought is this what I receive after nearly five years' service for my country? I was very bitter.'

Many other players returned home hoping, nay expecting, that their suspended early wartime contracts would be renewed, but like Wadsworth they were shown the door. However, thanks to a single-minded determination, Wadsworth himself would make a phenomenally successful return to football. After being given the heave-ho by his beloved Blackburn, he was so distraught he'd considered burning his boots and giving up the game aged just 23. But fortunately, his family persuaded him to carry on and he dropped through the leagues to get a contract with nearby tiny Nelson. Wadsworth quickly impressed and soon First Division Huddersfield Town were in for him. With the Terriers, Wadsworth went on to win three league championships, the FA Cup and the Charity Shield. He would also captain England and win nine international caps.

Jimmy Seed came from a footballing family. When he signed on for Sunderland before the war, his elder brother Angus was already playing for Reading and his sister Minnie would become one of the first stars for the Dick, Kerr Ladies team. Jimmy played in the reserves for a year and a half and was being tipped for promotion into the first team. But before he could make his full debut, Seed made a momentous decision. Writing in his autobiography, *The Jimmy Seed Story*, he recalled, 'Football had ceased to be the most important thing in life for me. Britain and Germany were at war and playing football was no longer such a thrill.'

Along with team-mates Tommy Thompson and Tom Wilson, he became the third Sunderland Tommy and signed up.

Fast forward to July 1917 and Private Jimmy Seed awakes choking. He is sleeping alongside nearly 1,000 Allied troops in a long street of bombed-out buildings in Ostend, Belgium, when a German plane flies overhead and drops mustard gas canisters. The chemical covers the rubbled street in a deadly mist, blinding, horrifically blistering skin, destroying lungs and killing. Alongside 700 other men, Seed would be one of the lucky ones. Though severely injured, they would survive the gassing. One hundred of their compatriots would not. Seed was shipped home for rehab and after spending many months recovering, he was sent back to the front in early 1918 – where he was gassed for a second time. His lungs were shot and this time around, the road to recovery would be a much longer one. Seed was sent to a sanatorium in Wigan to recuperate.

It was while returning to Wigan one Saturday morning after visiting his family that by total chance, Seed bumped into his Sunderland team-mates on a railway platform. He hadn't clapped eyes on most of them for years and they welcomed one another warmly. Stupidly, he allowed them to persuade him to play in a Victory League match – an interim set of fixtures put together before the Football League was able to start up again in earnest – that very afternoon. They were a man short and needed Seed to step up. Flattered that the first-teamers had such faith in him and convinced his recovery was going well, he agreed to play. It was an unmitigated disaster. The exertion of playing full-on football again nearly did for Seed. Choking, coughing and throwing up, his lungs and chest were burning. The last thing he should have done was play in a football match. That was hammered home further when alarmed Sunderland board members saw the state of health he was in and let him go.

When his recuperation finally ended, Seed went back to the pit where his working life had begun aged 14. He played some low-key pit football for Whitburn Colliery's team but had largely given up on the idea of playing professionally again. Then Seed was handed an offer that would change his life. He was asked to transfer down to the South Wales coal fields, so that he could work as a miner and play for the tiny Mid Rhondda FC in the coalmining town of Pontypandy. And then proof that miracles really do happen, he was spotted playing, rather brilliantly, for the little pit team by a Tottenham Hotspur scout. Spurs signed him up and by 1921 he was an FA Cup winner and earning the first of five England caps. After eight years at White Hart Lane, he moved back up north to sign for Sheffield Wednesday, where he captained them to back-to-back league titles in 1928/29 and 1929/30. Though he suffered lung and breathing problems throughout his career, Seed learned how to manage his disability and carved out a superb career.

One of Seed's fellow Sunderland reserve players, Norman Gaudie, did not sign up during World War One, even when compulsory conscription was introduced in 1916. Gaudie was sent his call-up papers but never showed up to enrol. A committed Quaker pacifist, he refused to take up arms. Other footballers who were conscientious objectors, such as Burnley's England international Edwin Mosscrop and West Ham's Leslie Askew, had also refused to fight but were granted exemption status and allowed to serve in non-combatant units working in factories and farms, mines and on port docks. But Gaudie refused to take part in any work that contributed to the fighting of the war. He told the military authorities that due to his religious beliefs he was 'bound to disobey any military orders in loyalty to those convictions, which are based on the spirit and teaching of Christ'.

Along with 15 fellow Quaker, Methodist and Socialist war dissenters, Gaudie was locked up in Richmond Castle in Yorkshire where it's alleged that the men, who became known as the Richmond Sixteen, were systematically beaten up and attacked by their guards. The men began to gain some degree of notoriety, which enraged secretary of state for war Lord Kitchener. He ordered them to be shipped to France and made to undertake non-combatant works on the docks, loading and unloading supplies and military material. If they refused their orders, the Richmond Sixteen were to be court-martialled and executed. All but one of the men refused to carry out the orders, so they were summarily court-martialled and incarcerated in military prison to await their deaths. The case caused a furore across large parts of British society with many seeing them as yellow cowards; many others, as men of deep religious and political conviction. In the end the matter went right to the very top, and to Lord Kitchener's fury, Prime Minister Herbert Asquith decided to commute the death sentences to terms of prison hard labour. On his release from prison some years later,

Gaudie would be utterly shunned by the sporting world and would never play competitive football again.

There were also the more fortunate ones. Hearts defender Paddy Crossan was hit by shrapnel in the leg and 'labelled' for amputation. Frantic for his footballing future, he pleaded with the German POW surgeon not to perform the operation. The medic relented and after further lengthy treatment his leg was saved. After the war, he played six more seasons for Hearts. Cardiff City's 20-year-old Fred Keenor took a shattering gunshot wound to the thigh and spent nearly two years on crutches. But after lengthy rehab he managed to walk again and then run, and finally became fit enough to play football once more. Keenor would go on to lift the FA Cup for the Bluebirds in 1927 and win 32 caps for Wales.

No one who was lucky enough to survive the slaughter was unaffected. All the young players who returned had been robbed of their innocence, the horrors of war forever imprinted upon their minds, a party to carnage and savagery they could never forget. But at least those who returned uninjured had their football. And the nation was more than ready for it. The leagues in England and Scotland began again in earnest in 1919. It was a soaring and inspirational joy for fans to experience life back on the terraces for the first time in four years, but it was hardly business as usual. The standard of play was poor. A generation of Britain's footballers had been robbed of their best years. Those not dead, badly injured or mortally traumatised by their wartime experiences returned to their clubs from the war not having trained for years. Most were unfit, some malnourished or recovering from trench foot and a staggering range of health problems caused by everything from typhoid and pneumonia to poorly treated venereal diseases. With precious little coaching many largely untrained and inexperienced teenagers, too young to fight in the war, were thrust into first team action, asked to learn 'the job' as they went along. It became a season of continual injuries to players, many of whom were never fully fit. Games often became a lottery, with players becoming exhausted as second halves played out. But at least football was back again.

The 1919/20 season's league champions were, for the first time, West Bromwich Albion, and their inside-left Fred Morris was the top scorer in the country with 37 goals. Aston Villa narrowly beat Huddersfield Town to lift the FA Cup, while Tottenham Hotspur were promoted as Second Division champions. The British public's thirst for the game was insatiable; the return of league football was greeted with record attendances at almost every league ground. Though it may be dwarfed today, Manchester United's average gate of 26,000 was more than double that of their last season of play in 1914/15. The Old Trafford match against Liverpool drew a crowd of 45,000.

But the simple truth was that the nation was well short of good footballers. And referees, coaches and trainers, many of whom had also died during the Great War. And the country was short of men. The 1921 Census revealed an astonishing statistic. For the first time in recorded history, Britain contained far more women than men. So many males died during World War One and then through the global Spanish flu pandemic that by 1921, for every 1,000 men there were 1,096 women. And that had a big impact on football. From the top leagues into non-league, football was struggling not just with quality but quantity. The talented shone through as they always do and quickly got signed up on decent wages. But up and down the football pyramid good but perhaps not brilliant players came back from war wanting more secure livings. Many survived the madness of the front by throwing themselves forwards, ever hoping, becoming engaged and marrying their sweethearts. The lucky ones who did return soon sized up their married futures. Being a footballer only promised a short and precarious career and many working-class men came back from war deciding to take jobs in factories and industries that would offer longer, regular careers. The government pledged servicemen first preference on available work and having survived the sheer horrors of war, many players were desperate for some stability in their lives.

Most clubs were not in a position to offer them that kind of job permanence. After years of war and no income from matches, they were skint, many hanging on to stay alive. At the time, all clubs depended financially on one single source of income – fans coming through the gate. Until clubs got a few seasons back under their belts earning money from matches, money was in short supply. It would be a long haul back to pre-war standards on many fronts.

Not that this particularly bothered the fans – they were desperate for football and wanted more professional clubs. In 1920/21 they got their wish when the new Third Division was added to the national structure. Made up of clubs from the south, north and the Midlands, the new division included the likes of future powerhouses West Ham, Leeds United, Nottingham Forest, Wolverhampton Wanderers and first champions Birmingham City. In 1921/22 it was all change again when the new Third Division was separated into two largely regional sections, split for the north and south. The number of professional Football League clubs now increased from 66 to 86. By 1923 everything began to change. Five years on from the end of the war, a new generation of fitter, better-trained young players started to make their mark on the game. This was the year when football truly began again.

2

Life in 1923

'In three words I can sum up everything I've learned about life: it goes on.'

Robert Frost, US writer and poet

IN 1923 footballers were local heroes who lived next door. The top players earned a fair bit more than the average wage but even they tended to live in the same areas as their fans. Some could afford to buy cars for the first time, thanks to the new production of cheaper small British cars such as the Austin Seven, the Sunbeam and the Jowett Seven. But many travelled to training and matches on the buses, trams, trains and trolley buses. This was back in the days when public transport was just that – a national system designed to carry the population around to work, the places they shopped and needed to travel to. Some players lived near enough to their grounds to take Shanks's pony and enjoy a short walk into home matches and training.

In ways that are perhaps hard for us to understand today when millionaire footballers live in gated communities a world away from their fans, players in 1923 had a common shared life experience with the supporters who paid their shillings every week to watch them play. They tended to come from the same working-class stock, started their working lives aged 14 in the same pits, factories and local industries and could instantly relate to the worries, concerns and day-to-day life of their supporters. Although transfers were increasingly on the rise after World War One, every team contained a hardcore of locally born players who'd come up from junior and reserve teams, pit, factory and church sides to play for their local first team. They were 'one of us' and there was huge local pride surrounding the success of footballers who hailed from nearby streets.

It was still a time when players went to the same pubs as their fans to celebrate or commiserate after a match and enjoyed the same cinemas and local cafes. Players who came from other clubs around the country on transfers were adopted into the same life, taking local digs, often living with fans who hired out rooms and instantly embraced into a working-class experience they knew well from their own backgrounds back home. In 1923, fans and footballers alike were feeling the pinch.

At the end of the Great War the country had been promised a 'land fit for heroes'. But by the early 1920s, and particularly in industrial areas, what many were experiencing was unemployment and short-time working. There were numerous miners' strikes over poor pay and dreadful working conditions. In the Scottish coalfields alone, 215 miners were killed in accidents during 1923, many from tunnel collapses and firedamp explosions. It was a hugely dangerous profession and to add insult to injury, mine owners had begun to cut hours and wages. Port cities and towns such as London, Glasgow, Liverpool, Newcastle and Hull employed armies of dockers to unload their cargoes by hand and these were notoriously impoverished communities. The men had no job security and were hired on a day-to-day basis. Depending on what cargo had arrived at the port, some or all of the men waiting to be chosen at the dock first thing in the morning would be given a precious day's work. Some were lucky to get a full week's employment, others just a day or two. In weeks and months when fewer ships came into port, work on the docks was hard to come by. Rather like modern-day zero-hours contracts, life was financially precarious for the dockers, and in bad months they had to knock the pub and football on the head.

All across heavy industry, much of it in the north, life was becoming hard. Faced by the ever-expanding trading empires of Japan and the USA, Great Britain was falling into industrial stagnation and in 1923 this was hitting a lot of clubs in their pockets. At the end of the season, South Shields' annual general meeting reported a loss of £4,990 while overdraft and bank charges amounted to £12,027. The meeting was told, 'The serious trade depression is stated to be responsible for the fall in receipts. Compared with the previous season, the gate money shows a decrease of £6,149.' Middlesbrough reported that gate receipts were down £5,398 as they recorded their heaviest deficit. At Burnley, the board reported, 'The receipts from [1922/23] matches show a very serious decline, being practically down one-third.' At nearby Bradford City's annual general meeting in June, chairman A.E. Briggs made a strong appeal for better support from the public. The meeting was told the bad news, 'At the end of the 1920/21 season there was a credit balance of £1,158, whereas now there was an overdraft of £8,907. The average home attendances barely exceeded 7,000.'

Even at Aston Villa, perennially one of the best-supported clubs in the land, a stormy annual general meeting was stunned to hear that finances were seriously on the decline at Villa Park. They were told that in 1922/23 the average home match produced receipts of £1,652, a decrease per match compared with the previous season of £225; the average attendance was 27,879, a decrease per match of 4,964. Directors blamed the situation on 'the depressed state of trade and so much unemployment'. Success bred profits for some clubs. Thanks to their promotion and FA Cup Final appearance, West Ham United posted record profits, but on the whole clubs ended the 1922/23 season with falling attendances, increased costs and worrying deficits.

For those fortunate enough to be in regular full-time work, the average wage in the Britain of 1923 was £5 a week. By comparison, the maximum wage in the Football League was £8 a week during the season, £6 in the off-season. In 1919 those figures had been £10 a week and £8 respectively, but, and despite strike threats from players, the Football League Management Committee voted to reduce the maximum wage to lessen financial pressure on clubs. In truth, only the top footballers earned the £8 a week, but players were generally well-remunerated compared to the rest of the country's workforce. On top of basic wages, players at most clubs were paid win and appearance bonuses and some had begun to make money from product endorsements.

There was massive demand for new homes. Virtually all towns and cities had their own Victorian-era, over-crowded slum areas of row after terraced row of run-down, dilapidated streets. Seventy per cent of homes had outside toilets, many shared, and inside bathrooms were rare. Eighty per cent of Britons lived in rented accommodation and most houses were owned by private landlords who spent little on upkeep, never mind updates. The 1919 Housing Act had ambitiously promised its homecoming heroes that the government would help fund the construction of half a million new houses by 1923. But as the economy weakened and funding was cut, only 213,000 homes were completed by December of that year.

Aside from football, the two most popular activities were going to the local pub and the cinema. In 1923, the average price for a pint of beer was seven old pennies. Prewar British beer had generally been much stronger, a pint of mild being around seven per cent ABV. Worried about the effect of drunkenness on workers in the key armaments industries, the factories and the mines, the wartime government of the day passed legislation to limit mild to around three per cent ABV.

In 1923, what most breweries were producing in the largest bulk, and the vast number of drinkers were consuming, was mild, which by modern standards was still fairly strong. It was also much darker in colour than before the war because people associated a deeper hue with high strength and stronger flavours, so extra sugars and caramel were added to the brew. Light ales and stout were still popular but breweries made most of their profits from mild. By the early 1920s, small street-corner slum pubs serving ale from jugs were being replaced with larger, smarter, purpose-built buildings with draught beer stored in cellars served from hand pumps. Though predominantly still male domains where women were not welcome in the bar, pubs increasingly offered other rooms, snugs, parlours and lounges, where wives, girlfriends and female family members were welcomed alongside their menfolk. The pub was becoming more broadly social. Many professional footballers and their partners and families would be a part of this.

Cinemas were big business. Even the smallest town had at least one picture house and in 1923, there were 4,150 of them across the United Kingdom. The cheapest seats – usually right at the front – cost just a few pennies, which made it a less expensive form of entertainment than watching a football match. In the early 1920s, and thanks to a major increase in the number of women and middle-class folk watching movies, the cinema chains began to build more palatial venues that offered everything from powder rooms, creches, cafes and liveried doormen. Benches and uncomfortable chairs were exchanged for red velvet seats and luxurious balconies offered uninterrupted views of the action from above. Vast new picture palaces opened around the country: The Majestic in Leeds; The Piccadilly in Manchester; and The Elite in Nottingham.

In Brighton, The Regent opened its doors and boasted seating for 2,200, a restaurant, cafe, tea room and a huge ballroom upstairs for dancing. The bigger cinemas employed small orchestras to accompany the silent movies. The smaller ones had cinema organists and piano players. In 1923, cinema-goers would thrill to the gothic other-worldliness of *The Hunchback of Notre Dame* starring the genuinely scary Lon Chaney as Quasimodo; the genius clowning of Old Stoneface, Buster Keaton, in *Safety First*; Cecil B. DeMille's epic *The Ten Commandments*; and two series of films about Fu Manchu and Sherlock Holmes, churned out at pace by Britain's biggest film maker, Cricklewood Studios.

The average British diet was fairly limited and basic. A loaf of bread cost nine pence. Sliced bread would not be introduced into Britain until the 1930s and overwhelmingly, Britons in 1923 preferred white to brown or wholemeal. People ate what they could afford. The more well-off middle classes would enjoy a Sunday roast dinner, and then through the week eat cheaper cuts of meat that required slower cooking. Beef and pork cuts were generally too expensive for working people, who stuck to cheaper meats including mutton, rabbit and offal, and often meat was cooked in stews and pies or sausages in toad in the hole to make it go further. Yorkshire pudding gave some welcome heft to a meal and was relatively cheap to make. Domestically produced salad vegetables and fruit were only available during the summer months, while citrus fruits, bananas and pineapples were relatively expensive, exported into Britain from around the empire. Cabbages, root vegetables and potatoes were key staples and could be pickled or stored throughout the year.

During World War One, local authorities were granted the power to confiscate land for growing food which became a boon to partial self-sufficiency for a lot of working families. By the early 1920s there were 1.5 million allotments in Britain, which supplied many homes with basic staples and a useful side income, selling on surplus fruit and vegetables to friends and neighbours. Those lucky enough to have garden spaces also grew their own and kept chickens for their eggs and sometimes a pig or two, fed on household waste.

Except for the rich, eating out was rare. Apart from the more continental fare served in posh city restaurants and upmarket hotels, genuinely good British cuisine was hard to find when dining out. In 1923 there was little to be had in terms of 'takeaway' or street food. Regionally, the south-west had its Cornish pasties. In London and the south-east, pie and mash shops were an affordable favourite. Cheap exotic food was to be had in Britain's oldest Chinatown in Liverpool. But overwhelmingly, the most popular food cooked outside the home was fish and chips. In the 1920s the average British family visited a 'chippie' at least once a week. Fishing on an industrial scale all around the British coast meant that fish was cheap and plentiful, and thanks to the ever-expanding rail network it could be transported quickly and efficiently around the country. Every other terraced street seemed to have a fish and chip shop on the corner and by 1927, there were 35,000 of them across the country. During World War One, the government deemed fish and chips to be so vital for national morale that it was one of the few foodstuffs that was not rationed.

Unless you were rich or middle class, holidays were a rare occurrence. Working people didn't get much time off from their labours in 1923. Thanks to the Bank Holiday Act of 1871 – sponsored by the Liberal peer Lord Lubbock, who became known as Saint Lubbock due to his bill's success – people in England, Wales and Ireland were given Easter Monday, Whit Monday, the first Monday in August and Boxing Day as official holiday days. In Scotland, it was New Year's Day, Good Friday, the first Monday in May, first Monday in August and Christmas Day. The Act did not include Christmas Day and Good Friday as bank holidays in England, Wales and Ireland because they were already recognised as common law holidays. Sundays were the one guaranteed day off each week and in 1923, most office, mill, factory and shop employees were required to work on Saturday mornings.

Most 'holidays' were days out, usually at the seaside. Thanks to the ever-expanding rail network and the establishment of organised charabanc trips, workers and their families from Manchester, Liverpool and the east Lancashire mill towns would flock to fast-developing tourist resorts such as Blackpool, Southport and Morecambe. Blackpool was truly the 'Mecca of the North'. London Midland Railways advertised it as 'for the classes and the masses' and during the summer months, sometimes laid on as many as 90 extra holiday specials a week to the seaside town.

In Leeds, Bradford, Sheffield and Doncaster, workers would head out to Scarborough – the home of Europe's biggest hotel, The Grand – Filey, Whitby and the Lincolnshire resorts of Skegness, Cleethorpes and Mablethorpe. Londoners would travel the 50 miles to Brighton or down to Clacton and Ramsgate. Sunday schools would often arrange bus trips to the seaside for children and their families and factories and mills would lay on organised visits for their workers.

The rare treat was a bank holiday weekend away, stopping at a local bed and breakfast for one or two nights. The facilities were often cramped and basic, with an entire family often sharing the same room. The holidaymakers would finish their breakfasts and then get thrown out on to the street for the rest of the day, not allowed back into their digs until late afternoon. Better still was hiring out a new-fangled chalet – usually wooden-built and temporary, but by 1923, many boasted water, electricity and cooking facilities.

Some workers were lucky enough to spend the entire week by the seaside. Employed by factories and mills that operated week-long annual shut-downs for cleaning and maintenance, they were given a precious week off and they did very much like to be beside the seaside. The trips promised sun (sometimes), sea and entertainment; by 1923, most of the seaside staples were in place. Amusement halls, better known at the time as penny arcades, had grown in popularity since the end of the war and lined the resort promenades. Bingo was big and one-armed bandits had started to come over from the USA. Pinball, bagatelles, fortune-telling machines and rifle ranges were all popular. Ice-creams, seaside rock and candy floss were comparatively cheap little luxuries for what Yorkshire coastal town residents called the 'comforts' (come for t'day). Many of the resorts had piers that boasted variety halls and theatres that regularly booked the country's most famous entertainers, singers and comedians for long summer seasons. By 1923, most people just wanted to forget the war and move on. But many couldn't. For men in particular, football proved to be a glorious distraction.

3

The Fans

'In his life, a man can change wives, political parties or religions. But he cannot change his favourite football team.'

Eduardo Hughes Galeano, Uruguayan
writer and novelist

FOR BETTER or worse many of us are born into our football clubs, and often it tells the story of a family. My dad Gordon supported Bradford City, so I did. My grandfather Fred Smith Close was a Bradford Park Avenue fan and had been since before World War One, so Dad supported City almost in spite, because they did not get on. The hard-working manager of a string of grocery shops, my grandad was appalled when my father announced in the early 1950s that he'd been accepted as a student at Bradford Art College – the very school that David Hockney would attend some years later. My dad was feckless, unrealistic, head in the clouds. People like us don't become artists.

Back in the days when there were no grants for students, my dad struggled through a year or so of part-time jobs to fund his degree before bowing to the inevitable and packing in his art course. As a working-class lad, he just didn't have the resources to take it any further. So he decided to see the world, joined the military police and served all over Europe, and also in Africa. Wherever he travelled, Dad proudly identified himself as a Bradford City fan, not Park Avenue. Definitely not Park Avenue. That was Grandad's team. The old man he had always clashed antlers with.

As myself and my two brothers grew up as kids in the 1960s and '70s our football loyalties were regularly battled over within the family. My father always had the upper hand because once he left the army and worked as a wrestler, he lived with us every day and he was, well, our dad. But when we would visit our grandad every week or so, he would put the pressure on by being wistful, spinning old and exciting footballing tales and generally trying to entice us into the Park Avenue brotherhood. He took me to a few games as a little kid and it was there that he became this man I did not recognise. In 'real life' my grandad complained about everything, was annoyed with anything that happened around him and gave little credit or praise to anyone he knew – particularly his son and his grandchildren. During matches at Park Avenue, he became a totally different man. He became a raconteur, an enthusiast. Many of his tales related to his years after World War One and into the early 1920s, the time when he was an ardent, ever-present Bradford PA fan.

He regularly regaled my two brothers and I about what life was like at Park Avenue in his heyday. He was a young, unmarried man at the time, working as an assistant manager in a grocer's shop and a bi-weekly regular at the old Park Avenue ground. The 1922/23 season was a good one to be a Park Avenue 'homie'. They ended up runners-up in the Third Division North just a few points behind Nelson, so missed out on promotion, the victims of too few wins on the road with just five. But their home record was remarkable and increasingly pulled in enthused fans as the season progressed.

It was swashbuckling attacking football, with Park Avenue scoring 51 goals in their 19 home games. In ten of those they scored three goals or more, hammering champions Nelson 6-2 and Accrington and Southport 5-1 respectively along the way. In their first 18 home games, they won 14 and drew four. On the final day of the season they lost out 1-0 to Wrexham to spoil a season-long unbeaten home record. My grandad remembers the crowd sizes growing exponentially as the months went by, particularly for local derbies and big games. He stood in among some packed crowds. It was these games that he remembered with almost total recall and sheer enthusiasm.

Most of the time, he said, the home crowd was packed in so tightly at his regular end that it was impossible for him to reach inside his coat to pull out a handkerchief. On one occasion he wet himself because it was impossible to find a way through the crowd to the toilets. Other fans would just unbutton their flies and relieve themselves down the back of the coats and trousers of the men squeezed together in front of them. When you could get to the toilets, they were for men only and my grandad said they were never properly maintained or ever cleaned and stank worse than any loo he'd ever used before or since. Grandad remembered the terraces not smelling much better:

'There wasn't deodorant in those days and a lot of blokes didn't scrub up well very regularly with soap and water. You'd be in among a crowd and it was all body odour and beer fumes. You'd catch a whiff sometimes and recoil, but to be honest, most of the time you were too absorbed by the game and being a part of the crowd.'

Later in his life and not long before he died, I once asked Grandad what being a part of the crowd felt like. He stared wistfully into the middle distance and smiled, which slightly took me aback. Grandad, for I'm sure a lot of good reasons, was never what you would call a happy man. In fact, in my family experience and bless his soul, you'd call him a grumpy old bastard, and didn't smile very much at all.

'You felt free,' he said. I questioned him further about what he meant. 'I don't know. You might have had a crap week at work or got an earful off the girlfriend or the wife. Or you were bloody hard up and had bills you were struggling to pay because that was life at that time. But at the match, you were free. Didn't have to think about anything.'

When you were a working-class man in 1923 there wasn't much to look forward to, and let's not get started on what women had to put up with. For the man in the street, when you realise that life is rigged against you, football is a simple and wonderful joy that connects you to the world in which you live. Then his face fell back to its default grimace, 'Then I got married and couldn't afford to go games.'

I asked him what my grandma thought about football and he sighed, deflected the direct question and replied, 'She played the piano.' And indeed she did, around the picture houses of Bradford, Leeds and Wakefield, accompanying silent movies. A man of his time, he felt awkward about his wife contributing to the weekly rent and outgoings, even though it was through something she clearly loved. Some women had got the vote and many more stayed in jobs they'd taken on during the war and were earning their own way. But for a lot of working-class blokes at the time, it was almost a shaming thing to become a man who wasn't the sole provider. That was my grandad.

Way before the days of replica shirts, the fan apparel of the day was the scarf but few clubs sold or merchandised them at the time. They were knitted by family members, in the colours of your club. In later years these were rather disparagingly referred to as 'granny scarves', but one can't imagine any one of them being knitted without a great deal of familial love. Circumstance meant my grandad couldn't wear one. In the working-class Bradford of 1923, money was short and people generally owned just the one scarf to protect against cold weather, not a collection of them. My great-grandmother was planning to knit him a thick woollen Bradford Park Avenue scarf in the club's colours, until one of the assistants in his grocer's store was angrily pulled up by the owner for wearing a similar one on a freezing day in the shop. 'Wear that in here and you'll piss off all our customers that are Bradford City,' he was warned. It spoke much about the local footballing rivalries that were steadily growing in the bigger cities around the country. Concerned about losing business, local shopkeepers kept as neutral as they could. Accordingly, Grandad went for an-employee-hoping-for-promotion uncontroversial grey.

Apart from local derbies, and Bradford Park Avenue had a good few that season, my grandad couldn't ever remember many away fans attending games. As a home fan he finished work around 2pm on a Saturday, usually a bit later as they got cleared up for the weekend, which gave him less than an hour to travel across Bradford to attend the matches.

He recalled, 'It must have been a bear pit for away teams. I remember us always making a lot of noise. A lot of fans in our end had rattles, which I found really annoying, particularly when they were being clacked around right in front of your face. Sometimes you got clouted. I hated the rattles. There was a lot of chanting and organised clapping. We'd pick up on things about their players. One might have been a bit overweight or had big ears, whatever it was. And one fan would start up a chant whenever one of their lads got the ball, like, "Fatty's on the wing, Fatty's on the wing." And within seconds, thousands would be joining in. It was uncanny how quickly everyone picked up on a new chant. It was a good laugh but it's only afterwards when you'd think, that was really disrespectful. You were chanting and shouting things at grown men you wouldn't dare to do if you met them in the street. I mean these were professional players so were probably used to it all, but if it were me I wouldn't have felt chuffed. Particularly if you had your wife and kids in the crowd. But that was how it was and you just sort of got caught up in it all.'

I think my late grandad's thoughts about the lack of away fans must be accurate. In 1923, the importance of home support was massive. At the end of the 1922/23 season 57.36 per cent of games were home wins; 24.03 per cent were draws, and just 18.61 per cent were away wins. Dozens of teams across the Football League had impressive home records. Out of the First Division's top ten sides, eight lost three or fewer. Nineteen of the top division's 22 clubs had home wins in double figures, including third-bottom Nottingham Forest who ended the season with 12 wins out of 21 at the City Ground. Wrexham finished tenth in the Third Division North yet lost only once at home. In the Second Division, South Shields were 13th and lost only three – as did Durham City, who had to apply for re-election in the Third Division North.

Yet a look at the season's away records is quite shocking. Out of the Football League's 86 clubs, only one, West Ham United, had away wins into double figures, with 11. Liverpool, Swansea, Portsmouth and Nelson managed nine apiece. Thirty-four clubs won only three or fewer away from home and of those, Hartlepools United, Wolverhampton Wanderers and Newport County didn't manage a single away win. Preston North End, Tranmere Rovers, Nottingham Forest, Ashington, Oldham, Wrexham, Merthyr and Reading only won one each.

It was a paean to fan power and support, but also spoke much about the social culture of the day. Unless they were travelling away to a local derby that was easily accessible by bus, train or rarely, car, it was impossible for fans to attend away games in 1923. Like my grandad, most workers in Britain had to work on Saturday mornings so getting from London to Manchester or Newcastle to Birmingham for a three o'clock kick-off was out of the question. My grandad didn't and couldn't attend a single away game in 1922/23. Most matches were attended by homies who made matches a screaming, chanting, shouting cauldron of frenzied local support. For nearly 60 per cent of games to be won by the home team with just over 18 per cent away victories tells its own story.

The legacy of war was still apparent. There was a distinctly military element to football that fans could relate to, even in its language and terminology, for they had all experienced the war as soldiers, sailors or simply civilians. Defending and attacking. Holding and capturing territory. Your boys wore different colours to show what side they were on and you had a deep belief that your team was 'good', theirs bad. You fought to win. In this case not for your country, but your town or your side of the city. For your neighbourhood and the people 'like you' who shared the same football club loyalties. If you lived in the north of Manchester you were City, in the south you were United. In Glasgow the loyalties were split down more deeply sectarian lines, with the Catholic and Republican side of the city diehard Celtic, and the Protestant and Unionist areas overwhelmingly Rangers. In rather more genteel Edinburgh, the rivalry between the Catholic Hibernian and the Protestant Heart of Midlothian was nonetheless just as intense. Small towns like Nelson, Ashton, Merthyr Tydfil and Aberdare took great civic pride in their professional local teams, and were loyal to the last.

The crowds were overwhelmingly male, and in 1923 represented a significant bonding experience within families. Fathers, sons, brothers and uncles all shared the matchday experience, right across the generations. Football was their universal language, a conversation they could all understand and happily discuss together. That they could talk about before, during and after the match. Share the joy of victory and commiserate together over defeat. Enthuse about their star striker's latest goals and complain about that big lump of a defender who always gets beaten for pace, because wherever you are, there's always one. For most adult men, 'the match' was the happy release at the end of a hard-worked week.

Some of the best-paid players became the envy of their team-mates by splashing out on buying cars, but they were few and far between. My grandad remembered regularly sharing bus seats with Bradford Park Avenue players who lived where he had just moved to in Heaton, a slightly up-and-coming area at the time, down to Park Avenue on their way to the match. Well before the days of gossip columns or social media, the players were always happy to give their thoughts about the game ahead and scurrilously pass on gossip about the manager, the coaches and other players. Grandad remembered one Park Avenue player whose name he failed to recall decades later, announcing to him he was going to ask for a transfer to Oldham Athletic because he'd been tapped up for better money and his wife was from Glodwick. 'But keep it to yourself, lad,' he was told. Today, that would have been online within seconds. These were very different days.

The facilities inside most Football League grounds were fairly bleak. Besides the aforementioned toilets, little was done to make the lives of fans in any way more than tolerable. Many grounds had one or possibly two stands where fans who paid more were allowed some covered respite from the rain, wind and snow – the greater majority bought the cheaper tickets for the totally uncovered all-standing terraces where there was no protection from the weather at all. Refreshments were in short supply and most grounds only offered hot beverages such as tea, Oxo and Bovril at stalls around the stadiums. Some of the bigger clubs sold pies, but the whole culture of takeaway food in the Britain of 1923 was totally in its infancy. Fish and chips at the end of your street was pretty much your lot. The very idea of selling food in a football ground was alien to most clubs. Why would it even occur? You came to watch football. If you wanted to eat, you brought a wrapped-up buttie or waited for your tea. Food and refreshments were generally served on matchdays in club boardrooms for the directors and their mates, but you had to be a member of the local great and good to enjoy such a privilege. And that was much more about businessmen glad-handing than any particular need for food.

The atmosphere in a football ground is of course created by the fans and in 1923, they had their own repertoire of songs, cheers and chants. Perhaps the oldest terrace refrain that's still sung today is Norwich City's 'On the Ball, City', a song that most believe was written in the 1890s by a man who would later become a director at the club, Albert T. Smith. Carrow Road would have resounded to the number in the early 1920s and was religiously learned off by heart by Canaries fans. Lyrically, it's probably one of the most eloquent football chants ever written. If football is the ballet of the masses this was proof it could be its poetry, too.

In the days to call, which we've left behind,
Our boyhood's glorious game
And our youthful vigour has declined
With its mirth and its lonesome end;
You will think of the time, the happy time,
Its memories fond recall
When in the bloom of your youthful prime
We've kept upon the ball
Kick-off, throw-in, have a little scrimmage
Keep it low, a splendid rush, bravo, win or die;
On the ball, never mind the danger,
Steady on, now's your chance,
Hurrah, we've scored a goal.
Let all tonight then drink with me,
To the football game we love
And wish it may successful be

As other games of old,
And in one grand united toast
Join player, game and song
And fondly pledge your pride and toast,
Success to the city club.

In terms of depth and lyrical dexterity, it's certainly a good few notches up from 'Ee-ay-adio' and 'Two, Four, Six, Eight'. For a taste of how the song is still sung in the modern day check out the Groundhopper Soccer Guides on YouTube, and specifically 'Norwich City's "On The Ball City" with lyrics'. It is a thing of beauty.

In the early 1920s, Portsmouth fans first began to raucously sing the 'Pompey Chimes' (sometimes known as 'Play Up, Pompey'). The chimes in question were sited in the nearby Guildhall clock, which would strike every quarter of an hour. Depending on kick-off times in 1923, at 3.45pm (in the deepest of winter months) or 4.45pm the chimes let the fans in Fratton Park know that full time was approaching, and whether the Blues were winning, drawing or losing, the crowd would sing 'Play Up Pompey' to let the players on the pitch know they only had a few minutes left to change the game or sit on the result. According to the *1900/01 Official Handbook of Portsmouth FC*, the original words to the chant were:

Play up Pompey,
Just one more goal!
Make tracks! What ho!
Hallo! Hallo!

But perhaps the most famous English club song of all time first graced the terraces in the early 1920s, the quietly keening West Ham anthem, 'I'm Forever Blowing Bubbles'. Written as part of the Broadway musical *The Passing Show* of 1918, the song soon became a music hall and songsheet hit in Britain and was adopted by West Ham because their young player Billy Murray had more than a passing resemblance to the curly haired youth who featured in a very famous Pears soap advertisement of the time and was promptly nicknamed 'Bubbles'.

In 2010, I was in the crowd at the Boleyn to watch the Hammers play Bolton Wanderers. The ground was not far off full, though it was frankly a lower mid-table clash between two at the time fairly mediocre teams. I'd bought my programme and my plastic cup full of plastic coffee, found my seat and awaited kick-off. This was my first time at the Boleyn and I loved the ground, its closeness to the tight terraced streets and shops of the East End, the very proximity to the source of its love and support. I was there with my former co-author and now good friend, eminent American sports history professor Chuck Korr, who wrote the definitive book about the Hammers' history, *West Ham: The Making of a Football Club*. As we sat in the stands and discussed the team selections, the state of the pitch and the beleaguered old stadium, bubbles began to rise from the stands around us. More and more and more. And as the bubbles spread across the pitch and floated up into the stands, the Hammers fans began to sing:

I'm forever blowing bubbles
Pretty bubbles in the air
They fly so high
Nearly reach the sky
Then like my dreams
They fade and die
Fortune's always hiding,
I've looked everywhere,
I'm forever blowing bubbles
Pretty bubbles everywhere
When shadows creep

When I'm asleep
To lands of hope I stray
I'm forever blowing bubbles
Pretty bubbles in the air.

Of course I knew the song, but I had never experienced it live
and impassioned, sung by fans who cared so much about their
club. It seemed to me the most beautiful of football songs. Not
aggressive, arrogant or self-serving, but wistful, thoughtful and
reassuring. And the very history of it touched me deeply. This
was the same song that West Ham fans had been crooning
together on the terraces since the early 1920s over 100 years ago
and then through generation after hopeful generation. For me,
it is the song that sums up everything that football is and can
be. Victories, disappointments, hopes, friendship, loyalty and
dreams, and a passionate determination that no matter what,
however high your team rise or how low they fall, you will
always be there. With your team. By the end of the rendition,
I had tears in my eyes. Call me emotional, but football is. It's
for fans.

4

Training and Tactics

*'A football team is like a piano. You need eight
men to carry it and three who can play the
damned thing.'*

Bill Shankly

IF YOU enjoy throwing medicine balls around, playing
leapfrog, doing star jumps and running endlessly around a
football pitch, then training at many clubs in 1923 would have
been right up your street. No, me neither. Apart from a new
elite of managers and coaches who were starting to look at
pioneering new ways of training and conditioning players, and
more of that later, the greater majority of clubs in Britain took a
rudimentary approach to preparing their teams. The prevailing
opinion was that you starved a player of the football during
the week so that they would be hungry for it on Saturday. As
a consequence, the ball was often a stranger during training
and little work was done on game play plans or improving
individual skills.

This was still the British way – keep players fit for matchday
and depend upon them to produce their innate talents during
the game. Despite new coaching and training developments
around the world, dear old Britannia continued to be a smug,

self-satisfied and complacent place to play football. If players wanted to hone and improve their own individual skills it was pretty much regarded as their own business, not the job of the coach. As every club at the time played a rigid 2-3-5 there was little talk about tactics week to week.

The tactics of the game and the way it was played in 1923 had hardly changed for 35 years. The first season of the Football League began in 1888 and its runaway winners were Preston North End, who became champions without losing a single game. 'The Invincibles' won the FA Cup that season too, beating Wolves 3-0, their tactically innovative manager William Sudell having developed a highly successful new game formation known as the 'Pyramid' – in simple terms, 2-3-5. By the 1890s it had been adopted by virtually every league club in England and soon spread around the world. And over the next four decades the view in Britain was very much that if it ain't broke, don't fix it.

So why was it so widely used? It spoke brilliantly to the footballing needs of the time. Two full-backs; three half-backs, comprising of one centre-half and two wing-halves; and five advanced players – two outside-forwards, two inside-forwards and a centre-forward. When defending, the two full-backs would zonally mark the opponent forwards' central trio, while the half-backs would fill the gaps, marking the opposition wingers or inside-forwards.

The key reason for this formation had everything to do with the offside law of the time, which said there had to be three opponents between the striker and the goal, and the Pyramid proved so successful it endured well into the 1920s. In 1923, it remained the formation used by most teams. It would be the formation favoured by the legendary Uruguay national team when they won the 1924 and 1928 Olympic Games and the inaugural World Cup in 1930. So it was 2-3-5 all the way. As Jonathan Wilson observed in his groundbreaking book,

Inverting the Pyramid, 'Quick or slow, with passing short, triangular or wing-to-wing or old-fashioned dribbling the pyramid would remain the global default until the change in the offside law in 1925 led to the development, in England, of the WM. Just as the dribbling game and all-out attack had once been the "right" – the only – way to play, so 2-3-5 became the touchstone.'

More of the new offside law and the WM formation later. There were though, English coaches who were developing new ideas and beginning a quiet revolution. Unfortunately, the football establishment in this country and the clubs themselves were so conservative, the most innovative were forced to coach abroad, including a man who would become the creator of 'total football' long before the Dutch sides of the 1970s. Step up Jimmy Hogan, who would also inspire the tactical genius of the legendary Hungarian team nearly three decades later.

Hogan was a decent enough footballer who played before the war for Burnley, Fulham, Swindon and Bolton as an inside-forward. He'd always planned to get into coaching and management and had been particularly drawn to the tight passing game and close possession skills of his Scottish team-mates at Fulham. From the turn of the 20th century and well into the 1920s, the Scottish Football League and national team regarded itself as superior in style and thought to the English Auld Enemy, whose clubs tended to be physical, play it long and often in the air. As more Scottish players moved south of the border, some English coaches began to take note of their tidier, possession-based play. Hogan was one of them.

He began to develop a new system based upon short passing and possession with players continually interchanging positions and 'playing out' for one another. In 1911, and in his early 30s, Hogan was offered the coach's job with the Austrian national team, where he worked in tandem with a Czech coach, Hugo Meisl, who shared the Englishman's more cerebral footballing philosophy. As Jonathan Wilson describes in *Inverting the Pyramid*, they 'believed that movement was necessary, that too many teams were rigid and so predictable ... both believed that it was necessary to make the ball do the work, that swift combinations of passes were preferable to dribbling.'

Hogan worked much more individually with players, showing them how to fit into his overall tactical plans. He worked on improving their ball retention skills, short- and long-range passing abilities and their positional awareness so they could best deliver his ideas. More than anything, he taught players how to read a game and adapt to change it. This would be the beginning of modern coaching. Hogan was in 1914 offered the manager's job at Budapest club MTK, who had become aware of his ideas and gave him *carte blanche* to develop his philosophy on their young team. Many of his new players were university students used to study and instruction, and they responded well to Hogan's almost intellectual approach. He was one of the first managers to use a chalk and blackboard to spell out his tactical thoughts to the players, tutoring them in new ideas about movement, possession and playing without the ball – all coaching approaches we know about today but were largely unheard of in the early 1920s. It was a match made in heaven.

Football had not been massively popular in Hungary. Once Hogan put his attractive and exciting new ideas into practice at MTK, other league sides saw the great sense of what was quickly dubbed 'the Danubian style' and tried to follow suit. Hungarian sports fans loved it, turned their interest towards football and attendances began to rise. But as the war progressed and borders changed, Hogan was judged to be a foreign prisoner of war and interned in Austria. Arms were twisted and deals done so that Hogan could return to Hungary, where he continued to manage MTK to great success. His influence on Hungarian football would have a profound and lasting effect. Disciples of his footballing philosophy would go on to play for, coach and manage the country's top clubs and the national team using his style of play. Ultimately, his foundations would produce the legendary Hungary team of the late 1940s and early '50s.

Hogan returned to Britain at the end of the conflict, hopeful that his successful new approach to tactics and coaching would find him a manager's job in England. He was horrified to discover that he had been virtually blackballed as a traitor by the FA for working in 'enemy' territory abroad during the war and was 'unwelcome' in the Football League. Hogan, who was seriously skint on his return, applied to the FA for a grant and was pointedly told that FA benefit money was only for footballing people who had served their country during the war. Many speculate that this was the moment that English football internationally began its slow and miserable decline. It had a revolutionary in its midst, a man who could have transformed thinking about our domestic football and driven change. But prophets are seldom heard in their own land.

Enraged at just how conservative the football establishment continued to be, Hogan returned to mainland Europe to give them the benefit of his new ideas and to simply earn a living. In 1923, Hogan was appointed manager of the Switzerland national team – the following year they would be coached to play well above themselves and end up as silver medallists in the 1924 Olympics Games football final. Hogan would finally make it back to these shores in 1934 as manager of Fulham. It would not last long. His senior players were highly suspicious of his new-fangled coaching methods and he was ousted after just 31 games in charge. He returned to Austria and helped them reach the final of the 1936 Olympics. After World War Two, he coached for a while at Brentford and then at Celtic, where a young midfielder called Tommy Docherty became mesmerised by his footballing philosophy. In an interview with BBC Sport, Docherty spoke of the huge influence Hogan would have on his own management career at Manchester United:

'He used to say football was like a Viennese waltz, a rhapsody. One-two-three, one-two-three, pass-move-pass, pass-move-pass. We were sat there glued to our seats, because we were so keen to learn. His arrival at Celtic Park was the best thing that ever happened to me.'

Hogan then moved on to work as a youth team coach at Aston Villa, where he had a massive influence on another future Manchester United manager, Ron Atkinson, who admitted:

'When Jimmy came to Villa he was revolutionary ... he would have you in the old car park at the back of Villa Park and he would be saying, "I want you to play the ball with the inside of your right foot, outside of your right foot, inside again, and now turn back on to your left foot inside and outside." He would get you doing step-overs, little turns and twists on the ball and everything you did was to make you comfortable on the ball.'

The greatest testimony to his huge influence on football came at Wembley in 1953. The Hungary of Ferenc Puskás and József Bozsik travelled to the home of football and utterly embarrassed England in one of the most one-sided internationals ever seen in this country. Not only did the Hungarians thrash England 6-3, they out-played, out-passed and bossed them around in every area of the pitch. A goal up inside the first minute thanks to a strike from Nándor Hidegkuti, Hungary were so fluid in their movement that England were left chasing shadows. Hidegkuti's marker Harry Johnston had a nightmare of a game, unsure whether to closely follow the deep-lying striker or hold his position and wait for the Hungarian to advance; Hidegkuti scored a hat-trick. This was an England team that contained major domestic stars such as Billy Wright, Stanley Matthews, Stan Mortensen and Alf Ramsey, but they were given a bitter lesson in how much football had moved on around them, by a team from a country of only a few million people. The myth of England's invincibility was crushed in the dirt of their own national stadium.

Worse was to come. Less than a year later, England travelled to Budapest for 'the return' and swiftly showed the 92,000 Hungarians in the Népstadion that they had learned nothing at all from their Wembley humbling. Playing the same tired old WM system, England were starved of possession and blown apart 7-1. The two games taken together were nothing short of a national humiliation. And speaking after the match, Hungarian Football Federation president Sándor Barcs told the press, 'Jimmy Hogan taught us everything we know about football.'

Forty years later an elderly Barcs would feature in the 1993 BBC documentary *Kicking and Screaming* to give his views on the slow demise of English football that had its roots in the early 1920s. He revealed, 'British football was isolated. They didn't like the continental football. They felt themselves the aristocrats of the game and that is why they were isolated … I will be impolite telling you this but we always differentiated between British and Hungarian football – what you played was industry and what we played was art.'

Barcs was not wrong. There was a complacent arrogance about English football that made it introverted and introspective. We invented the game, for God's sake, and were for ever its standard-bearers. The manner in which we played football was, therefore, naturally the way it should be played. Fans didn't graft away for long hours in factories, mines, offices and shops to watch pretty, short-passing football. They wanted blood and guts, up and unders and to be dramatically entertained for 90 minutes. They loved dribblers of the ball, flying wingers, brutal shoulder charges and goalmouth incident, elbows in the gob, football red in tooth and claw.

That was all good and fine on the domestic front, but this thirst for battle and brawn as opposed to brains and beauty, signalled the beginning of the end for English football's claim to be the epicentre of the sport.

Along with Hogan, a pioneering elite of British coaches went to work at clubs across Europe, frustrated at the domestic game's utter reluctance to progress and change tactically. In the early 1920s, former miner and Crook Town player Jack Greenwell was managing Barcelona through their first 'golden years'. One of the first British footballers to play in Spain – for Barca from 1912 to 1916 – he was then taken on as manager because of his innovative approach to coaching. Greenwell focused on playing a passing game and building attacks from the back and transformed Barcelona's fortunes. He went on to manage Espanyol, Valencia and Mallorca, and at the end of his career as a manager he became the first foreigner to helm Peru's national team. In France, former Falkirk and Morton player Victor Gibson would spend a decade managing Cette (later FC Sète) and become one of the first managers to embrace the talent and skill of non-white, African-born players, while winning the first French league and cup double. These were English and Scottish managers and coaches who had the bottle and the ambition, the vision and the sense of adventure to travel the world in pursuit of their dreams. To play football in a new way and test the boundaries of the sport. Meanwhile, in 1923 British players continued to play with 30-plus-year-old tactics and run endless laps around a pitch, play leapfrog, do star jumps and throw medicine balls at one another. The future would of course bring a sorry reckoning.

Football is a drama in two acts. From Shakespeare onwards, every true drama needs its antagonists, the baddies, the enemies. Hardmen were revered as long as they were playing for your team, and a strong feature of English play in 1923 was no-nonsense physical contact. Footwear was still glorified hobnail boots; shinpads were thick and highly protective. English football was a tough game. The shoulder charge was universally accepted as a thoroughly legitimate move and referees were by and large happy with raking tackles, whether players were going for the ball or the ankles. The culture of the day was that football was a hard, physical, contact sport. Muscling out your opponents was part and parcel of the game. Though they may not have enjoyed it, flair players, dribblers and star men accepted that they were targets and got little protection from referees. Every team had their hardmen, their job simple: take out the opposition's best players. This was a different form of football from today.

Goalkeeping was largely a thankless task. Opposition forwards were allowed to barge, shoulder charge and generally physically batter keepers with grinding regularity and the stopper depended hugely on protection from their defenders. Even if the keeper had the ball in his hands, opposition forwards were quite within their rights, due to the then current laws of the game, to regain possession by kicking him until he released it. Not surprisingly, they got rid of it pronto.

Being a goalkeeper in 1923 was also a fairly static affair. The 18-yard box was for defenders to work in – most keepers stood on their line and stayed there. They were paid to stop shots, not to dictate a game from the back. Once they had the ball safely in their hands, and with strikers clattering in upon them, the default was to boot it back as far up the field as they could. Few ever threw or rolled the ball out to nearby defenders or were ever asked to take the time to do any more than 'clear their lines'. There was no time.

The role of managers and coaches was also very different. West Ham's 1923 FA Cup Final player Jimmy Ruffell reminisced about the setup at Upton Park later in his life: 'Syd King was a good manager. But he left a lot of the day-to-day stuff to our trainer Charlie Paynter. It was Charlie that most of us talked to about anything. Syd King was more about doing deals to get players to play for West Ham. But he was good at that. He got us to the cup final and got West Ham promoted in 1923 so you can't ask for much more than that.'

5

The Kit

THE AVERAGE professional football in 1923 was a beautifully handmade piece of work. Inside was a rubber bladder. The outside, either a 12- or 16-panel ball made of brown padded leather, tied together at its apex with corded laces. The average weight of a modern football is 425g. The average ball in 1923 was only a little heavier at around 450g, but because they were made from padded leather they quickly took on moisture from the pitch and by the end of a match could easily weigh 100g more. If it was a game in the rain being played on a muddy surface, often double that. Heading a ball in bad weather conditions was a nightmare. Players often complained of severe headaches after such games and with a far greater awareness of head injury and the link to dementia and neurological disorders, it's worrying to speculate just how many footballers in 1923 later suffered severe illness and death because they headed heavy footballs in games – and day in, day out during training. One renowned centre-half, Burnley and England's Tommy Boyle, was renowned for regularly putting in extra training after each session, often spending more than an hour heading the ball relentlessly, time after time, from the halfway line into the goal.

New research throws even more worrying light on the possible consequences. A 2016 University of Stirling study showed that heading a football can significantly affect brain function and memory for up to 24 hours. Researchers fired footballs from a machine designed to replicate the pace, power and trajectory of an average corner and asked a group of players to head the ball 20 times. Their brain functions were tested before and after the exercise. According to a BBC report on the study, 'Researchers said they had identified small but significant changes in brain function. Memory performance was reduced between 41 per cent and 67 per cent in the 24 hours after routine heading practice.'

In 2019, the FIELD study, led by Glasgow University's Professor Willie Stewart, revealed that professional footballers were three and a half times more likely to die of neurodegenerative disease than age-matched members of the general population. Professor Stewart carried out new examinations on the brains of England internationals Jeff Astle and Nobby Stiles and concluded they had died not from Alzheimer's disease, but from chronic traumatic encephalopathy (CTE), which was caused by heading footballs. We'll come back to Tommy Boyle later in this book to see how life ended up for him.

A modern player would also have found a 1923 football very different to master with his feet. With the laces so prominently on the outside of the ball, bounce and movement along the ground was uneven and unpredictable. Tap a modern-day football accurately down a white line and on the white line it will stay. Not so a pill from 1923. Depending upon where and when the laces made contact with the grass, the ball would bobble off and away from the line. It also moved unpredictably in the air, making volleys and half-volleys often a matter of pot luck when shooting. But this was the type of football players used week in, week out and the best performers learned how to manoeuvre it on to the laces or away from them, depending on what type of pass, dribble, cross or shot they were setting out to achieve.

Shirts were close-fitting and made from tough, heavyweight fibres, usually cotton but sometimes, particularly for goalkeepers, wool and wool mix. In 1923, for outfield players they were mostly laced crew necks and invariably long-sleeved. Hand-embroidered club badges were made separately and then sewn on to the shirts. The dyes used in shirt manufacture were not colour-fast and after many months of boil washes, late-season kits looked distinctly washed out. Wags among the fans would often replace their chants of 'up the reds' to 'up the pinks'. Modern fans would find some club colours unrecognisable. From 1915 to 1923, the Tangerines of Blackpool were the white shirts and blue shorts; from 1922 to 1924 the Sky Blues of Coventry were the red and green quarters with white shorts; Crystal Palace played in claret tops with long pale blue sleeves *a la* West Ham; Watford played in black and white stripes; Brentford in white shirts and blue shorts; while Reading and Leeds United turned out in blue and white stripes.

In 1923, two of the biggest kit manufacturers, Bukta and Humphrey Brothers Clothing of Wilmslow (later to become Umbro), were based in the north-west, the centre of Britain's cotton industry. Bukta was founded in Stockport in 1879 and first made kits for Nottingham Forest and Newcastle United. By 1923, the firm supplied the shirts, shorts and socks to many of the Football League's First Division sides. Many smaller clubs used local clothing companies to produce their kits, often due to contacts on the board.

The rules at the time demanded that the away team had to change shirts in the event of a colour clash, but to save on the expense of buying extra kit, change shirts could be worn with the club's usual shorts and socks. Most clubs went for a neutral white away shirt, as this was long before the lucrative market of replica shirt sales had even been imagined. In 1923 there were no shirt numbers, never mind names on the back, and it would be many decades before kit sponsorship splashed company names on to the shirts and shorts. Up until 1909, goalkeepers wore the same-coloured shirts as the rest of their team. But a rule change to help referees – and fans – differentiate between the keeper and his outfield players decreed that the man between the sticks had to wear a different-coloured top.

Shorts were still pretty long, fashioned to just above the knee and made of sturdy cotton material. Socks were thick and woollen, fastened just below the knee with ties. Rain was ever the bain and once kit became saturated, it was heavy and uncomfortable. But that's what footballers were used to back in 1923. Clothes for men at the time were hardly free-fitting anyway. Most wore thick suits and starched shirts with tight collars, both at work and at home. Any kind of leisurewear was a dream away. Some clubs had started to introduce early tracksuits but most players trained in their usual match kit, or on particularly cold days, in woolly jumpers.

Boots were beasts. By 1923 they had become much more substantial affairs. Wearing heavy, well-padded, high boots protected the bones in the foot and the ankle. The thighs were sufficiently self-protected by flesh, fat and muscle. But the shinbones and lower areas around the knees had become a worryingly vulnerable area for professional footballers in a game that had become ever more physical by the 1920s. The boot of 1923 was a serious piece of footwear. Forget your sleek, streamlined modern-day 'slippers'; the shoe *du jour* was more like a workman's boot, reinforced toecaps and all, but with added screw-in leather studs. Made of thick leather, they were ankle-high and offered a lot of protection to the lower extremities and all for good reason.

Football in 1923 was not for the faint-hearted. Tackles were hard and the game was tough. It was accepted, by players and referees alike, that it was a contest based on physical contact. Today, the off-the-ground-hit-the-player-not-the-ball lunging tackle or raking challenge would at least garner a yellow card; more often a red. Not in 1923. All clubs had at least one 'enforcer' – hardman defenders that we'll cover in more detail later – whose job it was to 'take out' the opposition's most creative and dangerous players. Those players were most grateful for the protection of an ankle-high boot. The average boot was also durable in the extreme. Half-back Frank Moss, who played 283 times for Aston Villa and captained England five times in the 1920s, wore the same pair of boots throughout his entire career – and they were second-hand when he first got hold of them. Many players at the time bought their boots in smaller sizes and then stood in a hot bath allowing them to expand, the aim to mould the boot better to the shape and size of the feet. All boots were brown and kept in good repair through regular and liberal application of 'the footballer's friend', dubbin – a mix of oil, wax and tallow that came in tins and was used to waterproof and soften the leather. Many boots were locally made. Around Sheffield and north Derbyshire, boots for local teams amateur and professional alike, were made by small shoe-making companies in Stoney Middleton and Eyam. Some firms sold their products further afield. Burnley-based company King's supplied its 'King Boot' to various Lancashire sides.

Given football's tough tackling and heavy play, a must for the players of 1923 was a sturdy pair of shinpads. The football shinpad was invented by Nottingham Forest captain Sam Weller Widdowson in 1874, largely because he also played county cricket for Nottinghamshire. As a forward he was sick to death of being clattered by over-zealous defenders and didn't want to miss his cricket because of football-related injuries. He made his shinpads by very simply cutting down a pair of cricket pads to half their size and strapping them to the outsides of his football socks. From accounts at the time, Widdowson was no shrinking violet himself and could dish it out with the best of them. During his sole appearance for England, in 1880, he accidentally shattered the jaw of Scotland's John Campbell in a thumping aerial challenge. The *Nottingham Evening Post* once described him as his side's 'big weighty captain'. Blackburn and England player Jimmy Brown called him 'a very terror … the Reds beat us 6-0 and Widdowson didn't bother to go round our defenders; he went through them.'

Widdowson was roundly mocked for his invention by other players – until 1881 that is. Concerned about the number of players fracturing tibias, the FA introduced the compulsory wearing of shinpads into the official laws of the game. Widdowson was suddenly quids in, and set up a company to produce and market shinpads with fellow Nottinghamshire batsman – and Notts County co-founder – Richard Daft. The design became snugger so that it could be worn inside the socks and soon footballers everywhere were thanking Widdowson for his innovation. Widdowson later became a football referee, and as no stranger to innovation, he officiated in the first game where goal nets were used, at an exhibition match in Nottingham. He later became chairman of his beloved Nottingham Forest.

There's very little to be said about goalkeeping gloves, because in 1923 few keepers ever used them. It's hard to believe given how heavy footballs could become through the course of a game on a muddy pitch, but many keepers felt constrained wearing gloves.

Referees looked particularly dandy. Most wore smart blazers and jackets with white shirts and ties; some wore dicky bows. Long shorts, high socks and unless the pitch was very slippy when they'd don football boots, they'd wear smart, well-polished, hard-wearing brogues. Some wore trilbies or straw boaters.

The 'kit' for fans was scarves, rattles and rosettes. Many were homemade as most football clubs hadn't quite got their heads around the idea of merchandise and marketing in 1923. Is there a noise more irritating than the vuvuzela? Let me give you the football rattle; for the uninitiated, it was actually a little master of simple engineering, a handheld ratchet device containing a wooden gearwheel that clacked against wooden panels as you span it round. Originally used as bird scarers and fire alarms, rattles first started appearing as a noisy fan accessory in the 1880s, and by the 1920s they were an extremely common sight – and sound – in football grounds. The noise must have been unbearable.

Individual clubs began to ban the damned things throughout that golden age of full-on football hooliganism, the 1970s, as heavy wooden rattles proved to be very effective weapons too. So many a fan's hearing was saved. The average football rattle emitted between 90 and 100 decibels. By way of comparison, a lawnmower emits 90 decibels, a chainsaw 100. The vuvuzela? An ear-splitting 120 decibels, so I guess just in terms of sheer bloody annoyance the vuvuzela will always shade it over the old-time football rattle.

6

The Grounds

'There's no place like home.'

Sir Henry Bishop and John Howard Payne,
Home Sweet Home

IN 1923, English football started to think big. That year, the world's largest international stadium, Wembley, was opened and the nation's biggest ever club ground, Manchester City's Maine Road, was built. Both were proof that football was taking itself more professionally and seriously and starting to become more hard-headed about making money. And it was all thanks to two seemingly anodyne developments connected to the sport that this change came about.

The first major development was that clubs were allowed to become public limited companies. Again, on face value, this all sounds fairly prosaic. What it meant in practical terms was that clubs could start to raise and borrow money to develop their grounds or build brand new ones. Increase capacities and draw in more fans.

Before the turn of the 20th century, actually getting fans to pay on their way in to watch a match was a haphazard affair. Clubs had to put their trust in 'gatemen' who were charged with trying to stop fans as they streamed in through open entries into the grounds, taking cash and stashing it in money bags and sacks slung over their shoulders. Hundreds, often thousands of supporters, managed to sneak their mates into matches without paying, by quibbling over change or dropping coins or simply by distracting the gatekeepers with chat, conversation and challenges. And not to put too fine a point on it, not all football ground gatemen were what you might call honest coves. Many a weekend trip to the pub was paid for courtesy of Swindled FC. But in 1895, a new invention changed everything to do with football finance – the Salford-manufactured Ellison Rush Preventive Turnstile.

This new contraption crucially allowed clubs to halt each supporter one at a time, take their ticket money and then allow them into the ground. It may sound pretty simple and straightforward to a modern fan, but this new development helped increase clubs' revenue exponentially. What made the new turnstile design unique was that it featured a foot pedal, which allowed the attendant to lock and unlock the turnstile as each fan passed through. The pedal was connected to a tamperproof mechanism that counted every single spectator's entry, so gate receipts could be accurately matched up against the afternoon's takings. Turnstile operators soon learned that honesty was most definitely the best policy if they wanted to keep their jobs. A side benefit was that clubs were also able to accurately count their attendance figures, as previously, any calculations could only ever be best estimates. The enterprising Salford company also made a fortune using the same mechanism for the penny slots in public toilets. Ellison was given the contract to provide and install Wembley Stadium's 100 turnstiles, but well before then, they had become the go-to company for dozens of English and Scottish clubs who were either upgrading their grounds or building new ones.

Prior to World War One, most Football League grounds were a hotch-potch of bits and bobs of terracing and stands that had been built largely unplanned over decades. That all changed, largely thanks to a Scottish architect who football historian Simon Inglis describes as 'the man who designed the modern football terrace'. Archibald Leitch's influence was so great that by the 1920s 16 out of the nation's 22 largest stadiums had been built by, or had work done on them by, him. In his native Scotland, he was responsible for Ibrox, Hampden Park and Celtic Park; in England, Old Trafford, Goodison Park, Highbury, Anfield, Ewood Park and The Dell. He added new stands and buildings to Bradford's Park Avenue ground, Sheffield United's Bramall Lane, Bradford City's concrete Midland Road Stand, and the double-decker Kop at Leicester City's Filbert Street.

Many of his original grounds have now been demolished, re-worked or built upon, but a classic Leitch design still remains intact to this day at Fulham's Craven Cottage – the Johnny Haynes Stand. Built in 1905, its façade featured Leitch's signature red-brick style and it is now the oldest original stand in the Football League. Leitch had started his career designing factories, and all of his football grounds had an air of straightforward functionality about them. Most were built to similar house-style plans, featuring two stands down either side of the pitch, with uncovered terracing at either end.

His first major stadium commission was building Ibrox in Glasgow. As a Rangers fan himself it was a labour of love, and rumour has it that Leitch did the job for free. Tragically, the project ended in disaster. In 1905 the new Ibrox attracted its first capacity crowd for a Scotland v England international match. During the game a section of the timber-made terraces collapsed and 25 fans lost their lives. Leitch was devastated, and as well as nearly ending his career, it sent him back to the drawing board determined to improve public safety inside football stadiums for good.

The terrible tragedy haunted Leitch and drove him to invent and patent football's first tubular steel crush barriers. He designed and constructed terracing that featured fixed steps, designated aisles and highly strengthened foundations, all to bring a far greater robustness to ground design. These measures hugely improved safety and Leitch proved to the football world that his company could offer the very best in stadium building. They were rarely pretty but 'did the job' most fulsomely. Most had little seating provision and usually just one or two covered stands; the rest of the grounds were uncovered terracing completely open to the vagaries of the weather.

Leitch was never an establishment figure and throughout his career, he was little-known outside of the football world. When he died in 1939, not one national newspaper carried his obituary. His greatest annoyance and regret was that despite all of his vast experience in building football grounds, he was never considered for what he considered to be the 'top job' – constructing Wembley Stadium.

One thing that architects like Archibald Leitch didn't have to worry about was floodlighting. In 1923 there was no evening football; everything took place during the hours of daylight. There were some early experiments. In 1920, the ever-innovative Dick, Kerr Ladies team played an exhibition night match using a white football and a pitch illuminated by two World War One anti-aircraft searchlights. But it would not be until nearly 30 years later that Football League clubs began to install permanent floodlighting and fans could begin to experience the heady thrill of the night match. Instead, and to fulfil the annual league and FA Cup fixture list, all clubs played several daytime midweek games through the season. These were necessary but not particularly popular with the club boards. As most of their fans were at work during the day, the midweek matches, which became nicknamed 'the old fellows games', generally attracted much smaller crowds, ergo less revenue.

Leitch not only missed out on the Wembley Stadium project but was overlooked by Manchester City for their new ground on Maine Road. Since their formation in 1880, the Blues played at the Hyde Road stadium in Gorton. Though it had a capacity of 40,000 the place was a dump. Squeezed in between a maze of tight terraced streets, dangerous subterranean passages and railway arches it was, in modern parlance, a damned good place to get mugged in. The ground only had a single stand that was patched up and falling to bits and terraces on just two sides, made from cinders, gravel and waste. In one corner, a railway line passed through the stadium to a neighbouring boiler works and facilities behind the scenes were pretty dire.

City had been looking to leave Hyde Road for years and at one point had even considered a groundshare with United at Old Trafford. A fire that burnt down the main stand in 1920 hastened the decision to scout for a new site on which City could build a brand new stadium. They found it in Moss Side and though the footprint of the new ground, which was on an old claypit used for brick making, required significant amounts of draining and levelling, it offered the benefit of being on a huge 16-acre site. Before building work began, officials evicted a traveller camp from the land and urban myth or not, a curse was placed upon Manchester City – to wit, nothing shall ever come to the team that plays at this ground. Joe Mercer and Malcolm Allison obviously hadn't heard that one.

Curses aside, the building of Maine Road was a major achievement. The club engaged top Manchester architect Charles Swain to design the stadium, and because of their amazing success at building Wembley well ahead of deadline, Sir Robert McAlpine's builders were contracted to undertake the work. Like Wembley, it took only 300 days to build and cost the club £100,000. It contained just one stand, with a seating capacity of 10,000; the rest of the ground, great, high sweeping uncovered banks of terraces, which were constructed with 20 miles worth of concrete steps. This vast bank of terracing was originally dubbed the 'Popular End' but as time went by legendarily became the 'Kippax', forever the home of the City faithful. The 80,000-capacity stadium opened for business on 25 August 1923 when City hosted Sheffield United; 56,993 fans watched the Blues overcome the Blades 2-1.

So City had a brand new, grand blue stadium. But fans are seldom happy. In this case, many were narked about the location of the ground. It was two miles west of the old Hyde Road stadium and only three miles from the dreaded enemy at Old Trafford – effectively, 'out of area'. The Manchester City board, though, were not stupid. Ever looking to increase their fan base, particularly now they had such a huge stadium, they knew that the site was in a densely populated working-class area close to a vast new council housing estate. Hopefully it would lead to rich pickings on matchdays. Proof of their wisdom occurred later in the season when 76,166 packed into Maine Road to watch City take on Cardiff in an FA Cup tie – at the time, the biggest sporting crowd ever to gather in Manchester.

In 1923, the average cost of admission into a First Division match was one shilling, though clubs raised prices for glamour matches and local derbies – in 1923, the cheapest ticket for the FA Cup Final cost the princely sum of three shillings to watch Bolton Wanderers play West Ham.

Once inside the stadium, most Football League grounds were basic to the extreme. With so much uncovered terracing, fans had to be a hardy breed when winter winds, rain and snow swept across grounds. My grandad remembered regularly wearing at least four layers of clothes and two pairs of gloves just to keep warm at Bradford Park Avenue's winter matches.

'The worst was when it was raining,' he recalled. 'Stood for nearly two hours out in the open you got piss wet through and cold as old custard.'

Come the depths of winter, the average Football League pitch of 1923 may as well have inspired a new newspaper betting game – not Spot the Ball but Spot the Blade of Grass. Newsreels and photographs from the time regularly show players splashing through great puddles, slipping and sliding through thick mud, their kit caked and wet. Ice and snow were simply obstacles to be overcome, which all added to the blood and thunder style of play. It was rare for a game to be called off or abandoned mid-play in 1923.

During bad weather, the spectacles on display were often dire to watch. By December, many pitches had turned into mudbaths. Some grounds had rudimentary drainage systems but most were totally hostage to the weather. Few clubs had trained, full-time groundsmen and the upkeep of the pitch was mainly looked after by volunteers or local unemployed who forked over the turf before games in return for free tickets. In 1923 there were no training grounds at even the biggest clubs, so all the training took place on the match pitch midweek, adding further damage to the turf. The only available remedy for waterlogged pitches was to cover the surface with dozens of bales of straw or tons of coconut matting. Before one game, Newcastle United tried to improve the state of a frozen pitch by covering it with straw and then setting it alight. It then began to rain, turning the entire playing area into a sticky, charcoaled mess. They solved that problem by turning to the 1920s' default last resort – sand, and bloody lots of it. As the winter months delivered more and more rain, sleet, ice and snow on to pitches, most playing areas began to resemble extremely dirty beaches.

In 1923, there was one Football League ground that suffered from a peculiar left-field problem. Hartlepools United's – as they were called then – Victoria Park spent another season with a temporary main stand, as the club continued to badger the German government for some compensation money to pay for a permanent new build. The roots of this bizarre story began on the night of 27 November 1916, when a German Zeppelin flew over the North Sea from an airfield close to Hamburg and appeared in the sky above Hartlepool. Caught in searchlights, the airship was fired at from artillery on the ground but continued to fly over the town, dropping bombs on shops and houses. Accounts from the time differ over the number of casualties, but anything from two to four people were killed and 34 were injured.

Attack from the air was virtually unknown to civilians in 1916 and the sheer horror of being bombed from above sent the town into panic and chaos. One of the fatalities was a woman who died of a heart attack. Royal Flying Corps pilots were scrambled at the nearby Seaton Carew Aerodrome and a South African pilot, Second Lieutenant I.V. Pyott, was one of the first to reach the airship. Swooping down on to the Zeppelin from 9,500 feet, Pyott fired a flurry of incendiary bullets into the gas giant, setting it ablaze. Pyott got so close to the burning airship his face was severely scorched. The Zeppelin crashed into the sea and burned for half an hour off the coast before sinking. Second Lieutenant Pyott was awarded the Distinguished Service Medal for his actions.

During the attack, two of the Zeppelin bombs fell on the main stand at Victoria Park and smashed it to smithereens – and Hartlepools were bloody annoyed. Once the war had ended, Hartlepools stubbornly and doggedly tried to hold Germany to account for the damage and for years, continued to send letters to successive Weimar governments demanding £2,500 in compensation. To this day, the cheque has still not arrived.

7

The Building of Wembley

'If you build it he will come.'

From the movie *Field of Dreams*

IN LATE Victorian times, the Wembley area was still a largely undeveloped and rural part of London. Describing its 19th-century history in his famous 1973 TV documentary *Metro-Land*, Poet Laureate John Betjeman dismissively concluded, 'Beyond Neasden, there was an unimportant hamlet where for years the Metropolitan [line] didn't bother to stop. Wembley. Slushing fields and grass farms.'

Betjeman was being a little unfair, but perhaps because he was a man who had little interest in or knowledge of sport. Those 'slushing fields' contained a lot that was important to north Londoners at the time. The land on which Wembley Stadium would be built was owned by the Metropolitan Railway Company and already held huge sporting significance for north London. Since 1880 it had been the home to dozens of football and cricket pitches and was regularly used for cycling and athletics. A lake was used by local rowing clubs and in the coldest winters, ice skating. By the end of World War One, 100 sports clubs and thousands of amateur sportsmen and women regularly used the Wembley Park facilities. Certainly on a local level, it was entirely appropriate that the capital's biggest new sports ground should be built in an area so beloved by London's sports lovers.

But the actual footprint on which the stadium would be built had been the home to something very different; a structure that would become one of the capital's most expensive and disastrous follies, the little-known and long-forgotten Great London Tower. In aim and ambition, it was a Victorian forerunner of the London Eye – a structure that was planned to draw tourists from near and far and take them 1,200 feet into the air to enjoy views of all London.

It was the brainchild of Sir Edward Watkin, a visionary who epitomised the entrepreneurial Victorian energy that drove industrialists, inventors and creatives to build bigger, grander and higher. An MP and chairman of nine different railway companies, Watkin was one of the driving forces behind the growth of Victorian Britain's railway network. He was relentless in seeking opportunities to open new lines and stations and his companies constantly bought land to develop. But like all entrepreneurs, big ambition sometimes leads to failure. In the early 1880s he teamed up with a French Suez Canal contractor, Alexandre Lavalley, to form the Anglo-French Submarine Railway Company and commissioned plans to build the first Channel tunnel. Pilot tunnels were dug at Shakespeare Cliff on the south coast and at Sangatte in France. But thanks to strong political pressure and a series of hysterical press campaigns that worried the tunnel would seriously compromise our island kingdom's national security, it came to naught.

Undeterred by the failure of the tunnel, Watkin came up with a new and equally novel idea – to build Britain's tallest metal structure: an eight-legged tower that would contain two observation decks, restaurants, theatres and dance halls. The top of the tower, reached by a system of lifts, was to provide a fresh-air sanatorium and an astronomical observatory. Though an admirer of Gustav Eiffel and his talents and the recently opened tower in Paris, Watkin believed that Britain could do better. 'Anything Paris can do,' he proclaimed, 'London can do bigger.' He then had the bare-faced audacity to invite Eiffel to design it, but with patriotism in mind, the Frenchman politely declined the offer. So very deliberately Watkin demanded that the engineers design a tower that was 150 feet higher than Eiffel's iconic creation, rising to 1,200 feet. To draw tourists and Londoners alike to the tower, Watkin planned to build a new railway station nearby, Wembley Park Station. It was a part of a wider plan to expand the operations of his Metropolitan Railway Company in and around Greater London.

It was a hugely ambitious project and to raise cash for it, the railway entrepreneur launched a public subscription scheme. Unfortunately, the public didn't want to know and Watkin and his company were forced to fall back upon their own funds. To make it more affordable, the eight-legged design was scaled back to a cheaper, four-legged affair and work began on the tower. By September 1895, the base stage was built – the first 400 feet. But engineers soon discovered that not only were the foundations unsteady, the cost-cutting had caused serious problems. By building the structure on four legs instead of eight, each of the supports was taking on an increased pressure load that was already causing subsidence in the local clay soil. To fix the problem would cost a fortune. No further work would ever be done on the tower and the company behind it went bankrupt. The Great London Tower jokingly became known as the Shareholders' Dismay, then the Great London Stump, and inevitably, Watkin's Folly. The base section stood for a few years more, until it was dynamited and demolished.

As John Betjeman described it, 'The tower lingered on, resting and rusting, until it was dismembered in 1907.'

Nearly 20 years later, architects and engineers prayed that their grand new building project, the Empire Stadium, would not too become a white elephant. The Empire Stadium – later to be re-named Wembley – was never meant to solely be a football ground but an all-purpose general sports stadium that would include an athletics track. Its purpose, to be the main focal point of the 1924/25 British Empire Exhibition, which was a massive event aimed at promoting British trade abroad, strengthening the bond of Empire and generally 'bigging up' Britain's – albeit waning – greatness on the world stage. The Empire Stadium would hold special events to highlight the very best of British sport and athletics. Though the centrepiece, other exhibits being built around it were equally impressive. Also constructed especially for the event were the Palace of Industry and the Palace of Engineering – at the time, the two largest buildings in the world. Alongside them were 'pavilions' featuring the work and culture of 56 different colonies and dominions, plus numerous commercial kiosks and cafes and a 47-acre funfair. Among the more exotic attractions were a then rare Indian restaurant and a life-sized statue of the future Edward VIII made entirely from butter. Go figure.

The two key men behind Wembley Stadium's design and construction were, on the face of it, an odd couple. Architect Maxwell Ayrton was an avowed classicist, highly influenced by the design work of the ancient Greeks and Romans. He had started his working life as an assistant to the highly renowned architect Edward Landseer Lutyens, not only the creator of the Cenotaph in Whitehall but the British Embassy building in Washington DC and most of the public buildings in New Delhi. Lutyens was regarded by many as the greatest British architect since Sir Christopher Wren, so Ayrton had learned under the best. In true classicist style, Ayrton's designs often involved columns, pillars, arched openings and parapets and it was this touch of grandeur, history and heritage that the authorities wanted to draw on for their new Wembley Stadium.

By contrast, the project's structural engineer, Tottenham Grammar School pupil Owen Williams, was ultra-modern in his approach to design and construction. He believed that architecture and engineering must be inseparable and he based many of his works on new modernist ideas about building work. Owen was apprenticed to the Electrical Tramways Company while taking a degree in engineering at the University of London and was not classically trained as an architect. Crucially, what he also brought to the party was a deep knowledge and appreciation of a new building material, ferro-concrete. It was already much used in the USA for the construction of sports stadiums, the first being Shibe Park, home of the Philadelphia Phillies baseball team in 1909. In simple terms, it was slabs of concrete shot through with strengthening steel rods. Reinforced concrete's great advantage was that it could be erected much more speedily than normal stone, bricks and mortar buildings. Williams had set up his own engineering and design company specialising in the use of ferro-concrete and right next to Wembley, he had already started work on the Empire Exhibition's Palace of Industry Building – the first major public building in Britain where concrete was used for the exterior.

Why this pairing particularly interested Wembley Stadium's backers was that they wanted the ground to look iconic – but built quickly. Accordingly, Ayrton set about designing a grandiose façade of pillars, columns and arched openings for the stadium, all features that would normally have been brought to life through the use of stonemasonry. This time, however, his grand designs would be rendered in Williams's ferro-concrete. It led to some strange trade-offs – for example, structurally unnecessary hollow columns decorated the front wall of the stadium, only every third column containing a real column support. But it certainly looked grandiose.

Building magnate Sir Robert McAlpine won the tender to build the stadium and work began in February 1922. The first very substantial job was to level off the site, which involved digging out 120,000 cubic yards of clay. And in among that clay, workers dug out the foundations of the ill-starred Great Tower of London. Once the site had been cleared, the future King George VI, Prince Albert, strode out on to the flattened ground among a small army of dignitaries and glad-handers and ceremonially dug the 'first turf'. The *Daily News* sycophantically reported, 'The Duke turned the spade as if he meant business.' As a reward for his hard graft, Prince Albert, an inveterate smoker, was presented with a gold cigarette.

Over 1,200 labourers worked on the stadium, using 1,400 tonnes of structural steel, half a million rivets, 600 tons of steel rods for reinforcing 25,000 tons of concrete, and 14 miles of concrete beams to form the terracing. The whole construction was held up by a network of light steel girders. Work progressed at lightning speed and was finished in exactly 300 days and on budget. By comparison, construction work on the new Wembley Stadium began in October 2002 and was not finished until March 2007. The pitch was laid and seeded as early as September 1922 and by January 1923, much of the outside of the stadium had been completed.

Writing in *Athletic News* in early March, correspondent 'Tityrus' took a tour of Wembley and gave an approving and enthusiastic update about work on the building:

'Someone once said that babes and fools should never see any elaborate work until it is finished and can ravish the eyes. The stadium still resounds to the beat of the hammer and the bustle of 1,500 men toiling to equip this arena, but such amazing progress has been made in the last four months, that the staff of Sir R McAlpine, the contractor, will hand over the masterpiece on April 27, and quit the scene of their labours. The great fabric has been built. The interiors of the banqueting hall, the dressing rooms and other apartments, have to receive the last touches. Unless there is some extraordinary interruption, the new home for the final tie, the scene of the last struggle for the emblem of victory, will be ready.'

Due to be finished in early 1924, the stadium was ready for business way ahead of schedule. McAlpine and Sons was triumphant, 'For speed of erection, size, beauty, accommodation and permanency, it has never been equalled. And it is the work of British brains and British hands throughout.' A reporter from the regional *Western Daily News* proclaimed that Wembley resembled 'the chief amphitheatre of ancient Rome'.

It cost £750,000, the equivalent of somewhere around £46m today, and provided terraced standing for 91,000 fans and seating for nearly 30,000, made up of a mix of lift-up wooden seats 16 inches wide and planed wooden planks riveted to the concrete treads. The stadium featured a long, covered stand on either side of the pitch and open terraces at either end that contained a matrix of hundreds of safety barriers. Everything at Wembley had to be the biggest, the best and the most modern – veritably the national temple of sport. The iconic domed twin towers soared 128 feet into the skyline, surmounted by concrete flagstaffs capped with concrete crowns.

Concrete was king for the Empire Stadium, being as it was, one of the very first large buildings outside of the USA to be made entirely from the newly invented ferro-concrete. Around the pitch was a cinder running track exactly a quarter of a mile from start to finish. Its two longest sides would be used for sprint races and measured 220 yards in length, the longest in Britain. One important stadium feature that all modern fans would soon spot was missing was floodlighting. In 1923, there was no such thing yet as evening matches and everything was played in daylight. Floodlights would not appear at Wembley until three decades later.

At the time, construction industry magazine *The Engineer* was particularly taken by the part the labourers played in safety tests for the stadium. The 1,200-plus men were drawn up outside the venue and then marched in, in companies, and led to the banks of seats immediately behind the Royal Box. There, the workers were led through a series of exercises by resident architect and former army captain F.B. Ellison which involved standing up, sitting down, swaying from side to side and forwards and backwards, and then enthusiastically jumping up and down while shouting and waving their arms around. The men were then moved to other sections of the stadium and encouraged to repeat the exercise. Finally, they were asked to run up and down the many flights of steps.

The Engineer noted, 'It was quite obvious that the majority of these men had seen service in the war, for otherwise we do not believe it would have been possible for them to act in unison with such wonderful precision.'

With a capacity of over 126,000 it was the largest sports stadium in the world. Facilities included a banqueting hall and restaurants behind the chief pavilion, so that refreshments could be 'obtained at all times'. The dressing rooms were the most spacious in the world by size and contained the most up-to-the-minute physiotherapy equipment. Extensive foyer areas were tucked into the stands under the seating, with one foyer containing what was at the time the longest straight bar in the world.

As well as the twin towers, Wembley contained many other features that would become iconic. The famous 39 steps up to the Royal Box would soon become the subject of urban myths because of that seemingly random number – not rounded up to 40 or down to 35, but 39. An odd number in every respect. One theory was that either Owen Williams or Maxwell Ayrton was deeply religious, and the steps symbolically represented the number of books in the Old Testament. Others surmised that one of the men was a fan of John Buchan's swashbuckling 1915 adventure novel *The Thirty-Nine Steps*, a truly picaresque thought. Over 50 years later, BBC football commentator John Motson famously made reference to the urban legend. In the 1977 FA Cup Final Manchester United beat Liverpool 2-1, and as the Red Devils' captain Martin Buchan made his way up to receive the trophy, Motson commented, 'How fitting that a man named Buchan should be the first to climb the 39 steps.' Among the more benignly hopeful explanations is that in numerology, 39 is a tell-tale sign that life is going to turn around for the better, an optimistic hope for the new stadium. The truth is probably far more prosaic – 39 steps might just have perfectly fitted the size and design of the stand.

Key to the future success of the stadium would be its accessibility. A nearby rail and underground station had been built next to the ground, connecting Wembley to both Baker Street and Marylebone stations, offering ten-minute journeys from central London. An extensive new road network had been laid around and from the ground that connected to all the major travel arteries around north London: local transport companies had already planned an extensive timetable for new bus routes to serve the stadium. Tram lines into the centre of London ran nearby and to the immediate south-west of the stadium, over three acres of land had been turned into a car park for 300 cars and 130 charabancs and buses. It was boasted that no other sports stadium in Britain was better served in terms of transport.

Progress on completing the stadium had driven along at such a pace that the FA had shuffled plans forward to hold the 1923 FA Cup Final there. The national sporting body had a major investment in Wembley, having signed a contract to stage the FA Cup Final in the stadium for the next 21 years, so a lot was riding upon its success. Originally, the plan had been to hold the 1924 final there but everyone involved saw no reason not to jump the gun. It was still a gamble and something totally new and untried for football – a national stadium without a club attached. As well as cup finals, they planned to stage international matches there too, as well as athletics and field events. But would they be able to fill the stadium regularly enough for it to pay its way? Would the British people take it to their hearts? Only time would tell.

The 'odd couple' of Williams and Ayrton would go on to do much work together, including designing and building a series of Scottish bridges at Findhorn, Spey, Dalnamein, Montrose, Lochy, Brora, Crubenmore and Loch Alvie. For his work on Wembley Stadium, Williams was awarded a knighthood in 1924, aged just 34. He would go on to become the principal engineer on Birmingham's Gravelly Hill Interchange, better known as Spaghetti Junction, and as a designer, the Grade II-listed Daily Express Building in Manchester, built between 1936 and 1939, would be regarded as his finest architectural work. Along with a dedicated workforce that worked night and day on the project, the two men combined to create Britain's most iconic sporting stadium in record quick time.

So the countdown on Wembley's grand opening had begun. A series of further safety tests were successfully undertaken – one including an entire army battalion who were charged with marching together with heavy step, up and down and all around the terraces, giving the terraces a severe heavy battering. Three days before the FA Cup Final, last checks were done and Wembley received its safety all-clear. Little did its makers know, but they had created the stage for something utterly unexpected.

8

The White Horse Final

'A horse, a horse! My kingdom for a horse.'

William Shakespeare, *Richard III*

Saturday, 28 April 1923

4am. It began quietly, considerately. Back gates were eased gently off their latches, hobnail boots tiptoed as best they could through cobbled back alleyways and side streets on to the main roads into Bolton town centre. As men met their friends along the way, a low, excited hubbub replaced the near silence. As fans bumped into other fans and formed into larger groups, all pretence of considerate early morning behaviour was lost to the excitement of expectation. Shouting and chanting began, a proud force of football fans taking the first steps on their journey to London and Wembley and the hope of cup glory.

The streams formed into a great swelling river, an ever-growing phalanx of nearly 30,000 Bolton Wanderers fans wearing black and white scarves and rosettes marching into the town. The FA estimated that perhaps 5,000 would make the journey south. They could not have been more wrong. In Bolton, dozens upon dozens of empty charabancs lined the streets, readying to take the journey south, revving up their engines, their drivers eating early morning bacon butties bought from the many cafes that had opened early doors, keen to make a killing. At Bolton Trinity Street, rail staff braced themselves for four hours of madness as at platform after platform, extra early morning trains to Manchester Piccadilly began to pull into the station. Nearly a fifth of Bolton's entire population streamed into their carriages, on to the charabancs, crammed into cars.

5.20am. The first London-bound train pulled out of Manchester Piccadilly railway station. Ten carriages packed to the gunnels, fans squashed up against one another in the corridors. The smell of body odour mixing with the fruity belches of Friday night's beer. Some had bought a butty for their breakfasts, others a few bottles of ale to start the day with an alcoholic boost. Chants and songs began, to last the entire journey. Excited debates took place about the day ahead and the clear and obvious talents of their Wanderers team. But this game would be different. West Ham played in the Second Division so few Bolton fans had ever seen them play. They scoured the day's newspapers to see what they could learn about the East Enders. Train after train followed, packed with Bolton fans. From Manchester, the magnificent steam trains took three hours to get into Central London. From there, destination Wembley. The north was coming to town.

In its build-up coverage to the final, the *Western Daily Press* delivered a snide and classist verdict on the lengths ordinary football fans would go to – particularly from the north – to pay their way down to Wembley,

'The economist who looks around and deplores the amount of unemployment and poverty in the country can only hold up his hands in amazement at the very large sums of money that are spent on the by no means trivial expenses incidental to the witnessing of a great football contest. The gate money counts as little in the grand total. The travelling expenses eat up the major part of the expenditure. But this is good for the railways, so, perhaps, it would be discreet not to complain overmuch. Yet the aggregate sum, spent from first to last – and some of it falls into the hands of the Chancellor of the Exchequer – must be enormous. The whole thing is a phenomenon that baffles analysis.'

Fair to say, then, that in many quarters the joy of football had not yet touched the beady-eyed and conservatively judgemental English middle classes and the people who purported to speak for them. At the time, Britain was still a class-ridden society and outside the working classes and the lower middles, football was generally regarded as fairground entertainment, trivial and vulgar. Not that the London-bound Bolton fans could give a sod about the day's amateur cultural commentators – they were on the way to Wembley.

The first three finals after the war had been held at Stamford Bridge and drew moderate crowds. Having signed their 21-year lease to use Wembley for future cup finals and worried that the far larger new national stadium would struggle to fill, the FA launched an unprecedented and expensive advertising campaign in the local and national press. They were expecting more than 5,000 Bolton fans to attend, which proved to be a hopeless underestimate, and looking at West Ham's average Second Division home gate in 1922/23 of 22,000, their concern was that the world would see the nation's great new stadium, built especially for the Empire Exhibition, less than half full. Not a great look, a potential national embarrassment. The FA's ad offensive would clearly have an effect on neutral fans, who began to buy tickets for the final in their tens of thousands. But what actually happened on the day leapt way beyond anyone's imagination.

It was rare for a London club to appear in an FA Cup Final. In the previous 40 years, Tottenham Hotspur had been there twice, winning it on both occasions, in 1901 and 1921; Chelsea were 3-0 losers to Sheffield United in 1914/15. And that was your lot. So putting local footballing rivalries aside, fans from around the capital clearly decided to turn up on the day to show their support for a fellow London club.

The Hammers were a popular side, renowned for their relentlessly attacking attitude and wing play. They were a Second Division side, and British fans have, of course, always loved an underdog. On their way to the final they did not face a team from the top league and Bolton would be their first experience of England's *crème de la crème*. The Hammers' manager, Syd King, had grown a reputation as a talent spotter and wheeler-dealer and his side contained several promising young bargains expertly scouted from lower-division and non-league teams. The season before, he drew the wrath of fans by selling his star striker Syd Puddefoot, very much against the player's will, to Falkirk in Scotland for £5,000, a huge fee for the time and a measure of the power of the Scottish club back in 1923. Boleyn fans were outraged. Fan favourite and local East End boy Puddefoot was a veritable goal machine, scoring 107 in 194 games for the club. But King was nothing if not shrewd, and supporters soon began to realise there was a very clear method in his madness.

He happily took the Falkirk money and among the nucleus of fresh players he signed were Vic Watson from Wellingborough and Billy Brown from Hetton, both for the princely sum of £25 and massive future fan favourites. His influential captain George Young, a brilliant on-field organiser, was poached from First Division Bolton for just £100. His talented young cup final side cost just £2,025 to assemble – only six of his players were signed for more than £50. And as a result of his clever dealings, 1923 proved to be a landmark year for West Ham United.

For many football fans in London and the south-east, the Hammers had become their 'second team'. In 1923 the rivalry between teams from north and south was becoming ever more intense. The attitude in the industrial north was we make all this nation's money, and London bloody keeps it and spends it. And they're bloody jealous of our football teams' enduring success. Since 1900, Blackburn, Everton, Liverpool, Manchester United, Newcastle United, Burnley, Sunderland and The Wednesday – not yet named Sheffield Wednesday – won the First Division 16 times between them. The other two titles during that period went to Midlanders Aston Villa and West Bromwich Albion. In London, football fans were sick of chippy northerners continually winning bragging rights for, well, winning everything. The attitude down south was, if my team can't be there, let's turn up and cheer on the Hammers against those flat-vowelled buggers from 'oop north'.

Bolton had never won the FA Cup before, or the Football League for that matter. They'd been a First Division team for decades, had lost the FA Cup Final in 1894 and were third in the top league in 1892 and 1921. But by 1923, Syd King's opposite number Charles Foweraker had put together a machine of a team. As pragmatic and persistent as King's side were swashbuckling and attacking, the Bolton side were an expertly well-put-together jigsaw of pieces that dovetailed and fitted in with one another to form a complete picture. It wasn't a particularly pretty portrait, but it had a total clarity from front to back and in between.

Wanderers would finish the league season in a respectable mid-table position, but in their one-off FA Cup matches they were ruthlessly efficient. On their five rounds to the final against fellow First Division teams Sheffield United and Huddersfield Town (beaten in a replay after a draw), Second Division Leeds United and Third Division Norwich and Charlton, Bolton conceded just two goals and scored nine. They were learning to become one-off game FA Cup grinders which they would perfect to great success throughout the rest of the 1920s.

They had a group of defenders who knew one another inside out, most of whom had played together at Bolton for years. Goalkeeper Dick Pym was known as 'Pincher Pym' because of his skill in grabbing the ball away from opposing attackers' heads and feet. Full-back Alex Finney never made it into an England shirt but was consistent, solid, a player who put his body on the line for the team. Central defender Jimmy Seddon won six England caps and played 375 games for Bolton as an uncompromising, hard-tackling stopper. Ex-Atherton Collieries player Bob Haworth was only 5ft 7in tall but tough as old boots, a ruthless defender. Harry Nuttall was Bolton through and through, his dad having been a groundsman and trainer for the Trotters. Because the men knew one another's games so well, they were tactically astute, happy pressing high together or falling back much deeper, keeping their shape in a final they-shall-not-pass bank of dour defensive defiance. The aces were up front. In David Jack and Joe Smith, Wanderers had one of the most fearsome strike partnerships in the Football League. They scored 300 goals playing together for Bolton and on the pitch they played hand in glove. On the way to the final Jack had scored in every round.

Two teams with very contrasting styles were set to take the stage in front of King George V and his royal entourage, to contest the first match at the biggest sports stadium in the world. No one could have predicted how the day would play out.

The forecast was for a warm and sunny Saturday, perfect playing conditions on a brand new pitch, and Londoners were desperate to see and celebrate the capital's impressive new stadium which rose above north London like a cathedral. And they did in their teeming tens of thousands. The cheapest tickets on the day cost ten shillings and sixpence (52.5p today). To put that in its historical context, at the time a gallon of petrol cost three shillings and five pence halfpenny (17.5p today). Pretty much three gallons of petrol to watch the match of the season. As the morning of 28 April progressed, London's roads, trains and underground system started to become gridlocked. Nothing new in the present day. For a Saturday morning in 1923, it was virtually unprecedented. Something extraordinary was starting to develop.

10.30am. Seventeen-year-old West Ham fan George Kerr left his home in Boleyn Road, Barking, to catch the 11am special bus to Wembley.

He later recalled, 'I booked my seat on a London General Omnibus … it was scheduled to leave Barking at 11am but actually left at 11.30am. But who cared? With a 3pm kick-off, there was no worry, or so we thought … when we were two or three miles from the stadium we got a shock. We were told by some coming away from the stadium that it was no good going on because the gates were closed, but we pressed on. The buses finally stopped about three-quarters of a mile away from the stadium which was about as close as they would get.'

10.45am. After a brisk early morning journey down south on the nation's pre-motorway A roads, the Bolton Wanderers team coach arrived in the north of London. It was immediately caught up in heavy traffic, stuck en route to Wembley. Their determined Bolton-supporting coach driver persevered and managed to get the squad to a mile away from the stadium, looked at the roads ahead thronging with fans, and discussed what to do next with the management staff. The decision was made that they were 'stuck', so the players and staff grabbed their bags and equipment, got off the bus and spent the next half hour walking and weaving their way together through the flood of fans towards the new stadium. It was at a snail's pace. The Bolton players were continually stopped by their own fans, and though they were happy to chat, shake hands and sign autographs, they were desperate to get inside the ground so they could start preparing for the most important match of their lives. As David Jack later recalled, 'As we tried to get our way into Wembley, I was already aware that this was going to become an extraordinary day.'

11am. The gates opened for the first time at Wembley Stadium. Ground staff had been well-drilled and trained to expect if not exactly a sell-out, then a reasonable crowd. New state-of-the-art turnstiles had been installed around the ground and their operators knew that most fans would be turning up with tickets bought in advance. A large amount of ticket holders had turned up early but there continued to be a steady and well-organised through flow of fans being happily shepherded into the new stadium. But more and more pay-on-the-gate supporters began to arrive.

Midday. According to a report in *The Guardian*, written by 'our London Staff', from 12 o'clock onwards there was a steady pour of people through the turnstiles but everything worked smoothly. *The Guardian*'s reporters stayed outside, interviewing fans and gaining material for colour pieces. The mood of the ever-growing crowd was good-natured and expectant. It was a beautiful day. Pre-match interviews done, the reporters made their way into the ground. One wrote:

'I entered at 1.35pm and found no difficulty in climbing up to my place in the press gallery at the top of the stand on the north side, above the Royal Box. But even at that time I saw that the outer terrace [outside the ground] was thronged by a great crowd of men, who seemed to be rushing to and fro trying various entrances ... one noticed that there were few officials about to give directions, and the policemen at the doors were unfamiliar with the workings of the new stadium [inside the ground].

'Looking down from the press gallery there seemed at 1.45pm to be no more room for anybody. It was the most stupendous crowd I had ever seen, for the simple reason that no other building exists which can accommodate 125,000 people. It was a solid slope of pink faces arranged in a wide ellipse surrounding an oval of exquisite green turf … there was no reason to expect anything but the most impressive match on record. People were seen still pressing in through the openings in the outer wall, but they seemed to be miraculously finding room somehow. The journalists sharpened their pencils and prepared to record the match.'

But as the press settled down, transcribing their shorthand notes from pre-match interviews, they were largely unaware of how dangerously and rapidly matters were escalating outside the ground. The new stadium was brilliantly well served by public transport, ultimately too well, and as thousands flooded in, many thousands more largely ticketless fans quickly arrived on trains, buses, trams and Shanks's pony to further swell the hordes still struggling to gain access to the match. It was a disaster waiting to happen.

1.45pm. Instructions came from increasingly concerned officials that all gates should be closed.

As Hammers fan George Kerr finally managed to slowly and laboriously pick his way through the hordes of supporters, he hit a full stop 50 yards or so away from the ground. From there onwards it was like a mass, manic, writhing game of sardines:

'I saw the turnstiles had been built into wooden structures that were about eight feet high, the turnstiles themselves were locked and deserted but bodies were climbing over them like monkeys and I quickly followed suit … I got behind the crowd and was soon being pushed forward by others who got behind me. I was literally pushed into the ground.'

The sheer force of the crowd smashed open one of the closed turnstiles. The police and ground officials were so concerned about the fast-growing potential for threat to life that the turnstiles were re-opened and fans allowed in without having to show tickets or pay on the gate. In they streamed but now there were 20,000-30,000 angry fans massing behind those at the front, relentlessly pushing forward and causing dangerous pressure points all around the new stadium. Some found planks, ramped them up against the lower outside walls and created new entries into the ground. The sloping terraces were supported by a mass of iron girders, some 20 feet high, and thousands of others precariously climbed the girders to get over the top of the walls and then jumped down on to the already packed crowds below, causing hundreds of injuries. It was complete mayhem and the authorities found themselves completely out of control of the situation. The local mayor estimated that there were just 200 police officers on duty at the ground.

Though the stadium was already dangerously over-full, tens of thousands more supporters forced their way in and on to the terraces, bloating the crowd ever further. It must have been terrifying to be trapped inside this pressure cooker; new bodies endlessly surging forward from behind by the second, pushing and pressing others forward. People losing their footing, tripping over, trampled underfoot. Panic, confusion and no way out. Eyewitnesses recalled screams for help and the whimpering of fans accidentally pushed to the ground and stepped all over.

Chillingly, older fans would have keenly remembered the 1902 Ibrox Stadium disaster, when a new stand collapsed during a Scotland v England Home Championship game, killing 25 and injuring over 500 supporters. Some at Wembley may well have been at the 1902 match and witnessed the carnage first hand.

Small children were being passed over people's heads to protect them from the crush. But the elderly, infirm and disabled were left utterly prone as thousands more forced their way in behind them. It was a tragedy of potentially massive proportions just waiting to happen. Something had to give.

2.20pm. Reporters in the press box began to notice a curious bulging of the crowd across at the far corner by the western goal. The 'bulge' suddenly burst out from the stand and spread along the touchline. Hundreds of fans had literally been forced out on to the pitch by the thousands crowding in behind them. Short minutes later, and with a terrible weight at their backs, a mass of fans were pushed out of the stands and on to the touchline around the opposite goal. More followed at numerous pressure points around the inside of the ground, until eventually that excruciating pressure forced 10,000 or so fans out on to the pitch itself. The chaos was now at its most confused and worrying height. And yet among the mob of fans on the pitch, music could still be heard. With unfathomable stiff British upper lip, the Guards Band stood their ground in the centre circle surrounded by an ever-growing mob of fans and continued to play on.

3pm. Kick-off time. King George V had settled himself in the Royal Box, which was draped in scarlet and entwined hosannas of hothouse flowers. But the match did not kick off. There were now even more fans on the pitch. Urgent calls for mass police reinforcements had gone out, but the officers who had been put on duty to keep order at a huge new ground, that none of them knew, had bravely started to try and push the crowds back off the pitch and on to the touchlines. In comparison, herding cats would have been a far simpler affair. They tried linking arms together with a dozen or so other officers at strategic points on the pitch and then walked steadily against a section of the crowd to force them back. Instantly, they simply disappeared into the sheer mass of bodies, soon lost inside the bubble. And then on came the horses.

Led by former soldier PC George Scorey on his mount Billy, Horse 62, the nine mounted officers were charged with edging the crowds backwards towards the touchlines. Ironically, PC Scorey and Billy should never have been there. A couple of hours earlier they had been patrolling the West End, the constable keeping an avuncular eye on the matinee theatre-goers and shoppers. Sweltering in the sun, PC Scorey decided it was time for a cuppa and he took a tea break at Rochester police station. But once there, he was sent straight back out on to the streets. His superiors told him that things were 'starting to get ugly' at Wembley Stadium and ordered him there immediately to help control the crowds. PC Scorey had to ask them for directions as he had no idea how to get to the new ground.

Four and a bit miles later, PC Scorey arrived, his war medals on his chest, and marshalled his forces. Slowly and patiently, the horses nudged and pushed fans away from the pitch. It was partially successful, but only for a while.

As they viewed the chaos and confusion from the back of the tunnel, the Bolton players must have felt a curious sense of déjà vu. It is a little-known fact that they had experienced something a little similar in their FA Cup semi-final against Sheffield United at Old Trafford weeks before. The record books say that the game attracted the stadium's record attendance at the time of more than 72,000. What they don't show is that the ground sold far more reserved and on-the-day tickets than could be fitted into the ground. Thousands were turned away as the crowd began to swell disturbingly in number in and around Old Trafford. Eventually, over £2,000 was refunded to disgruntled fans, many of whom marched over in high dudgeon to Manchester City's old Hyde Road stadium to watch a Central League reserve match against Leeds United – the biggest crowd for City's second string. With kick-off approaching, Old Trafford was fast becoming dangerously over-full.

A reporter from what is now the *Yorkshire Post* – still known in 1923 as the *Yorkshire Post and Leeds Intelligencer* – described the scene:

'The pressure in some of the popular parts was severe to the point of danger. Ambulance men had a busy afternoon in treating or removing the fainting cases, but so far as I have been able to learn there was no really serious casualty. It was perhaps fortunate that the crowd broke bounds, and relieved the pressure. More than some little inconvenience and delay occurred through encroachments on the touchline, but with tactical management and the stately parading of two handsomely mounted policemen, the game went its course.'

Déjà vu indeed. Back in the Wembley dressing rooms, the players were edgy and confused, eagerly awaiting the latest news from the pitch. My former co-author Chuck Korr interviewed Hammers winger Jimmy Ruffell shortly before his death, and the player remembered the moment it was decided they should go out on to the pitch:

'The dressing room door opened and in walked one of the King's representatives. He told us that George V said it was about time they got on with the game.'

The players made their way out of the tunnel, shocked to see the mayhem close up. Soon, they were literally in among it, sucked into the crowd. Ruffell recalled, 'Most of the people at Wembley seemed to be Londoners. Well, the ones I saw seemed to be. As we tried to make our way out on to the field everyone was slapping us on the back and grabbing our hands to shake them. By the time I got to the centre of the pitch my poor shoulder was aching.' Ruffell had just narrowly passed a fitness test on a shoulder injury that threatened to keep him out of the final.

The arrival of the players did, however, seem to have an effect upon the fans, who seeing their heroes in kit and ready to play, began to collectively realise that with no pitch there would be no game. And that's why everyone was in the stadium. Phalanxes of supporters in the centre of the pitch began to copy the initial police action, linked arms in their hundreds and then their thousands, and step by step slowly marched backwards, nudging the fans behind them towards the touchlines. Miraculously, this spontaneous operation worked. The pitch was cleared. Fans massed inches behind the touchlines, but ever teetering, tremulously on the brink.

The national press were keen to celebrate the importance of the day, but couldn't help but point a finger over the fiasco that was unfolding. A correspondent for the *Daily Mail* described the stewarding as 'useless' from the off and wrote that officials in and around the ground 'seemed to know nothing'. Fans had not been directed to any specific areas and roamed the stadium wherever they wished.

3.45pm. The match finally kicked off 45 minutes late. To say that this was not a situation conducive to playing a game of football would be an understatement. Rule Five of the old FA match regulations was being broken virtually every few seconds, as fans encroached upon the field of play. Thousands of boots had trampled up the turf and the hooves of police horses dug up great clods and sods; the pitch was a furrowed mess. The noise in the stadium was ear-splitting, a constant roar, and it was impossible for players to hear one another's shouts, let alone instructions from the bench.

Every few minutes members of the crowd on the touchlines would get an accidental shove from behind as fans surged forward and spilled on to the pitch, getting in the way of players and officials. The linesmen couldn't even see the touchlines, never mind operate down the outer sides of the pitch as normal. They spent the game actually on the pitch, running the line down either wing, which was bad news for West Ham's outside-forwards Dick Richards and Jimmy Ruffell, whose usual style was to maraud aggressively down either wing. In the first few minutes of the game, they often found themselves 'in traffic' with not just opposition players but linesmen and fans, whose outstretched legs accidentally threatened to trip them up.

Pragmatic as ever, Bolton immediately narrowed their play towards the centre of the pitch. David Jack, who'd scored in every round, found wide-open space to score the opener after just two minutes because his West Ham marker, right-half Jack Tresadern, was trapped in the crowd, unable to get back on the pitch after taking a throw-in. Jack's hammer shot struck a fan who was pressed against the back of the net, unable to move, and it knocked him unconscious. Matters became yet more chaotic after 11 minutes when another dramatic crowd surge sent hundreds spilling out on to the pitch. The match was stopped as members of the Red Cross stretchered off the injured and police attempted to clear the pitch once again.

Bolton remained on top throughout the first half, stifling West Ham's attacking talent by switching to a line of five half-backs when the Hammers had possession. Unable to find a way through the crowds to the dressing rooms, the players stayed on the pitch, and after a few minutes they changed ends and kicked off again.

West Ham began the second half strongly and created a couple of good goalscoring chances. But eight minutes into the half, the wind was well and truly knocked out of their sails by a second controversial Bolton goal. Outside-forward Ted Vizard fed the ball into the box to Jack Smith who cracked it first time past goalkeeper Ted Hufton. The West Ham players were furious, claiming that the ball had not crossed the line but hit a post and rebounded back out into open play. To add insult to injury, they angrily pointed out to the ref that in the build-up a Bolton fan had stepped over the touchline and kicked the ball to Vizard when it was actually going out of play. Referee David Asson waved the dissenting players away and the goal stood. For the rest of the match, neither side managed a serious shot on goal and Bolton ran out 2-0 winners.

On at least one occasion during the game, Hammers captain George Kay asked the referee to abandon it. At any other time and in any other circumstance, the match would have been called off. But not to play on would have caused a riot. And after working so hard to get fans off the pitch and raising expectations so high, the authorities had backed themselves into a corner. The afternoon's chaos was not exactly the worldwide PR success the British government was looking for in opening the globe's largest stadium, the centrepiece of the Empire Exhibition. But to abandon the match would undoubtedly have made matters far worse. Miraculously, no one died among the chaos. Although doctors and Red Cross workers treated well over 1,000 injured fans, only 22 had to undergo further hospital treatment. And apart from the entrances being stormed and turnstiles wrecked, the new stadium had shown itself to be a safe and sturdy structure way above and beyond the call of duty.

West Ham were unhappy losers. Their trainer Charlie Paynter's verdict on the match was, 'It was that white horse thumping its big feet into the pitch that made it hopeless. Our wingers were tumbling all over the place, tripping up in great ruts and holes.' The truth is First Division Bolton had dealt far better with the extraordinary conditions and adapted their tactics cleverly and continually to counter any threat from the Hammers. The gap between the top league and the one below was already evident in what we see today between the Premier League and the Championship. That extra bit of professional nous allied to an extra abundance of individual skill throughout the Wanderers side won it on the day.

PC Scorey and Billy became national icons. Black and white newsreel and press photos of their work at the centre of the action led to the game soon becoming dubbed the 'White Horse Final'. The irony is that Billy was a grey, and it was only the quality of black and white photographic film at the time that made the horse appear washed-out and white. A further irony – the FA gave PC Scorey tickets to each subsequent FA

Cup Final, but he never attended, having no interest in football whatsoever.

That there were no deaths was down to luck and circumstance. Quoted in *Kicking and Screaming: An Oral History of Football in England*, eyewitness Sydney Woodhouse described his thoughts about the chaos, 'Had there not been free access to the pitch from the bottom of the terraces, the casualties would have been colossal. I think the crowd safety was due to the behaviour of the crowd and the absence of any barrier preventing people getting on to the pitch … and that was the whole saving grace. Otherwise I think hundreds would have been crushed, literally hundreds.'

Athletic News did not hold back in its condemnation of what it described as 'a fiasco'. Its redoubtable correspondent 'Tityrus' delivered the newspaper's verdict and didn't pull his punches:

'It was miraculous that the destination of the cup was decided, whether the conditions were perfectly fair to the teams I take leave to doubt. In days of old, this match under the conditions that prevailed would have produced a protest from the defeated. Under modern government, if this had been a tie between two clubs in an earlier round, one of them would have been called upon to pay a fine of £300 or £500. Who will suffer for the colossal blunders of the management of this final? Already there has been a committee of inquiry into the general conduct of the British Empire exhibition and a drastic report. Is there to be a report into this disgraceful fiasco at the stadium? There ought to be, and the responsibility placed on the right shoulders. The spectators made an exploration into Blunderland and what scores of thousands saw of this game was beyond me. I repeat that it was a miracle that the match was played. No thanks are due to the officials of the stadium.'

All points forcefully and well made, but any investigations into the chaos soon became mired in fudge and much governmental obfuscation. The crowd chaos led to much debate in parliament about crowd safety at football matches. But after much harrumphing and toing and froing, all the MPs could agree upon was to make future FA Cup finals all-ticket affairs. Truth be told, in 1923 the safety of predominantly working-class football fans was not high on the agenda of politicians or it seemed, the footballing establishment.

History will always remember the match as the White Horse Final. But it should perhaps be better remembered because of the actions of one very brave and decisive man, and I don't think it's ever been fully acknowledged. It is not often that football books eulogise the work of referees, but if it had not been for the courageously nimble quick thinking of David Asson the game would never have gone ahead – and then who knows what mayhem might have occurred. Imagine yourself in the same position. One poor bloke in the middle, among over 200,000 confused, potentially angry fans, up against a situation no man had ever faced before in sport. Around him was a massive riot in the making. Surely it would have been far easier to just abandon the game? His blood pressure must have been through the roof, but he tried to remain calm throughout and ensured the game was played, putting in a man-of-the-match performance, all things considered.

Among the melee and the madness, Asson approached the two captains and said, 'We are only three here.' This was a reference to himself and his two linesmen, and a plea that he needed their help. He got it. Both managers gave him all due respect, the players too. They didn't agree with every decision he made during the match, but it was thanks to his determination and persistence that the first Wembley game was played. I truly wish that I could tell you more about David Asson but astonishingly there is little to be found about his life. This is curious and frustrating to me, because this was the man in the middle of a maelstrom who kept his nerve so that one of football's most important games would literally get over the line. Truly the day's unsung hero.

Bolton's players stepped up to the new Royal Box to receive the FA Cup for the first time from the king himself, where they were handed their nine-carat gold winners' medals. They lived it up for the next few days, enjoying a luncheon in their honour at the House of Commons, followed by an official civic reception back in Lancashire, where tens of thousands lined the streets to welcome them home. Bolton was a proper hardcore football town that had seldom tasted success. Wanderers had skirted triumph a few times in the past – FA Cup losers and some good league positions – but this delivered the dream, their first major success. Bolton was drunk for days.

West Ham were staying sober. They had to lick their wounds and regroup. Only 48 hours after the final, the Claret and Blues had to play their penultimate game of the season, still well and truly in the promotion frame but knackered from their hard work at Wembley, carrying several players who'd narrowly passed fitness tests. In a tough, attritional match they beat Sheffield Wednesday 2-0 and went into the final game of their Second Division campaign against Notts County, with all to play for. The prize, promotion to the First Division for the first time in West Ham's history. After the crushing disappointment of Wembley, could Syd King's team deliver?

9

First Division

'It was the best of times, it was the worst of times.'

Charles Dickens, *A Tale of Two Cities*

TRUE FOOTBALL fans are rightly enthused by the Liverpool of Jürgen Klopp, with their total full-on footballing style and amazing achievements. Before that, the success of the Kenny Dalglish years when Anfield witnessed football at its most dashing; and before that, the European and domestic triumphs achieved by the uncomplicated genius of quietly spoken Bob Paisley, the great organiser and motivator. And before them all, of course, the legend that was Bill Shankly. An utterly driven man who took his wife Nessie to watch a reserve match on their honeymoon, Shanks is rightly regarded as the man who dragged Liverpool back into the big time after decades of mediocrity.

But they had been top dogs before – and that was in the early 1920s. Way back then was when the first great Liverpool team were starting to build an amazing legacy. In 1923, the simple facts were that Liverpool won the championship for the second year running – the first back-to-back champions since the 19th century, a great story and achievement within itself.

But this time around the tale continued a bizarre sub-plot – at its heart, one man: Liverpool manager Dave Ashworth.

The pipe-smoking, heavily moustachioed Ashworth was a rare beast, having been a top Football League referee before going into management with Oldham Athletic in 1906. He was highly successful and well-loved there, taking the Lancashire Combination side into the Football League and then into the top division within two years. Following a spell before and after the war managing at Stockport County, he was taken on as Liverpool boss in 1920. Like many clubs, Liverpool were hamstrung by the effects of World War One on their players. Most of those who did return hadn't played competitive football for years or carried the legacy of wartime injuries, both physical and mental. Ashworth took over as manager in 1920 and led them to a second successive fourth place, eight points behind champions Burnley. By 1922, they were league champions.

During the summer prior to the 1922/23 season, Ashworth took his men on an all-expenses-paid tour to Italy, to show the wider world, and particularly the rest of Europe, that Liverpool were now among football's royalty. They were joined on the trip by Burnley, who the season before had finished third. This would be the first time that Liverpool had undertaken a foreign pre-season tour since a 1914 trip to Sweden.

The two squads boarded a train from Lime Street Station down to London and then on to Dover to take a ferry over to Calais and further trains to Paris and Milan, the headquarters for their joint tour. Apart from those men who had fought in World War One, few Britons had ever travelled abroad. In 1923, only six per cent of the population held passports, including most of the Liverpool and Burnley players who had to be quickly 'signed up' to make the trip. But this was a statement. We are England's best, ready to take on anyone. In truth, it was as much holiday as pre-season tour, a thank-you for a highly successful season. On arrival the Liverpool players relaxed on a boat trip around the islands of Lago Maggiore, the second biggest pre-Alpine lake in Italy. The following day they were taken by cable car up Monte Mottorone to take in majestic vistas of the Italian Alps. They stayed in one of Milan's finest hotels, enjoyed a lot of good food and more than the odd Peroni.

On the football side, Liverpool and Burnley kicked off their tour by playing one another. Burnley ran out 1-0 winners. Liverpool left-half and England international Tom Bromilow wrote a column for the local press as a record of the trip. Tom was not impressed by Italian football. After one of the 'friendlies', he wrote, 'I have never played in such a game wherein so much hacking, kicking and pushing was tolerated. In fact, the home side indulged in everything but biting.'

But Liverpool's – and Burnley's – pre-season tour seemed to set them up well for the season ahead. There were no personnel changes at Anfield and Ashworth was highly optimistic. 'We ought to have a very good season,' he told the local press. 'There is perfect harmony from the boardroom to the dressing room and that goes a long way.'

Ashworth's prediction was soon borne out. By December 1922 Liverpool were top of the league, two points clear of Sunderland, the division's top scorers with 44 goals. All did indeed seem to be in perfect harmony at Anfield. But from total left-field, Ashworth dropped a bombshell. Though well on their way to back-to-back championship wins he announced he was quitting the club to manage bottom-placed Oldham Athletic. Liverpool fans were aghast. His timing was extraordinary. He quit Anfield soon after Liverpool had beaten Oldham, home and away, over the Christmas period, so could see first-hand what a state they were in.

Imagine Pep Guardiola or Jürgen Klopp on top of the Premier League, streets ahead by the turn of the year, suddenly deciding to quit their jobs and take over at bottom clubs

Norwich or Watford. This effectively is what Ashworth did at the end of 1922. Some speculated that having enjoyed a happy and successful eight-year spell at Oldham before the war, Ashworth couldn't bear to see his old club in the doldrums and wished to return to help them stay in the First Division. The truth was far more personal. Ashworth's home life was far from straightforward. His two daughters were both disabled and the Ashworths lived in Stockport. The daily, 86-mile, two-way commute to Liverpool had become too much for Ashworth and his family, and Oldham was only 11 miles up the road or rail.

Sixty-year-old board member Matt McQueen took temporary charge, thus becoming the first ex-Reds player to also manage the club. The Scottish international had played over 150 times for Liverpool and his home was next to Anfield. He'd been out of the active side of the game for a while and the next few months saw the Reds playing in fits and starts. In their last 15 league games they hardly hit title-winning form, winning six, drawing five and losing four, but thanks to Sunderland hitting a similarly indifferent patch, McQueen managed to shepherd them home for a second successive title. The Wearsiders' last 15 matches saw them win eight, but also lose six.

Though originally appointed as caretaker, McQueen would stay on as manager for a further four years, only retiring after losing a leg in a car accident, which continued to cause him health problems until his death in 1944. Anfield's Centenary Stand now covers the site where McQueen's house once stood.

Most of the Liverpool squad were championship winners from the season before and knew each other's game inside out. It was a team full of quality. At the heart of the side was one of the toughest players in football, the Bootle hardman, Walter Wadsworth. On playing alongside him, team-mate Donald MacKinlay later recalled in an interview with Liverpool's *Anfield Wrap*, 'I remember one match ... when Wadsworth injured a leg and I saw blood coming out of his boot. I told him to get some attention to it and his reply was, "Whose blood is it, yours or mine?" and went on playing. I think the game was tougher in my day.'

Their goalkeeper Elisha Scott added, 'As a sheer stopper, I have never seen anything approaching Wadsworth. Too little of the credit for the championships is laid at his door. He certainly was robust, I'll admit, but nothing more. I have seen him fling himself ten yards over the ground to stop forwards applying the crusher.'

Opposition players regularly gave Wadsworth a wide berth and tried to play more towards the other wing. By many accounts, he was definitely a clogger and a fouler, but it was his massive body strength that put opponents off going one on one with him. His shoulder charges, totally legal in the day, were swift and brutal, and with tree trunk legs Wadsworth was often the immovable object around which forwards would seldom pass. One of Wadsworth's slogans was, 'Ball may pass me, but man never.'

It wasn't just opponents who had to watch their step with Wadsworth. On 1 December 1923 Liverpool played Sheffield United at Bramall Lane. Wadsworth was goaded by a Blades fan sat in a stand next to the touchline and totally lost it. Soon after, he wrote an article about the incident in the *Topical Times* and was less than repentant:

'Let me state here and now, that I hit a spectator, I admit it. I think I was justified because a spectator called me something that I will allow no man to call me … I hope the action I took will lead to the offenders realising that they cannot lean over the railings and offer vile insults at footballers.'

Two seasons later, Liverpool played Newcastle United at Anfield in February 1925. Newcastle forward Tommy Urwin threw mud at Wadsworth, who in return punched him full in the face. He was banned for the rest of the season.

McKinlay and Scott were also key to Liverpool's success. Scotland's Donald McKinlay was club captain in 1923, having joined Liverpool as a teenager way back in 1910. Though only 5ft 9in tall, he was an uncompromising, hard-tackling player and an expert dead-ball specialist. He would play over 400 games for Liverpool, mainly at left-back, but was so versatile in his reading of the game that he also turned out at Anfield as a wing-half, a centre-half and right across the forward line. Ulsterman goalkeeper Elisha Scott was at Liverpool from 1912 to 1934 and still holds the record as the club's longest-serving player. Like McKinlay, he was only 5ft 9in tall, small for a goalkeeper even in 1923, but Scott had a tremendous leap, much of it learned in his Belfast youth footballing days when he played as a centre-forward for the Belfast Boys' Brigade. Over their two championship-winning seasons, Scott would make 81 appearances from a possible 84.

But this was to be Liverpool at their peak. The average age of the squad was 29 and a good number of the players were well into their 30s and nearing retirement. During their last five games they played Herbert Chapman's Huddersfield Town twice and it was a sign of things to come. Town more than matched the Reds in both games – drawing 0-0 at Leeds Road and 1-1 at Anfield, which gave Liverpool the point they needed to retain the title. Town would end not far below them in third. The following season would see both teams pass in opposite directions. Huddersfield would be crowned league champions for the first time; Liverpool finished down in 12th place, losing more games, 16, than the 15 they won. It would be another 24 years before Liverpool captured the title again.

Sunderland ended as runners-up, six points behind Liverpool. In the previous two seasons the Wearsiders had finished a mediocre 12th and aware that he needed to rebuild an ageing squad, manager Bob Kyle had been busy in the transfer market. By 1923 the only survivor of the Sunderland side that won the 1912/13 First Division title was the indefatigable Charles Buchan. But he was certainly the man to keep. Now 31, the England international ended the 1923 season as the First Division's top scorer with 30 goals. For seven out of the nine seasons he spent at Roker Park, Buchan was Sunderland's leading scorer, and to this day he still remains the club's record holder with 209 in 379 matches.

Already a Sunderland legend, Buchan was not your average footballer. He'd trained as a teacher and was articulate and argumentative, refusing to suffer fools gladly. In 1921 Buchan had been one of the players' union ringleaders behind an abortive footballers' strike, called because the Football League proposed to cut the maximum wage from £10 to £8 a week and £6 in the off-season. The strike would never happen, because too many timid players left the union for it to be effective. Buchan had never been afraid of confronting the establishment but this made him a marked man among the conservative stick-in-the-muds at the Football League and the FA. Though a great player and consistently a prolific goalscorer, Buchan would only be picked six times for England.

In total, seven out of the top ten teams came from the north – underneath Liverpool and Sunderland, came Huddersfield Town in third and Newcastle United, Everton and Manchester City below them. Arsenal were the highest-placed club from London and the south, ending up 11th. Northern dominance was evident throughout the league. Thirteen out of the 22 clubs hailed from Yorkshire, Lancashire and the north-east. From the Midlands were Aston Villa, West Bromwich Albion, Birmingham City, Nottingham Forest and Stoke City. Arsenal, Tottenham Hotspur and Chelsea came from London; Cardiff City from Wales.

Up and down the First Division, several players had excellent individual seasons. Though Birmingham finished a disappointing 17th, their star striker Joe Bradford ended up top scorer for the second season in a row with 18 league goals to his name. He would go on to top Birmingham's scoring charts in all but one First Division season between 1922 and 1933. Bradford scored 249 goals in 414 appearances for Brum and not surprisingly, is still their all-time top scorer. Just for good measure, he also scored seven goals in his 12 full England appearances. His team-mate, veteran defender Frank Womack, had a good, solid season celebrating his 15th year as a player at St Andrew's, but as ever, didn't trouble the goal stats column. The truth was Womack was well on the way to setting what would be an astonishing Football League record that still stands today. He left Birmingham for non-league Worcester City in 1928 after making 491 league appearances for City without scoring a single goal.

In only their second season in the top flight, Cardiff finished ninth, largely thanks to their own goalscoring machine Len Davies, who scored 28 goals in all competitions, including 19 in the league. Davies also got the winner in Cardiff's 3-2 Welsh Cup Final win over Aberdare. Like Bradford at Birmingham, Davies would end his career as Cardiff's all-time top scorer with 179 goals, scored between 1919 and 1931.

As a delicious side note, Davies would finally leave Cardiff to sign for what may well be the Football League's strangest club, Thames AFC, and one that someone should write an entire book about, so bizarre is their story. But, dear reader, for the purposes of our book, we must keep this journey short. Let me take you into modern-day east London. Make a turn off the busy bustle of Prince Regent Lane in London's Custom House into a quieter network of suburban streets. For speedway fans, it's a place of homage, the streets named after some of the sport's greatest riders and luminaries. Former world champions Bluey Wilkinson and Jack Young are celebrated on Wilkinson Road and Young Road; rider and manager Arthur Atkinson in Atkinson Road; and famed rider Tommy Croombs in Croombs Road. There are a couple of closes named after speedway promoter and manager Jonnie Hoskins and rider Aub Lawson.

The footprint of this small estate has an extraordinary history. It was the site of the long-ago demolished West Ham Stadium, which was for many years the largest sports club ground in England. With a capacity of 120,000, it was home to one of the nation's most popular speedway teams, the Ammers, who would regularly pack in crowds of 80,000-plus. It was for many years the venue that put on greyhound racing's biggest events. But it was built to house a long-forgotten football team, Thames AFC. Created to compete against the other London footballing giants, the hugely ambitious club was financed by a collection of the capital's great and the good and peers of the realm, in the centre of, at the time, the world's most populous city and in a sports-mad area of east London. What could possibly go wrong?

Thames duly joined the Southern League in 1928 and two years later were elected to the Third Division South. In the close season they splashed the cash, signing not only First Division royalty such as Len Davies but ex-England international and former Tottenham favourite Jimmy Dimmock, the man who scored Spurs' winner in the 1921 FA Cup Final, and Arsenal's hugely experienced Harry White. They would finish their first Football League season third from bottom, but did manage to set an impressive new record – they smashed the lowest attendance figure ever recorded at a professional match in England. On 6 December 1930 just 469 fans paid to watch Thames play Luton Town – in a stadium that of course, held 120,000. During their first season Thames averaged just over 1,000 fans per game and soon they were losing money hand over fist. At the end of their second Third Division South season they finished rock bottom and were so deep in debt that they decided not to apply for re-election, so were officially wound up. Len Davies had long since jumped ship, returning to Wales and Bangor after his one depressing season at the West Ham Stadium.

From the very start, it was the maddest of missions to manufacture a football club. Within a few short miles of the ground, well-established clubs such as West Ham, Millwall, Clapton Orient and Charlton had already mopped up local loyalties and support. Thames' embarrassingly short stay in the Third Division South showed they were singularly unsuccessful in poaching fans from rival clubs. Proof that money can't always buy success.

Oldham finally fell on their sword when they took on West Bromwich Albion at Boundary Park, needing a win to stand any chance of escaping relegation. The Latics had only scored two goals in their past ten matches, so the omens were not good and almost inevitably, the game ended in a 0-0 bore draw. *Athletic News*'s coverage read more like an obituary than a match report.

'Prior to Saturday there was a possible chance of Oldham Athletic retaining their place in the First Division, but their failure to secure full points on the occasion of the visit of West Bromwich Albion has apparently settled their fate. But even prior to Saturday, their supporters had already given up all hope, for less than 7,000 paid for admission to see the game with Albion. Moreover these faithful followers felt keenly the position of affairs, for a quarter of an hour from the finish they left the ground in droves. To be candid, neither side deserved a goal and I must say it was the most innocuous league game I have seen this season. Neither side was worthy of a point and yet both got one because of the goalless draw. I do not suppose either team would have scored had they played until dusk.'

Dave Ashworth had not been able to work his magic again at Oldham. Despite recruiting a raft of new players, nothing gelled on the pitch for Ashworth. After the war, life had been a struggle for Oldham in the top division. In the three seasons prior to 1923 the Boundary Park side had finished 17th, 19th and 19th respectively but 1923 would be the year that survival was beyond them.

Stoke City occupied the second relegation place. An ambitious club, they had been promoted from the Second Division the season before and spent good money on improving their squad. It would not be a happy return to the big time. After eight games, they were already rock bottom with two points. Desperate to stay up, Stoke went into the Christmas period splashing out on a clutch of new players including highly regarded Sunderland half-back Joe Kasher and Blackburn's flying winger Bert Ralphs. Things improved for a while and from early January into February they lifted themselves a few rungs up the table with five wins out of seven games. From there on in they hit a dreadful run of form. During their last 15 games, Stoke only managed three wins. In the last ten they scored only three goals. From week to week, manager Arthur Shallcross constantly chopped and changed his team. In all, he used 30 players during the season's 42 matches and only five of his squad managed to play more than 30 games. There was no consistency, no meaningful partnerships on the pitch and with four weeks of the season to go, Shallcross was given the push after four years as manager. Former England international Jock Rutherford was brought in but it was too little too late. Rutherford ended up having a major row with the board and he himself quit before Stoke's season came to its sad, disorganised end.

Nottingham Forest defied the stats, escaping relegation by four points in third from bottom, despite having the season's leakiest defence with 70 goals conceded in their 42 games, and the First Division's second-worst scoring record with just 41 goals, only six more than bottom club Oldham.

Unsurprisingly, champions Liverpool were the season's best-supported club with an average gate of 33,492, watched in all league and cup home games at Anfield by 793,192 fans. Second were Arsenal with an average Highbury gate of 30,762, followed by Everton with 30,262, Chelsea with 30,167, Tottenham Hotspur with 30,031, and Aston Villa with 28,857. However, a telling statistic that said much about the worsening economic climate in Britain is that every single one of these clubs was losing fans – some, like Chelsea, were haemorrhaging them. In the previous season, 1921/22, the Blues' average home gate was 37,646 – over 7,000 more per match. Spurs were down over 5,000 and Liverpool over 2,500, despite once again being champions. The downward trend continued in 1923/24 with the Reds' average gate dropping by another 3,000 to 30,381; Tottenham's dropped again to 28,400 and Everton fell to 29,185.

10

Second Division

'Up the Hammers.'

A regular comment from the stands

WHEN IT comes to fixture lists, fate sometimes plays little jokes. Coming into the final Saturday of the season, West Ham, Notts County and Leicester City all needed a win to be crowned as champions. Leicester were up against Bury, while West Ham were at home – against Notts County. The latter encounter matched up a free-scoring Hammers side that had already netted 63 goals that season against a Scrooge-like Notts County defence. County had been the season's steady-eddies, starting and finishing the campaign well with very few blips in between.

Key to the Magpies' success was the form of right-back Bill Ashurst and their two goalkeepers, Albert Iremonger and George Streets. Ashurst was having such a fine season that he became one of a rare breed – a Second Division defender picked to play for England. He made his debut against Sweden and would win a further three caps. Iremonger was an extraordinary player. A first-team regular since 1905, he was generally regarded in his day as one of the best keepers never to play for England. He was described as having 'hands like the claws of a JCB and was a seven-foot-tall monster'. In truth, he was 6ft 5in but must have seemed bigger because of his highly muscular frame and his loud, outspoken approach on the pitch. Famous for arguing the toss with match officials and booming endless instructions to his team-mates, he was now coming towards the end of his playing career and pretty much shared the starting spot with his long-time understudy Streets throughout the 1922/23 league season. Between them, they kept 23 clean sheets. Iremonger also played county cricket for Nottinghamshire and had two brothers, James and Harold, who were regulars at Nottingham Forest. James also played cricket for Nottinghamshire to stunning effect as an all-rounder, ending his Trent Bridge career after scoring 21 first-class centuries and taking 619 wickets. Albert would leave County two years later to play for Lincoln after making 564 appearances, turning out in his last Magpies game aged 40. He became such a local legend in Nottingham that a road behind the Meadow Lane ground was named after him.

The Hammers' season had all been about momentum. As well as their extraordinary run to the 1923 Cup Final, the Boleyn side gave the Second Division much of its excitement that season. Yet their campaign had started disastrously with just three wins out of their first 15 games, leaving them languishing down towards the bottom. On 11 November 1922, West Ham drew 0-0 at home to Leeds United to start an amazing 32-game league and cup run that would see them lose just once, in a Boxing Day match against Manchester United. Manager Syd King played a high-risk strategy throughout, rarely resting any of his regular starting 11. By the end of the season knocks, strains and pains were starting to add up and the week before the Notts County game, five of King's players narrowly passed fitness tests to turn out in the Wembley final.

Leicester were enjoying their best season since the turn of the century and coming into the final day they were the top scorers with 65 goals. New manager Peter Hodge had bought wisely during the summer, his recruits crucially including the Duncan brothers from his previous club Raith Rovers. The older John was a quick-footed goalscoring inside-forward and Thomas a pacy right-winger. Leicester started the season like a runaway train, as did John Duncan. On the first day of the season he scored two on his debut in a 5-4 away win at Stockport County's Edgeley Park. The following week, he scored again in a 3-0 home win against Rotherham County. The free scoring continued and after ten games, Leicester were top, chalking up seven wins, two draws and just one defeat. But as autumn turned into winter, the sparkling early form began to fall away. From early December into mid-February, Leicester lost eight, drew two and won only four. Thanks again to John Duncan's goals, they rallied over the next month or so and by 19 March 1923, and after 33 matches, they were top with 42 points. Notts County were third with 40 points and West Ham down in fifth with 37. But Leicester had another stutter into the final straights and their away game against Bury would be a tough one. The Lancashire side had been in and around the top six all season, largely thanks to a powerhouse home record. Before the Leicester game they had lost only twice at Gigg Lane. The stage was set for a dramatic three-way final-day showdown.

The top-of-the-table clash at the Boleyn Ground was a total war of attrition in front of a packed crowd. County scored after 20 minutes and then set about doing what they did best – defending deep. No matter what West Ham threw at them, the Magpies held firm right into the closing minutes. Up in the Midlands, Leicester v Bury finished earlier than the London match. The *Daily Graphic* described what happened next:

'The news of Leicester's loss was signalled from the veranda of the directors' pavilion whilst a fierce struggle was going on around the Notts goal. Immediately there was a cheer which swelled into an almighty roar as it was taken up by the crowd around the ground. For the moment the players were confounded and the play seemed to hang in suspense, but immediately the loss of enthusiasm became apparent. It was a thrilling scene. An interesting touch was added when Donald Cock, the Notts County centre, found the opportunity on the field to shake hands with George Kay, the West Ham captain.'

Both clubs had ensured promotion, Notts County as champions. For West Ham it would be their first time in the top league – the greatest of consolations after losing at Wembley. All testament to the great job King had been doing for West Ham since the turn of the century as player, secretary and manager. In 1923, the local *East Ham Echo* described him thus: 'Syd King is West Ham and West Ham is Syd King.' He would consolidate them in the top tier for nearly a decade before their relegation back to the Second Division in 1931/32. The following season they would struggle badly losing nine games on the bounce and on 5 November 1932, King was called before the board to explain why things were going so badly on the pitch. At the meeting, King, who was known to enjoy a drink or three and had been warned about it by management on numerous occasions, was 'drunk and insubordinate' and suspended for three months. In January 1933 he was sacked, his reputation in tatters. A month later, King was dead at the relatively young age of 59, after having drunk a lethal cocktail of alcohol and corrosive liquid.

Leicester would lose out on promotion by goal average – and much to his chagrin, John Duncan missed the Bury match through injury, the only time during the season that he would be absent. He would though end his first campaign at Filbert Street as top scorer with 20 goals; brother Thomas would chip in with six. Two seasons later, John's 34 goals would help power Leicester into the First Division as champions, but Thomas went on to pastures new.

In the close season of 1923/24, Leicester signed young non-league right-winger Hughie Adcock from Loughborough, who proved to be stiff competition for the Scot. The younger Duncan only managed a dozen or so league games and moved on to Halifax Town, then Bristol Rovers and non-league Kettering Town. Thomas's daughter Elsie went on to marry Don Revie. John would play on at Filbert Street for another six seasons and then later become Leicester's manager.

Despite the final-day dramas, it was an underwhelming season in the Football League's second tier. The majority of sides were much of a muchness, and only 18 points separated champions Notts County from relegated second-bottom Rotherham County. Notts ended the season on 53 points, and with a fairly unremarkable record for champions. Eleven of their wins were 1-0 victories and they only managed 46 goals in their 42 games. At home, the Magpies scored 29 goals – three less than bottom club Wolverhampton Wanderers. Runners-up West Ham and third-placed Leicester were both only two points away on 51 points. In fourth, Manchester United sat on 48 points, only six more than 12th-placed Hull City.

Down at the bottom, Wolves' relegation put the lid on a sad postwar decline. As recently as 1908 Wolves had been FA Cup winners, beating Newcastle United 3-1. Since 1919 the Molineux side had lurched from one slump to the next. In 1919/20 they ended up 19th in the Second Division, a single point ahead of the bottom three re-election places. In 1920/21, a long season of struggle saw them finish a relieved 15th. In 1921/22 Wolves managed 17th, just four points clear of the drop zone.

With no significant new signings made for the 1922/23 season, the writing seemed to be on the wall. It started badly and then got worse; in their first 15 outings, Wolves won just twice. December then brought them six losses on the bounce including a 7-1 hammering at Coventry City. Between 6

January and 31 March, they won just once. Other lowlights included losing 7-0 away at Leicester, 5-0 at Crystal Palace and taking a 4-1 home beating from West Ham. Despite a rally towards the end of the season when four wins out of the last six games brought the slightest veneer of respectability to the campaign, they ended up nine from safety on a miserable 27 points. Wolves' away record was the worst in their entire history; five draws, 16 defeats and not one single win all season. In 21 away games they managed just ten goals and conceded 51. All in all, not a good year to be a Wolves fan.

They were joined in the two relegation places with some degree of inevitability by Rotherham County. The South Yorkshire club had come up from the old Midland League into the Second Division at the end of the war and had struggled ever since. In the previous three seasons, County had finished 17th, 19th and in the 1921/22 campaign, 16th – ironically, their highest league position. As a football fan, it is of course the hope that kills you. After a poor start to the season, Rotherham had isolated little purple patches that briefly brought optimism into the Millmoor collective. In late October and early November they won three games on the bounce against Hull, Coventry and Crystal Palace, and drew a couple more. During those weeks, striker Albert Pape went on a run of eight goals in five games. In late February, early March they got back-to-back wins against Fulham and Notts County. A last push in their final ten games saw them hit moderately acceptable mid-table form with four wins, a draw and five defeats, but it would never be enough to save them from the drop. They ended up one agonising point adrift of Stockport County and Clapton Orient. Two years later they would merge with Midland League club Rotherham Town to become the Rotherham United we know today.

Port Vale finish 17th, two points off the relegation places, perhaps achieving the Second Division season's truly 'great escape'. In pre-season they had lost most of their experienced players, who'd moved on to other clubs because the Vale board were demanding pay cuts. New players were signed but not of any great calibre. The truth is the club were skint and with dwindling attendances, matters only got worse as the season progressed. Their attendances were 50 per cent down on the 1920/21 season and by May 1923, Port Vale recorded a punishing loss of £2,400 and a panoply of fines imposed upon individuals within the club by the FA, all found guilty of making illegal, under-the-counter payments to players. It was a miserable season for Vale, but somehow, and against all the odds, they stayed up. They only scored 37 goals, the second-lowest in the division that year. Only South Shields, with 35, scored fewer – but the north-east side ended with a seriously respectable home record of 11 wins, seven draws and three losses to place them three points above Port Vale. The Valiants' top scorer Tom Butler managed only nine goals from 42 matches – no other Vale player scored more than four. But after a poor, poor season, the players gave it a last-gasp go and their win and two draws in the final four games proved a squeak enough to keep them up.

Several players up and down the division had a stellar season that year. Top of the pile was Blackpool forward Harry Bedford. He played all 42 games for his club and ended not only the Second Division top scorer but also the leading scorer in the entire Football League with 32 goals – over half of Blackpool's tally of 60. His exploits were rewarded with an England call-up, and as a Second Division player, he duly made his debut against Sweden in a 4-2 friendly win in Stockholm – becoming the first Blackpool player to pull on an England shirt in the process.

Bedford started his professional career as a 19-year-old at Nottingham Forest in 1919, where he scored eight goals in 14 appearances. Blackpool liked the look of the tyro goalscorer and signed him up for £1,200 – he did not disappoint. In 169 games for the Tangerines the young striker scored 114 goals. In 1925 Blackpool cashed in to treble their money, selling Bedford on to Derby County for £3,900. He didn't disappoint the Rams, either, scoring 142 goals in 204 league appearances. Somewhat of a forgotten hero, Bedford finally ended his career in the early 1930s as one of the most prolific Football League goalscorers of all time. After leaving Derby, he went on to play for Newcastle, Sunderland, Bradford Park Avenue and Chesterfield, and overall scored 326 goals in just 485 games. On retirement, and like many other players at the time, Bedford became a licensee and ran several pubs in and around Derbyshire.

It was a good year for Fulham forward Frank Osborne. The Craven Cottage side finished mid-table in tenth and despite playing in front of a creaking midfield – team-mate James Croal was 38, Andrew Ducat 37 and Danny O'Shea 36 – and alongside 40-year-old Fulham stalwart Walter White in his retirement year, Osborne scored ten goals among the club's meagre 43. It certainly impressed the England selectors, who promptly picked him for two internationals against Northern Ireland and France. Frank Osborne thus became the first Fulham player to be capped by England.

From the very start of the season, Leeds United were many people's favourites for promotion thanks to the meanness of their defence. The previous campaign had seen them finish eighth, but their defence had been superb. Captain Jim Baker and young Ernie Hart were a formidable centre-back pairing, and along with goalkeeper Fred Whalley, full-backs Duffield and Frew, they conceded a fairly miserly 38 goals, the equal third-best record in the division. The same back five kicked off the 1922/23 season and after 12 matches they had let in just nine goals. But Leeds still found themselves mid-table with five wins, three draws and four losses. United's problem was scoring goals – only ten in the first 12 matches. Manager Arthur Fairclough tried to solve the problem by dipping into the transfer market, but the 25-year-old player he signed couldn't even get a game in his then current club's first team. The Leeds faithful were totally underwhelmed – until the new man arrived. His name was Percy Whipp and there was good reason for him being a permanent understudy.

Whipp played for Sunderland and the man who also operated in his centre-forward position was a certain Charles Buchan, England's top striker. But Fairclough had scouts regularly monitoring the player in reserve games and, seeing a lot of potential in the Wearsiders' second-string striker, signed him up for £750; very soon, the Elland Road fans would be roundly applauding his shrewd pursuit. Whipp arrived in the city the day before United's home game against West Ham, and cheerfully told the Yorkshire press that he'd never been to Leeds before and knew little about the club. Twenty-four hours later, he was the toast of the city after scoring a hat-trick on his debut in a 3-1 win. After his first 12 games in a Leeds shirt, Whipp had scored ten goals and the fans had taken the Gorbals-born Scot to their heart, nicknaming him the 'Arch General'. A player described by the local press as 'possessing rare cunning', Whipp ended his first season at Elland Road as Leeds' top scorer, netting 15 goals in 29 games. Unfortunately the rest of the Leeds side couldn't quite match his effervescence; their season ended with a poor run of just five wins in 18 matches and they trailed home a disappointing seventh. But in Percy Whipp they had found a new star and the following season, he would prove to be a key and vital player in their first Second Division championship-winning campaign.

It was a very bad year indeed for Coventry and their hitherto well-respected captain George Chaplin. Earlier in his career while at Bradford City, defender Chaplin had gone through hell and back, losing over two years of his football career to chronic tuberculosis and nearly dying in the process. In 1923, he lost his entire future in the game after being found guilty of match-fixing.

The story began three years previously, when Coventry were voted into the Football League for the first time in their history. They found the leap from the Southern League into the Second Division an excruciatingly difficult one. Apart from Chaplin and a handful of other experienced players expensively signed in the close season, City were woefully short on all-round genuine professional quality and it soon began to show. They lost every single one of their first nine games and didn't manage a win until Christmas Day, when they narrowly squeaked past Stoke City 3-2. Results improved a little in the new year and throughout the spring, but come the last week of the season they were still in serious trouble. The woeful Grimsby Town had already finished rock bottom, many points adrift, so the second re-election place was now a two-horse race between Coventry and Lincoln City. Lincoln were two points ahead, but with just one game left to play, against the classy Huddersfield Town. Coventry had home and away matches against fifth-placed Bury, who were on a good run of form. Out of the 15 games they'd played before the Coventry game, the Shakers had won ten, drawn three and lost just twice. Nobody gave Coventry much of a chance in either game.

Coventry had invested heavily to get into the Football League and a lot of their board's money would have gone down the Swanee if City had lost their Football League status after just one season. So a treacherous plan was hatched by chairman Dave Cooke, who persuaded Chaplin to tap up a carefully targeted group of Bury players. Before the final two games were played, Chaplin was despatched to Lancashire with £200 of Cooke's money in cash. Five Bury players, two club directors and a club official all agreed to collude in making sure that the Shakers would 'go easy' on Coventry in the clashes, and so they did.

The first game at Highfield Road ended in a 2-2 draw. City fans were grateful for the lifeline but were also surprised at how poorly the usually classy Bury had played. The second game at Gigg Lane saw a shock 2-1 Coventry win, which meant they would stay up. But from early in the encounter, Bury's home fans were immediately suspicious. The core of their team was playing totally out of character. Consistent throughout the season, they were now giving the ball away, mis-directing passes and jumping out of tackles with depressing regularity. Rumours ran around the ground that something was afoot. From that afternoon, a whispering campaign began. Players talked to other players, fans passed on the rumours and the domestic game was alive once again with depressing allegations of match-fixing.

With their customary alacrity, it took the FA three years to launch an inquiry. Meanwhile, the blameless Lincoln had lost their Football League status and were struggling to stay in business in the Midland League. Chaplin denied all charges against him, which two decades later he would admit was a lie. Along with chairman Cooke and Coventry director Jack Marshall he was, however, found guilty and all three were banned from football, in any capacity, for life. The five Bury players, two directors and club official were similarly barred. Referring to the second match, one of the Bury players reportedly told the inquiry, 'Coventry played so badly we had trouble allowing them the result they needed.'

It brought a sad and tragic end to the career of a previously highly respected and admired footballer – a decent man who many in the game had predicted would go on to become an inspiring coach and manager. From what we know, it's hard to judge whether he fell prey to greed, stupidity or loyalty to his club and chairman or a mix of all three. Whatever, it destroyed his football career and his reputation. It would also bring the Second Division season to a sad end. The cheat tag would hang over Coventry City for years.

11

Third Division South

*'There is just so much hurt, disappointment
and oppression one can take ... the line
between reason and madness grows thinner.'*

Rosa Parks

IN 1923, the world of football contained just two genuinely professional leagues: one in England and the other in Scotland. As we will discover later, many new so-called amateur leagues around the globe contained a legion of clubs who made comparatively huge payments, under the counter, to secure the services of their country's best players, plus houses, cars and even plots of land. It was known in various nations as 'shamateurism', 'brown amateurism' and in some countries, just good old plain corruption. The lesser players turned out for peanuts, truly amateur.

In Britain, it was not the same. Whatever way you want to slice it, British football was a more honest affair that gave so many players a genuine opportunity to make a living out of sport. Our ever-expanding leagues took talented young sportsmen out of mines, factories, mills and hard physical labour, because to grow and improve our leagues, we introduced paid professionalism into the game. This was

123

probably the last genuine revolution that we contributed to world football.

We were the first nation to offer working-class men a different, more exciting journey in life. To lift them from the inevitability of hard labour in their local town and city, a future hitherto predetermined by their situation, their class and location, following on to do what their dads, brothers, cousins and uncles all did. After the end of World War One, the Football League was expanded and more and more talented young working-class men increasingly had an escape route from the inevitability of their lives into something totally life-changing, something good, something ambitious. In the lower leagues, no one was being paid a fortune, but for most they were earning a good bit more than their previous manual jobs to play a game they loved. Football became freeing. It became for the players who walked out of the pits and quit their jobs in the mills and factories, a new joy.

When football kicked off again after World War One, the Football League immediately grew from 40 to 44 clubs to create two equal divisions of 22. The failure of Glossop to be re-elected meant that five new clubs would join the new Second Division – West Ham United, South Shields, Rotherham County, Coventry City and the re-formed Stoke City. From there, the league's expansion continued apace. In 1920 the leading clubs from the Southern League were invited to form a third level, which was expanded further the following year by being split into a regional Third Division North and Third Division South of 22 teams in each. These would soon prove tough divisions to get out of, with just the champions of both going up to the Second Division. This was a particular gripe for clubs in the Third Division South, because a lot of big sides such as Portsmouth, Ipswich and Nottingham Forest had joined it from the old Southern League. But it allowed clubs to turn professional, or mostly pro alongside part-time players and amateurs.

The two teams relegated from the Second Division were assigned to the most appropriate league geographically, with many Midlands teams yo-yoing between the regionalised third tier to maintain an even balance.

The 1922/23 Third Division South champions were a steamrollering Bristol City, but this would be the beginning of the yo-yo years for the West Country Robins. From 1912/13 it had been a decade of swimming respectably along in and around the Second Division's mid-table waters. But in 1921/22 disaster struck. It was a league full of mediocre sides and at the end of the season, only six points separated the bottom 11 clubs. Bristol City found themselves down at the bottom, missing out on survival just a point behind Coventry. They arrived in the Third Division South for the first time with pretty much the same squad, highly tipped to be champions at the first ask. They didn't disappoint, ending 1922/23 with a scintillating run of 15 wins and two draws. At home they were virtually unplayable, recording 16 wins, four draws and only one defeat, scoring 43 goals and conceding just 13. They immediately bounced back to their natural home of the Second Division. Or perhaps it wasn't. The following season Bristol City were relegated back to the Third Division South, and the yo-yos continued through the following decade.

Runners-up in 1922/23 were Plymouth Argyle – as they were in 1921/22, and would be four more times over the next five years. The perennial nearly men, Argyle were so near, so close, so many times throughout the 1920s. Their second place in 1922/23 was particularly cruel as they ended the season with a superb unbeaten home record of 18 wins and three draws. A key member of their team was a loyal one-club player who would stay with Argyle for 14 years and a man who in 1923 was Britain's one and only black footballer. Jack Leslie was born in London to a Jamaican father and an English mother and after banging in over 250 goals for amateur side

Barking Town, he was signed up by Plymouth when he was 22 years old. He bagged his first professional goal in 1923 against Gillingham and over the coming years would form a formidable strike partnership with outside-left Sammy Black. They played together 327 times, scoring an amazing 319 goals between them.

Leslie was much beloved by the Plymouth fans and his reputation grew to such a point that as a Third Division player he was given an England call-up – and then he wasn't. After publicly naming him in the 13-man squad to play against Ireland in October 1925, and without apology or explanation, the FA removed his name from the list. This extraordinary and shameful story started innocently enough, when Leslie's manager Bob Jack proudly sat him down to share the great news of his selection. Jack, who was the father of Bolton's 1923 FA Cup Final scorer David Jack, couldn't have been hearing things wrongly because well-respected regional newspapers like the *Western Daily Press*, *Liverpool Echo* and *Birmingham Gazette* all named the same list of 13, which included Leslie. This was news, because not only was it rare for a Third Division player to be selected for England, but it would have made him the first black player to get a full international call-up. Leslie, his family and friends and the Plymouth fans were jubilant – not just a groundbreaking moment for Leslie and his loved ones but a great honour for Argyle.

Then everything went silent, until a week or so later the FA issued a revised team sheet which they again issued to the press. This time, Leslie's name had been omitted. He was not injured and had not been suspended. Just dropped without explanation. In his own words, 'All of a sudden everyone stopped talking about it. Sort of went dead quiet. Didn't look me in the eye. I didn't ask outright. I could see by their faces it was awkward. But I did hear, roundabout like, that the FA had come to have another look at me. Not at me football but at me face. They asked, and found they'd made a ricket. Found out about me daddy and that was it. There was a bit of an uproar in the papers. Folk in the town were very upset. No one ever told me official, like, but that had to be the reason. Me mum was English and me daddy was black as the ace of spades. There wasn't any other reason for taking my cap away.'

Some suggested that FA bigwigs had got nervous about picking a third-tier player. Yet the Third Division South's Charlton Athletic centre-half George Armitage played in the October 1925 international against Ireland. National and regional newspaper pundits universally regarded Leslie as a seriously good footballer and there had not been a scintilla of surprise when he'd been selected for the original squad, playing though he did for a lower-division side. It's inconceivable that the 14-man FA selection committee could have been unaware that he was black, so the only conclusion can be that external pressure was brought to bear on the FA to reverse his selection in the squad.

To this day, no one knows precisely what happened behind the scenes, because the FA lied, obfuscated and refused to explain, even claiming that he'd never been picked in the first place. It was all a mistake, a miscommunication. What seems totally obvious is that Leslie was denied a potential England cap simply because of the colour of his skin. The gates would be slammed shut and Leslie was never considered to play for the country in which he was born again. It was one of the most shameful incidents in the history of the FA – and in the early 1920s they were guilty of quite a few, as we will see later. On the same afternoon that England played out a dull, dreary draw against Ireland, Leslie scored twice in Plymouth's 7-2 hammering of Bournemouth & Boscombe Athletic. Screw you, FA.

Many decades on, Jack Leslie is still revered in Plymouth. A public campaign is currently under way to raise money for a permanent memorial in the shape of a bronze statue of him outside Argyle's Home Park ground – one and a half times as big as the man himself. The truth remains that in a fair, non-colonial, non-racist world, Leslie would have rightly been the first black footballer to play for England – and should have added many more caps thereafter. But the footballing establishment in 1923 were deeply conservative, prisoners of their time and its prejudices, deeply suspicious and fearful of anything or anyone different or maverick. It's why they also had a hard time with Fred Pagnam, a courageous character who continually refused to doff his cap to the powers-that-be.

In 1923, the Third Division South's top goalscorer was Watford's 32-year-old striker Pagnam, a man with a remarkable past. Stats-wise he enjoyed an incredible 1922/23 campaign, scoring 30 goals in 38 games for a side that only finished tenth. Watford managed 57 goals in total, with Pagnam scoring more than half of them. The grammar-school educated son of a bank manager, Pagnam was not your average footballer. Rather like running away to join the circus, he defied all family advice to follow his dream. Pagnam's father was furious at his choice, adamant that he was throwing away a good education and a potentially lucrative future in the world of finance. But Pagnam was never anything but self-willed. Articulate and highly principled, he had been brave enough to stand up against one of English football's worst and most notorious corruption scandals.

In 1915, Pagnam was playing First Division football for Liverpool. He was a big hit at Anfield. The season before, he'd scored an astonishing 26 goals in 31 appearances and become a great fan favourite. On Good Friday 1915 he ran out on to the Old Trafford pitch smouldering with anger and disgust. Pagnam knew that a core of players on his own side had arranged to throw the match as Manchester United would have been relegated if they'd lost. Worse still to Pagnam was that

Sunderland legend Charles Buchan.

The bronze statue of Lily Parr in Manchester's National Football Museum.

Brazil's first football superstar Arthur Friedenreich.

PC George Scorey on his white horse Billy, clearing the crowd at the 1923 FA Cup Final.

Jack Leslie, cheated of an England place

Clapton Orient's Owen Williams.

The Ham Cheeses – coach Syd Paynter, left, and manager Syd King, suited and booted for a West Ham training session in 1923.

Clapton Orient players enjoy the traditional half-time refreshments – oranges and water from enamel buckets.

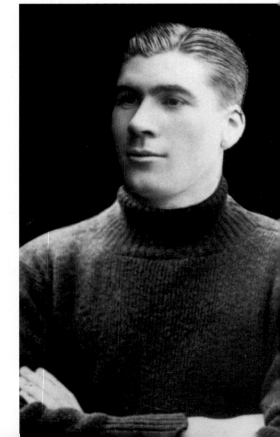

Liverpool's legendary long-serving goalie Elisha Scott.

Cigarette card of Bolton Wanderers FA Cup Final winning team.

Amateur football's ultimate purists, the Corinthians.

West Ham's FA Cup runners-up and promotion-winning side.

players from both sides were using the scam as an opportunity to personally make a lot of money from illegal bets on the game. Pagnam let his team-mates know in no uncertain terms that the whole deal stank and he would have nothing to do with it.

The fix was that United would be allowed to win 2-0. Pagnam told his team he'd do everything in his power to score and ruin their dirty bets. Halfway through the game, Pagnam broke free, shot for goal and hit the crossbar. Players rounded on him furiously and his team-mates made sure he wasn't passed to again. Once Manchester United reached the agreed scoreline, a farce of a match played out with the ball spending more time in the stands than on the pitch. United got their manufactured 2-0 win and escaped relegation by a single point. As a result, Tottenham and Chelsea were, unfairly, relegated.

National newspapers smelt a rat, as did the FA, who immediately launched an official investigation. Pagnam and United's George Anderson both bravely broke the dressing room 'omerta' and testified against their team-mates. Pagnam told the FA he'd shared a taxi to the ground with Jackie Sheldon, and during the trip, his captain offered him £3 to be part of the fix. Seven of the ringleaders – Liverpool's Sheldon, Thomas Fairfoul, Bob Pursell and Tom Miller and Manchester United's Sandy Turnbull, Enoch West and Arthur Whalley – were found guilty and all given life bans. Neither club was found to be culpable in any way, the FA totally satisfied that they knew nothing about the players' plot. Not surprisingly, Pagnam was not popular with many of his team-mates.

In 1919 he signed for Arsenal in a £1,500 deal. Pagnam was an immediate hit at the newly built Highbury, scoring 26 goals in 50 league games. But Arsenal were struggling to pay for their new stadium, and when Second Division Cardiff City came in with a £3,000 offer for Pagnam the Gunners' board decided to cash in one of their major assets and double their money. Once again Pagnam stepped up to the plate, scoring eight goals in Cardiff's last 14 matches, helping power them to promotion into the top league. But the first half of the 1921/22 season was not a success for Pagnam and back in the top flight he failed to score a single goal in his first 13 games. There were rumours of behind-the-scenes fall-outs with fellow players and coaching staff and the Welsh club took a big financial hit by selling Pagnam on. Not to a fellow First Division side, nor even a second-tier club. Third Division South club Watford stepped in with what for them was a record £1,000 fee. For football pundits of the day, it was an audacious move by the Hornets but a baffling one. Why would one of the top division's leading scorers drop down the pyramid to a club who had never risen above the bottom level?

It was a coup for Watford, and Pagnam quickly showed why they'd signed him. Still only 31, and despite his recent lean spell at Cardiff – the only one in his entire career – he netted 17 goals in 27 games for the Hornets in the 1921/22 Third Division South season. His 30 goals in 1922/23 included three hat-tricks during a run of five matches. In March 1923, *Gem* magazine had no doubts about his enduring skills, 'A harder or more whole-hearted player than Pagnam would be difficult to find, and he seems as strong as a horse.'

But by all accounts, Pagnam continued to be a difficult character to work alongside. He was described at the time as 'a nonconformist whose personality was not universally popular'. During his time playing with the Hornets, he was forced to apologise to the directors because of his behaviour towards some of his team-mates.

It was not a good year for the Welsh in the Third Division South, with Aberdare and Newport County ending up as the bottom two. At that year's end-of-season Football League AGM, clubs voted on who should be re-elected or indeed elected into the following season's competition. Fans of Aberdare and Newport breathed heavy sighs of relief as both garnered an overwhelming 45 votes each; Boscombe took 28 votes, Llanelli nine, and Pontypridd eight. A frustrated Torquay United received not one single vote, and Aberdare and Newport were duly re-elected. But Boscombe would also join them, which pointed out the complications of trying to balance two essentially regional leagues, when two clubs were relegated each year from the fully national Second Division – and only one promoted from each of the third tiers.

In 1922/23, Rotherham County and Wolves were both relegated down into the Third Division North. That levelled the division back up to 22 teams. With Third Division South champions Bristol City going up into the Second Division, that left it one club short. Step forward Boscombe. Just to confuse things a little further, weeks after being elected to the Football League, Boscombe changed their name to Bournemouth & Boscombe Athletic.

In many ways, Aberdare and Newport benefited from the massive churn there had been in recent years, 'lifting up' previously smaller-league clubs into the expanded Football League. It would have been hard, if not unfair, to expect those new clubs to instantly establish themselves as professional sides if they were only given a season or two to prove themselves. As it was, Aberdare and Newport improved massively the following season, both ending up mid-table. Though for Aberdare, the 1923/24 season was not without its problems. On 7 November an accidental fire raged through the main stand and offices of their ground, which also destroyed the players' kit. An appeal for help led to the donation of boots in various sizes from all over Wales, and for their next home game against Brighton they turned out in amber-and-black-striped shirts given to them by nearby Newport, as opposed to their usual claret and blue.

12

Third Division North

'When the gods wish to punish us they answer our prayers.'

Oscar Wilde, *An Ideal Husband*, 1895

NELSON IS a small former mill town four miles north of Burnley in east Lancashire. In 1923 it had a population of just 39,000 people, and against all the odds, their football club became champions of the Third Division North. For the purposes of this book, we could just go through the facts and stats of the one and only honour season in their short history. But buried beneath every simple story is a much greater and wider narrative thread. And there's a strange thing about small, seemingly unremarkable towns and their football clubs that you may only have vaguely heard about, because the deeper you dig the more remarkable they become.

Here are a few facts about Nelson that you probably didn't know. In 1918, to mark the end of World War One, local confectioner Thomas Fryer invented the jelly baby. A couple of years later, his Nelson-based company created Victory Vs. Nelson was the birthplace of one of Britain's most innovative, most successful and unsung coaches and managers of all time, Jimmy Hogan. In 1923 he was effectively being blackballed by

English football. Because of its strong left-wing affiliations, Nelson was known as 'Little Moscow'. The cotton mills in the town were heavily trade unionised and many local workers had joined the Communist Party. Though small in size, Nelson was a place that fought big for workers' rights and apart from the mill owners and their managers who lived in the big houses up the hill, was almost exclusively a working-class town.

Yet prior to the Industrial Revolution, Nelson did not exist – a rare Victorian community that came into existence from virtually nothing. It was a town built on cotton weaving and by the time of the 1921 Census, 88.9 per cent of the adult population, around 17,000 people in total, worked in the local mills. By 1923 its population made Nelson the smallest community to have a professional football team. Nelson were tiny minnows in the game, having just fought their way into the Third Division North the season before after years playing in regional leagues. Their first season in the big time had been a struggle. Hovering in and around the bottom places throughout the campaign, Nelson limped home just four points above the re-election places in 16th.

Their ambitious young player-manager David Wilson decided upon drastic action and for their second season he got rid of 13 members of his squad and recruited extensively. Wilson proved to be a shrewd operator in the transfer market, thanks largely to two things. He'd arrived at Nelson from Oldham Athletic where he had played over 400 matches – and he was still a current player. Wilson had played against everyone and everybody, knew all of their respective worths on the pitch and was canny enough to work out which of them he might manage to attract to the tiny, highly unfashionable Nelson. Allied to his own knowledge, Wilson had three other brothers who were playing professional football at the time: Andrew, for The Wednesday and Scotland; James at St Mirren and Preston North End; Alec played for Oldham and Preston

North End. Wilson endlessly picked their brains about players they rated and who might do a job for him at Nelson, and he got them to put out feelers to footballers they played alongside or knew. With great attention to detail, he pieced together a squad of players who would do Nelson proud.

At the core of his title-winning team were several hugely consistent performers. Twenty-three-year-old Scotsman John Black was a particularly key player for Nelson. With astonishing versatility, he was able to instantly fill gaps caused through injury or suspension and during the championship-winning season he played in four different forward positions, at half-back, and at full-back. No doubt he would have happily gone in goal if the keeper had been injured, but Nelson were well served in that department. Joseph Bird played all 40 games for the side that season and though small for a goalkeeper, standing only 5ft 9in tall, he was renowned as an agile shot-stopper.

Centre-half Ernie Braidwood was also an ever-present throughout the campaign, the rock upon which Nelson's defence was built. Six-footers were rare in the early 1920s, so it was no surprise that cartoonists in the local newspapers depicted Ernie as the 'Skyscraper'. He rarely had an off-day during the championship-winning season and not surprisingly, gave virtually nothing away in the air. Wing-half Ted Broadhurst was Nelson's 'water carrier', a tireless, never-say-die performer. He would become a fan legend at Seedhill first as a player, then as a coach and trainer, and in the 1922/23 season missed only two league games. Nelson were also astute on the transfer front. In February 1923 they strengthened their squad, signing inside-forward Dick Crawshaw from Halifax Town for £100. After scoring on his debut in a tight 1-0 win over Wigan, Crawshaw helped power the club towards the title with five key goals in the final dozen games.

One player Wilson most determinedly wanted to hang on to after their first league season was diminutive inside-forward

Joe Eddleston. In a poor campaign, Eddleston ended up top scorer with 17 goals. He was once again the top scorer when the championship was won, bagging 22 goals in the league. The 5ft 5in Eddleston stayed at Nelson for five years, scoring 97 goals in 183 appearances. They ended the season on 51 points with 24 wins, three draws and 11 defeats, four points clear of their nearest rivals Bradford Park Avenue. Seedhill had been turned into a fortress and Nelson ended the season with a stellar home record of 15 wins, two draws and two defeats, scoring 37 goals and conceding just ten. Wilson himself, now aged 38, turned out as a player nearly 30 times that season – and would not retire from playing at Nelson until he reached 40.

Come the close season, Nelson were in seventh heaven. New work on Seedhill bumped the capacity up to 25,000 and facilities for players and staff were greatly improved. If the players thought that winning the championship had made their year, more was yet to come. Over the summer the board paid for them to travel to Spain to play a string of friendly matches. While there, and somewhat astonishingly, the little Lancashire upstarts became the first English club to beat Real Madrid on their own ground. They prevailed 4-2 with two of the goals coming from the in-form Dick Crawshaw. To make it a truly successful trip, Nelson went on to beat Real Oviedo 2-1. So they would go into the following season on a high. Sadly, and such is football, it did not – could not – last. In the second tier of English football for the first time in their history, they would pull one of their biggest ever crowds – 12,000 – for their first match, a 1-1 home draw with Clapton Orient. It would take them another eight games to get a win, 2-0 at home to Stoke City on 29 September. Nelson battled hard throughout the season but were well out of their depth.

The Third Division North runners-up in 1923 were Bradford Park Avenue, just four points off the champions

Nelson but no cigar, as only the divisional winners were promoted. My grandad had been going regularly to Park Avenue before World War One and these had been, as far as things go, the glory days. At the end of the 1914/15 season the club achieved their highest league position, ninth in the First Division. In the dull hotchpotch days of unplanned, build-upon-build football grounds their Park Avenue stadium was a thing of beauty, re-designed by the age's top sports architect, Archibald Leitch, and featuring an unusual double-decker stand that served both the football ground and the adjoining cricket pitch, used for decades by Yorkshire County Cricket Club.

After the war, my grandad was witness to a slow decline. In 1921 Park Avenue were relegated from the First Division and the following year experienced an even more dismal season, relegated once again, into Third Division North. For 1922/23 the board pledged to stop the rot and start the climb back up the leagues. They made some handy close-season signings and throughout the campaign, and like Nelson, were virtually impregnable at home with 14 wins, four draws and just the one defeat. But similar to their previous two relegation seasons, Avenue remained shaky on the road with just five wins, five draws and nine defeats, which left them short of promotion. It would take some years before Bradford Park Avenue would rise again above the bottom division.

Elsewhere in Third Division North, 1923 was not a particularly happy story for a clutch of clubs. Sadly, one team decided to voluntarily leave at the end of the season. Though finishing a very respectable 11th and with one of the division's best home records, of 13 wins, two draws and four defeats, Stalybridge Celtic, to the shock of their fans, decided to call it a day as a professional club and resigned. One of the founder members of the Third Division North just two years previously, they decided to move back down into the smaller regional Cheshire County League.

With an average attendance that season of 5,480, the board surprisingly decided that they didn't have enough local support to justify having a Football League team – despite the fact that on 17 January 1923, Stalybridge played West Bromwich Albion in an FA Cup first round replay at Bower Fold in front of 9,753, their record attendance. At the end of 1922/23 Stalybridge's average attendance was certainly one of the lowest in the division, but hardly shoddy. It was a contentious decision to quit professional football that hit local fans hard. They'd stuck with them through the years of amateur regional football and now having a professional league club had become a matter of local pride. As often happens, it had put their town on the map. Whatever, it remains a mystery that the club suddenly lost all impetus and ambition despite doing fairly well in the Third Division North. The sad consequence was that Stalybridge lost its professional team and the Football League was robbed of one of its most well-appointed grounds, the wonderfully scenic Bower Fold, set as it was on a green, verdant hillside deep within the Pennines, surrounded by woods, forests and rolling pastures.

It was not a good year for the north-east, with Durham City finishing bottom and Ashington one place above them. Both were forced to apply for re-election; both were successful. Durham's brief sojourn in the Football League would be short and not very sweet. Only formed in 1918, they were elected to the Third Division North in 1921 and actually finished a very respectable 11th. But their Holiday Park ground was anything but. One of the most basic grounds ever to grace the Football League, its only facility was a low, wooden-seated stand. Crowds were low and the ancient cathedral and university city never really took football to its heart. They finally got kicked out of the league in 1928.

Little did they know it in 1922/23, but Durham City had a huge star in the making turning out for their reserves. A miner during the week, local lad George Camsell would break into Durham's first team and turn professional the following season then score 20 goals in just 21 games. From there, he never looked back. One of the most remarkable goalscorers ever to play in English football, Camsell went on to sign for Middlesbrough and in the 1926/27 season he scored a remarkable 59 goals – including nine hat-tricks – in 37 league games. The following season, Everton legend Dixie Dean would beat his record tally by one, but Camsell was just getting started. He would be Boro's top scorer for the next ten seasons, bagging 344 goals in 453 appearances. Perhaps as remarkably, he played nine games for England and scored 18 goals. After he retired, Camsell became a scout for Middlebrough and discovered a young man called Brian Clough.

The previous year, Ashington finished a very respectable tenth. A founding member of Third Division North and home of the northernmost team ever to play in the Football League, Ashington was an extraordinary football and sporting talent pool as the home to Jack and Bobby Charlton and their footballing cousins Jackie, Jim and Stan Milburn; Newcastle United striker Jimmy Richardson; future Burnley manager Jimmy Adamson; Leeds United goalkeeper John 'Safe as Houses' Potts and dozens of other Ashingtonians who left to play for a myriad of Football League clubs. Add to that cricketers Steve and Ben Harmison, Olympic gold medal rower Katherine Copeland and European Tour golfer Kenneth Ferrie, and it's clear that for such a small and remote town, Ashington has always had an amazing sporting pedigree. Unfortunately, in terms of football, its best players never stayed for long, being snapped up by the bigger fish in the pond.

Perhaps unsurprisingly, Durham were the division's worst-supported club with an average home gate of 2,108. The next-worst were Stalybridge Celtic with an average gate of 3,874 and alarmingly, this meant that the club had haemorrhaged nearly a quarter of its home support from the previous season, when the average gate at Broadhurst Park was 4,979. This sharp fall in attendances was mirrored right across the division for clubs that hailed from industrial and mining areas increasingly affected by the economic downturn.

13

The Battle of Britain

'O Flower of Scotland, when will we
see your like again?'

Roy Williamson of The Corries

INTERNATIONALLY, BRITISH football in 1923 was still a comparatively small and local state of affairs. The World Cup would not be launched until 1930, there were no remotely meaningful international European tournaments and match-ups against other countries outside Great Britain were exclusively conducted on a friendly or exhibition basis. The lack of international competition at the time was exemplified by the fact that a friendly between England and France in Paris in April 1923 would be the first time that the two countries would actually play an official senior international together. Scotland would not play an international game outside the British Isles until 1929.

There was, however, one major tournament that did exist and yearly, it consumed the passions of fans the length and breadth of the British Isles. Launched in 1883 and the oldest international tournament in the world, the British Home Championship was rightly nicknamed the 'Battle of Britain' – played between England, Scotland, Wales and Ireland

(Northern Ireland from the 1950s onwards), an annual tussle aimed at gaining the bragging rights to be named the best national team in Britain. In 1923, England still rather loftily regarded itself as the greatest footballing nation. The truth is that it wasn't even the best in Great Britain.

Over the course of a season, all four teams would play one another once, the final games usually being at the end of the domestic campaigns. The fixtures were organised so that each country would play a home game and two away one season, and then two at home, one away the next. Inward-looking British fans and pundits alike regarded it as nothing less than the top international championship competition on the planet, its annual winners therefore de facto world champions.

Though this somewhat oversells the tournament, it was truly competitive. Despite the fact that England had by far the biggest and deepest of professional leagues among the four sides, they hadn't managed a single tournament win since before World War One. In 1919/20 Wales would be winners; for the following two tournaments, it would be Scotland who came out on top. In 1923 England were desperate to regain the title. Two simple facts continued to have them on the back foot. Number one was the overwhelming strength of Scottish football and Scottish footballers in general. The Scottish Football League's powerhouse was Rangers and under the leadership of the club's most successful manager, Bill Struth, the Gers would win 14 league titles between 1920 and 1939. But this was not the two-horse race that the Scottish Premiership is today. Celtic at the time were a strong and talented team, but so too were Airdrieonians, Aberdeen, Kilmarnock, Falkirk, Hibernian, Dundee and St Mirren. In addition, ever since the Football League had turned professional, English clubs were packed full of Scottish players who were often superior in technique and skill compared to their English counterparts, thanks to Scotland's 'invention' and development of the 'passing game'.

Secondly, most of Wales's and Ireland's best footballers also turned out for the best English and Scottish clubs, playing in Britain's most competitive games week in, week out. Ireland's regular right-back David Rollo was a mainstay at Blackburn Rovers; William Emerson was a regular at Burnley and Ernest Smith at Cardiff City; David Lyner played for Manchester United, Robert Irvine for Everton and Patrick Nelis at Nottingham Forest. The Welsh squad included Bolton Wanderers pair William Jennings and Edward Vizard; Ivor Jones at West Brom; Edward Parry at Liverpool and Port Vale's Edward Peers. Wales were certainly no makeweights either, having won the 1919/20 British Home Championship with players who would form the core of their 1923 squad.

But Scotland were in the ascendency. The Thistles had won the previous two championships and key to their hopes in making it a hat-trick were two players who were in amazing club form as strikers. Thirty-two-year-old Andy Cunningham would soon end his career at Rangers after scoring 162 goals in just 350 games, averaging nearly one every second match. His partner-in-crime was Andy Wilson, who across the two seasons prior to the tournament had bagged an amazing 51 goals in 77 games as Middlesbrough's star striker. Together, they formed a formidable strike force.

England went in with a blend of older and internationally inexperienced players, sometimes a mixture of both. FA Cup Final loser John Tresadern of West Ham would make his debut aged 33. Huddersfield Town's goalkeeper Edward Taylor and Liverpool stalwart Ephraim Longworth were both 36; Chelsea's Jack Harrow 34; West Brom's Joseph Smith, 32. Over the three games, England would use an astonishing total of 25 different players, handing debuts to no fewer than nine of them.

Though the England fans and the squad themselves seemed desperate for success, there was a sense that the FA largely shrugged their shoulders when it came to the 1923 championship. They had had recent fall-outs with England's best and most prolific striker at the time, Charles Buchan, who despite scoring 30 goals that season for Sunderland was not selected for a single British Home Championship game in 1923. As a prominent member of the players' union he had clashed with the football establishment over their insistence in reducing the maximum wage from £10 a week down to £8. This was a man who did not suffer fools gladly and was not afraid to speak up for himself and those around him. A deeply conservative organisation, the FA did not like troublemakers and overlooked him. In doing so, and not for the first or last time, the dinosaurs at the FA would shoot themselves in the foot. There have been so many times during our footballing history that fans, players and clubs have justifiably felt that our national body has let us all down, by spending more time high-handedly opposing rather than supporting the people who really mattered in our national game. This was just another one.

The games were fitted in between domestic fixture schedules, with the 1923 British Home Championship actually starting in 1922. On 21 October England played Ireland at West Bromwich Albion's The Hawthorns, the match pulling in just over 20,000 fans. Not a huge crowd, but truth be told, the match most English fans wanted to watch was against the Auld Enemy, Scotland. Those present witnessed an encounter witheringly described by *The Times* thus, 'Nearly 20,000 people watched the game without becoming enthusiastic. There was no reason why they should do so.' By all accounts it was a disappointing game with a high wind blowing straight down the middle of the pitch spoiling a lot of the play. England attacked relentlessly but few players were able to shoot straight because of the weather conditions. It would be Chambers who was the difference between the two sides, one player who managed to get two decisive shots on target.

On 3 March 1923, Ireland went down to their second defeat, this time 1-0 to Scotland at Belfast's Windsor Park. According to *The Scotsman*, 'On the run of the game, Scotland scarcely deserved to win for the Irishmen played very well indeed, and [William] Harper, the Scottish goalkeeper, had far more work to do than [George] Farquharson of Ireland.'

Striker Andy Wilson scored from a fortunate rebound after a double Farquharson save, but otherwise struggled to make any impression on a solid Irish defence marshalled by 39-year-old veteran Bill McCracken, who'd just retired from club football to become Hull City manager. In his many years at Newcastle United, the wily campaigner was credited with, if not actually inventing the offside trap, pretty much perfecting it. So successful was his defensive ploy that it led in 1925 to a change in the offside law – two instead of three defending players had to be between the foremost attacker and the goal line. Rare indeed that a footballer's tactical shrewdness has changed the laws of the game.

Two days later, England travelled to Cardiff City's old Ninian Park ground looking to jump above Scotland with a win. Though the crowd of 12,000 was disappointing, the game was most certainly not, *The Times* calling it an 'exciting, interesting match'.

The first goal of the game came flying off the boot of Welsh captain Fred Keenor from 30 yards out on 17 minutes. Keenor would become an all-time great at Cardiff, where he would play over 500 games and be captain in 1927 when the Bluebirds became, to date, the only non-English club to win the FA Cup.

He also led Cardiff to an FA Charity Shield win and four Welsh titles, and a life-sized statue of him currently stands outside the Cardiff City Stadium. As a Wales player, he featured in three of the nation's British Home Championship wins in 1920, 1924 and 1928.

Keenor was a hard-tackling terrier of a defender and made his debut at Cardiff just before the outbreak of war. Fighting as a member of the Footballers' Battalion at the Battle of the Somme, he was so badly injured that it looked highly unlikely that the young Welshman would ever play football again. Keenor suffered a severe shrapnel wound to the thigh and for months, it was touch and go whether or not his leg would require amputation.

England chalked up a lucky equaliser on 36 minutes when a weak shot from striker Harry Chambers kicked up off the mud and deflected past Wales goalkeeper Edward Peers. After the break, West Ham's Vic Watson charged down an Edward Parry clearance and shot beyond the diving Peers to send England 2-1 ahead. With minutes to go, fate decided to equal out the luck on the day; Edward Taylor palmed out a shot and it fell straight into the path of Ivor Jones, who slotted past the goalie to make it 2-2. Honours even.

For Wales, the draw would mean a final game playing for the wooden spoon against Ireland. Both sides felt themselves unlucky, having played well in their first two matches, and thought they'd deserved more. So the meeting at Wrexham's Racecourse ground on 14 April 1923 had an edge to it. Tackles flew in for the first ten minutes of what promised to be a feisty affair, but Wales were strangely off their best, often giving the ball away. By half-time Ireland were 3-0 up with two goals from Everton inside-forward Bobby Irvine and one from forward Billy Gillespie. After a stolid second half, that's how the game would end. Gillespie would be a stalwart for both club and country. His Sheffield United career, war-interrupted, stretched from 1913 to 1932. On his retirement as a player, Gillespie became manager of Derry City throughout the 1930s, where he was held in such high esteem, the Northern Ireland club changed their colours to red and white stripes in honour of his long career at Sheffield United. For Ireland he won 25 caps and scored 13 international goals. On his debut for Ireland in 1913, he scored two goals, giving them their first victory over England.

The Home Championship decider came along three days later, when Scotland played England at Hampden Park. The equation was simple – England needed a win, Scotland just a point. Though 71,000 turned up, it was regarded by the SFA as a poor crowd by usual standards. The price of admission had been raised to two shillings and thousands of Glaswegians, narked with the increase, voted with their feet. They missed out on a match that *The Times* described with an understated and refreshing absence of hyperbole as 'fast and interesting throughout'. England took the lead on 21 minutes when Sheffield United's Fred Tunstall crossed for Burnley's Robert Kelly to head home from close in. Tunstall, a former pony driver in South Yorkshire's coalmines, would become one of the Blades' most long-serving players, turning out 437 times. Two years after this match, Kelly would break the British transfer record when he moved from Burnley to Sunderland for £6,550.

Six minutes later, Scotland were back level when a mistake by West Ham's John Tresadern let in St Mirren's Denis Lawson. His shot was saved at full length by Edward Taylor, but the keeper could only push the ball into the path of Andy Cunningham who slotted home from close range. In what was becoming an end-to-end game, England gained the lead once more just before half-time.

Another impressive run and centre by Tunstall was headed home by Vic Watson, a player who was given precious few opportunities to shine for England. He won only five international caps, scoring four times, and yet despite scoring 325 goals for West Ham in league and cup throughout the 1920s and early 1930s was given little chance to establish himself in an England shirt.

Ten minutes after the break, there was another crucial error by the England defence, this time the culprit being Huddersfield's Sam Wadsworth, who let in Wilson for an easy tap-in. Honours were even but the point proved enough for Scotland to win the title for the third season running.

Scotland's Wilson ended up as the tournament's top scorer with four goals, which continued an amazing run of form for his country. In a Scotland shirt Wilson gained 12 caps between 1920 and 1923 and scored an impressive 13 goals. Like many players of his generation, he missed out on greater honours because of World War One. He was also yet another player who'd been invalided home. For the rest of his playing career, Wilson wore a specially made glove to mask and protect a withered hand and forearm that had been shattered by enemy fire at Arras. Due to recurring problems with the injury, Wilson's arm eventually had to be amputated. It didn't stop him achieving a single-digit golf handicap, regularly making century breaks at snooker and despite being Scottish, playing lawn bowls for England.

England overcame their disappointment by playing their first senior international against France on 10 May in front of a packed 50,000 crowd in Paris's Stade Pershing. With England running out 4-1 winners, the standout story was double scorer Jackie Hegan. He'd made his England debut earlier in the year against Belgium, also scoring twice, in a thumping 6-1 win. Even for 1923 Hegan was a total anomaly. While his team-mates turned out professionally for top First Division sides like Liverpool and Bolton, the Sandhurst-trained army officer played as an amateur for Corinthians. An outside-left, he first appeared for the top amateur club in 1919 after turning up as part of the army team they were due to play. Corinthians found themselves three players short, so Hegan was 'lent' to the London-based team. He would stay with them for the next 14 years, scoring 50 goals in 167 matches. He won a further two caps later in the year, against the Belgians again and Northern Ireland, making him one of the last amateurs to play for a full England side. He also ended up England's top scorer in 1923 with his four goals.

Ironically, the celebrations following his first goal against France tell us much about the culture of English football officialdom in 1923. England's captain on the day, Charles Buchan, wrote about the incident in his autobiography: 'After half an hour's play, Hegan scored the first goal for England. As captain I was so delighted that I ran across and shook Hegan's hand. Though I never thought about it for the rest of the game, I got a severe reprimand from the FA member in charge of the team after it was over. It seemed that hand-shaking was one of those things that wasn't done.' Or more specifically, the snobbish FA official disapproved of a professional player shaking the hand of a 'gentleman amateur', a non-professional. Making excuses for their team's defeat, the French press made much of the fact that their team was amateur and that England were largely a team of 'highly paid players' of one amateur and ten professionals versus 11 French amateurs. As we will discover later in this book, the French team was far from amateur, packed full as it was by players who earned a very good under-the-counter 'ghost' living from their clubs.

In October, it was back to Home Internationals business for England as the 1923/24 tournament kicked off its first match in Belfast. Hegan would win his fourth and final cap, but his team would start the campaign with a poor 2-1 defeat at Windsor Park. The *Sunday Post* gave a succinct account of the game: 'The Ireland v England match at Belfast, which was witnessed by 25,000 people, was remarkable inasmuch as what was reckoned only a second-rate Irish team successfully held, and finally beat, the cream of English football. Liverpool, Blackburn, Rangers and Celtic all declined to allow Irish players time off, and Ireland had as a consequence to select six substitutes. Therefore while not a true test of international games, the match was remarkable for Ireland's splendid display and victory.'

One of Ireland's six substitutes was an obscure young footballer called Tucker Croft, who played for a tiny and long-defunct amateur Belfast club, Queen's Island. It would of course be Croft who scored the winning goal late on in the second half. The *Sunday Post* commented, 'Such a scene as followed was never witnessed probably in Belfast since Ireland first beat England here in 1913, but all said and done the Irish victory by 2-1 was thoroughly deserved.' Ironically, the man who had scored the two goals in that 1913 win, Billy Gillespie, was key to this Irish victory and subsequently named in many press reports as the man of the match. It would be Hegan's last international but he would continue to play as an amateur for Corinthians until 1933, his final match an exhibition against a Combined Danish XI.

England's quest to win their first British Home Championship since before the war started badly in October 1923 and then flipped totally belly-up in the spring of 1924. Ending up with no wins, one draw and two defeats, a dismal England took home the wooden spoon in fourth place. It would be a resurgent Wales who took the championship with a clean sweep of three wins; tournament favourites Scotland were mediocre runners-up, chalking up a win, a draw and a defeat, with Ireland coming third again with one win, against England, and two defeats.

In 1923, the English footballing establishment, players and fans still regarded themselves as football's pioneers, the only proper professional league, though Scotland would have disagreed. They could not have been more wrong. Around the globe, the world of football was beginning to change. It would become the year when England's delusions of grandeur first started to be revealed for the smoke, mirrors and illusions it had become. It was not for a lack of money, hard work and endeavour, but a paucity of imagination and a reluctance to look outwards and take on new ideas.

14

North of the Border

*'Of all the small nations of the Earth, perhaps
only the ancient Greeks surpass the Scots in
their contribution to mankind.'*

Winston Churchill

IN 1981, workers on a major renovation project at Stirling
Castle carefully removed an oak-panelled ceiling in a bedroom
that was once used by a young Mary Queen of Scots during the
16th century. To their surprise, they discovered a grey leather
football lodged in the rafters that experts – and the *Guinness
Book of Records* – believe is the oldest leather football on the
planet. Tests confirmed that it was made sometime between
1540 and 1570 and though unorganised kickabout football had
been played long ago in everywhere from China to medieval
Europe, this remains the oldest panelled leather, pig bladder
ball still in existence. Half the size of a modern football, it's
believed to have been used by the young Mary and her court
friends in frenzied kickabouts in Stirling Castle. It is perhaps
apt that this was found in Scotland.

England is generally regarded as where modern football
was 'invented' – and for a lot of good reasons. The facts
are incontrovertible: the world's first actual football club

was Sheffield FC; the globe's first fully organised football tournament was the Football League; the first professional clubs began in England. But there is an extremely compelling argument that from the late Victorian period onwards and well into the 1920s, by far the biggest influence on the development of world football as we know it today, its method of play and tactics, came not from England but from the Scots. It all began at Queen's Park Football Club, who developed a short-passing game that would become the default setting for Scottish football.

In 1923, football in Scotland was well and truly the people's game, its greatest and most loved live entertainment. The big-city teams like Rangers, Celtic, Hibs, Hearts, Aberdeen and the Dundees were regularly pulling in large and passionate crowds. Before Wembley and Manchester City's Maine Road opened in 1923, the three biggest football stadiums in the world were all in Scotland – Hampden Park, Ibrox and Celtic Park. For a country of only 4.5 million, it contained in 1923 two professional divisions plus a dizzying network of junior and amateur leagues that stretched from Dumfries in the south to John O'Groats in the far north. Scots had brought football for the first time to a host of South American countries and by the 1920s, their managers, coaches and players were changing football throughout continental Europe.

Rangers celebrated their golden anniversary by becoming Scottish champions, and under their inspirational boss Bill Struth they ended the campaign with an unbeaten home record and overall, 23 wins out of 38 league games. The team who pushed them all the way in 1922/23 in runners-up spot would prove to be their major rivals for the next four seasons – and they didn't hail from the green and white side of Glasgow. Airdrieonians came from the small town of Airdrie, 12 miles east of Scotland's second city. In 1923 it had a population of less than 25,000 and the season before Airdrieonians had finished 16th, just five points above the relegation places. The campaign before that, Airdrieonians were mid-table in tenth. Their best league finish had been third in 1912/13, so this was not a club with any particular pedigree. The major reason they suddenly became such a force in Scottish football was down to good luck and good judgement in signing three young attackers from smaller clubs, Hughie Gallacher, Bob McPhail and Willie Russell, who quickly became the country's most feared strike force.

At 15, Gallacher was playing amateur football for local junior sides and working ten-hour shifts at Hattenrigg pit in North Lanarkshire. Though precociously talented, senior teams passed on signing him because of his diminutive size. Seemingly weedy in stature and standing just 5ft 5in tall in his stockinged feet, it wasn't until Gallacher was 17 that the newly formed Queen of the South took a chance on him as a professional player. After a season playing for the Dumfries club, a host of other teams were soon in for him. His next destination would be Airdrieonians' Broomhill Park, where he would team up with more new signings – 17-year-old inside-left Bob McPhail and 21-year-old inside-right Willie Russell.

Despite his size, Gallacher was a keen amateur boxer and tough and uncompromising on the pitch – he needed to be. Defenders soon grew to loathe him. Fearless and fast, he ran relentlessly at opponents and with his immaculate close control and dribbling skills was almost impossible to knock off the ball by fair means. So foul it was, one crunching, illegal challenge after another. After many matches he would trot off with his legs, socks and boots covered in blood. As a youngster he started the 1922/23 season in and out of the first team – by its end, he was Airdrieonians' regular first-choice centre-forward.

Alongside Gallacher on the left was the even younger McPhail, lightning-fast, supremely comfortable on the ball and 'football wise' well beyond his tender years. To the right was Russell, a tough-as-teak inside-forward who would soon become 'the great provider', the master of the assist.

But much, much more was to come. The following year, they would win Airdrieonians' one and only major trophy honour, the Scottish Cup, and once again be Division One runners-up, again behind Rangers. Gallacher would be named man of the match in their 2-0 Scottish Cup Final win against Hibernian. Of the showpiece, McPhail would observe, 'The terror-like attitude of Gallacher caused havoc with the Hibs defenders. He and Russell were easily our best forwards.' In 1924/25 and 1925/26, Airdrieonians would finish as Division One runners-up for the third and fourth times in a row.

In their time at Airdrie, Gallacher would score 100 goals in 129 matches and McPhail 75 in 114, and though more the provider than a prolific goalscorer, Russell scored a very handy 37 in 127 appearances. It was, however, inevitable that the three amigos would all move on to appear on bigger stages. Gallacher played with a swagger on the pitch and was not shy off it. A feisty character, he was often fined and suspended for arguing with referees, team-mates and club staff. Married at 17 and separated a couple of years afterwards, he liked a good scrap, was never a stranger to controversy and had a justifiably high opinion of his footballing skills. He was arrogant, but understandably so.

Gallacher became so popular at Broomfield Park that the fans threatened to burn down the ground's wooden stand if he was sold. But it was inevitable that he would demand a bigger stage. So go he would, snapped up by Newcastle United for what at the time was a massive £6,500 fee. He more than repaid them. Gallacher scored twice for the Magpies on his debut and then bagged 15 in his first nine matches. From there he went on to score 143 goals in 174 games for Newcastle, before moving on to Chelsea, Derby, Notts County and Gateshead where he continued to net with unerring regularity. At the end of his long career, Gallacher had scored 367 goals in 545 games. He also won 20 caps for Scotland, scoring an amazing 24 goals in the process.

McPhail was poached by rivals Rangers for a hefty £5,000. At Ibrox he would become an all-time great, scoring an astonishing 261 goals in 408 games from inside-forward. For Scotland, he would win 17 caps and score seven times. Like Gallacher, Russell would move south of the border to a major English club; in his case Preston North End, where he would spend six years.

In 1923, champions Rangers were becoming a Rolls-Royce of a team under Struth. The former assistant manager had taken over the top job in 1920 under tragic circumstances. The then hugely popular boss William Wilton, who had won the championship nine times, died in a boating accident when the yacht he was on got caught in a storm and smashed against Gourock Pier on the Clyde. Struth was a renowned disciplinarian and demanded that his players wore suits, shirts and ties to and from training. He spent little time on the coaching side of things, but was laser-focused on the culture of the club, developing what soon became known as the 'Rangers Way' – self-discipline, discipline as a team and respect for the club. Players who did not live up to his high standards were swiftly moved on out of Ibrox and he was shrewd in the transfer market, always looking to sign what he deemed to be 'true Rangers types'. Struth went on to win the championship 18 times, winning 14 titles in 19 years up to the start of World War Two. In 1928 he managed Rangers to their first league and cup double.

In 1923, and similar to unexpected new rivals Airdrieonians, Struth had assembled a ferociously talented forward line. Andy Cunningham signed for the Gers from Kilmarnock in 1915 and only played a handful of games before going off to war serving as a lieutenant in the Royal Field Artillery. On his return he was in and out of the first team, but by 1921 he had played well enough to become regular pick as centre-forward. In 1922/23 he scored 11 goals and proved to be the perfect foil for new strike partner Geordie Henderson, who would finish the season as top scorer with 23 goals.

Celtic finished in third place, four points behind Airdrieonians, and nine shy of champions Rangers. It was a rare, disappointing season for the green and whites. The season before, they'd been crowned champions after losing just two matches along the way, but with pretty much the same squad 1922/23 fell flat. Celtic were beaten 11 times in the league and to add insult to injury, Rangers did the double over them, winning 2-0 at Ibrox and 3-1 at Celtic Park. For once, manager Willie Maley just couldn't get them firing on a consistent basis.

By 1923 Maley was already a legend in Scottish football. Made manager in 1897 aged just 29, he put together a young side largely signed from nearby junior clubs that between 1905 and 1910 won six consecutive titles, and the first league and Scottish Cup doubles. His management style was unorthodox to say the least. He took no part in training, watched every game not from the touchline but in the directors' box, never gave team talks before or after matches or at half-time, and had little to do with the players. His squad would learn who had been picked to play on a Saturday by reading the local newspapers. But his hands-off style seemed to work. Now though, he would have to work out how to best a resurgent Rangers.

It was not as if his 1922/23 team was short on stars. Irish striker Patsy Gallacher formed a lethal partnership with nippy right-winger Andy McAtee, and long-time captain Willie McStay was on great form that season. Some key young players were starting to come through into the first-team squad, including an 18-year-old who would go on to become the all-time leading scorer in top-flight British football. Jimmy

McGrory made his debut on 20 January 1923 in a 1-0 away defeat to Third Lanark. His first goal came two weeks later in a 4-3 defeat against Kilmarnock at Rugby Park. This would be followed by a further 549 in 546 competitive first-team games. Known for his bullet headers, McGrory was soon nicknamed the 'Human Torpedo'.

Celtic did end the season on a high however, overcoming Hibernian 1-0 to win the Scottish Cup for the tenth time. According to the redoubtable 'Tityrus' in *Athletic News* the Hampden crowd did not witness a thriller:

'The greatest virtue of the match was that it was decisive. The football public have reason to be deeply grateful that the game was brought to issue. Another such match would, I should think, exhaust even the patience of God's most patient and methodical race – the Scots. There were 80,000 people prepared to cheer good play. They had few opportunities of expressing their appreciation, for the match was the tamest of the tame contests that I have seen for a long while.'

Falkirk finished fourth with an unbeaten home record but ironically, it was the sheer volume of home draws – ten out of 19 games – that kept them out of the top three. Falkirk were a big deal in the 1920s. In 1922, they broke the world transfer fee record, paying West Ham United £5,500 for their prolific striker Syd Puddefoot – the star himself earned a generous £380 signing-on fee.

Queen's Park's club motto is 'Ludere Causa Ludendi' – to play for the sake of playing. In 1923 they were still determinedly and proudly amateur and being based in the wide catchment area of Glasgow were able to attract the very best of central Scotland's non-professional talent. Postwar, this had kept them in the top division until 1921/22 when a poor season saw them finish second from bottom, four points shy of safety and relegated into Division Two. Queen's Park soon showed that they were too good for Scotland's second tier and bounced straight back as champions, scoring the most goals (73) and conceding the fewest (31). They lost only five times all season, winning 24 and drawing nine. Clydebank too were on the bounce back. In 1921/22 they'd finished bottom of Division One, 12 points from safety. They'd suffered an atrocious season, conceding 103 goals and scoring only 34. With just six wins all season they went down into Division Two. This time around, their fans enjoyed a much happier campaign.

Looking a little further down the final Second Division table is like taking a glimpse into a long-lost footballing past. Bathgate finished fifth, Armadale sixth, and Broxburn United in eighth. They were all small-town clubs from West Lothian, home to collieries and their related heavy industries – and all would be out of the Scottish Football League or out of business by the end of the 1920s. The sad truth was that playing professional football was becoming unsustainable in a region where the mining industry was in steep decline and local unemployment steadily rising. Match attendances began to dwindle and the West Lothian clubs were struggling financially. With some ingenuity, Armadale suggested offering the unemployed admission into their games at a reduced sixpenny rate, but this was vetoed by the SFL. Their next potential money-making idea was to establish regular greyhound racing at their Volunteer Park ground, but when the SFL discovered that some of the racing would take place on the pitch they put a stop to that too. Armadale stumbled on until the 1932/33 season and then managed just 17 games before being expelled for failing to provide match guarantees to visiting teams.

Broxburn United had always struggled financially and it was long the view locally that it was unrealistic for a town of just 3,000 to sustain a league club. Broxburn depended on the oil shale industry and allied to a decline in local employment, their already small home gates dwindled further. In 1926 they were forced to drop out of the league.

Other clubs from the 1922/23 Division Two season are also long gone, consigned to the history books. In Edinburgh, St Bernard's were always the much smaller little brother to Hearts and Hibs. That's not to say they were without early successes. In 1895, three of the Edinburgh clubs enjoyed a clean sweep of all of Scottish football's major trophies. Hearts won the Scottish Football League for the first time, Hibs were Division Two champions, and St Bernard's beat the now-departed Renton 2-1 at Ibrox to lift the Scottish Cup for the one and only time in their history. In 1900/01 and 1906/07 they were Division Two champions. But after World War One, St Bernard's found it impossible to make any dent in the far bigger fanbases of Hearts and Hibs and struggled on in Division Two into the 1930s. But come World War Two they were 'mothballed' and never re-opened as a professional club.

Lochgelly United, who finished the season a respectable tenth, hailed from a small mining town in West Fife. The following season would prove to be a disaster. After again suffering the effects of dwindling home gates, they found it impossible to hang on to their better players. Lochgelly finished bottom and along the way set two totally unwanted Division Two records – the most defeats (30) and the fewest goals (20) scored in a season. In 1928, they disbanded.

Stirling-based King's Park came 12th and would stay in Division Two for many more years. But after their Forthbank stadium was bombed by the Luftwaffe in World War Two, they never played as King's Park again. Their place in local fans' affections would be taken by the newly created Stirling Albion. Vale of Leven ended up bottom and were already on the slide in 1923. Falling attendances led to financial troubles which forced them out of the league the following season, and they would free-fall through regional district leagues before going out of business altogether in 1929.

15

The Amateur Game

*'Every professional should remain always in
his heart an amateur.'*

Alfred Eisenstaedt, photographer and
photo-journalist

VICTORIAN BRITAIN is where the game began, the early
matches played by Oxbridge University and public school
'gentlemen'. It took a good few decades for the game we know
today to become more fully formulated, its early rules developed
and agreed. From the very beginning, one thing was for certain
– the game was an amateur one and the newly formed FA put
an absolute ban on paying for playing. But as in any competitive
sport, clubs and their fans wanted to win, so it didn't take long
before the better-supported and more well-off sides began to
offer 'under-the-counter' payments and benefits to attract the
best players into their ranks. It split English football down
the middle and effectively caused a schism between the more
working-class clubs in the north and the middle-class amateur
clubs of the south.

Eventually, the FA realised they had to act and under
pressure from big clubs mainly in the north and Midlands,
they met in July 1885 at the Anderton Hotel in Fleet Street, to

formally vote in favour of giving the go-ahead to paid professional football. It was not unanimous and there was much heated debate about what football should be and represent. In the end, 32 FA members voted for the change and 15 voted against. From that day onwards there became an ever-increasing formal divide between professional and amateur footballers. At a stroke, the FA had pulled back the dusty velvet curtains of English football and revealed the reality of the true-life drama that was really being played out behind the scenes. The sport would never be the same again. Money would become the be all and end all and those who had the most would become kings. The decision they made would become one of the greatest triumphs of capitalism and allow men to become rich upon the sport. That one single decision in football history led to Cristiano Ronaldo earning more in a week than most people earn in a decade. Little did the FA representatives realise over their brandy and cigars back in 1885 that their decision would be the point at which many believed that the true spirit of football died.

In the early years of the FA Cup, the winners were 'gentlemen' teams such as Oxford University; Wanderers, a club of former public schoolboys based in London; Old Etonians; Old Carthusians, former members of the Charterhouse public school; and Royal Engineers, an army team. After the FA ruling on professional football, only one non-league club would ever win the FA Cup again – the Southern League's Tottenham Hotspur, who beat Football League team Sheffield United in 1901. It became clear that the great schism was putting genuinely amateur teams at a huge disadvantage and as a consequence, the FA Amateur Cup was launched in 1891, with 81 clubs entering the inaugural tournament. Old Carthusians beat Casuals, a team of players from Britain's universities and public schools, 2-1.

From then onwards, the winners and finalists generally came from the two heartlands of English amateur football –

the North Eastern and Northern League and the south-east's Isthmian and Athenian Leagues. The winners of the 1921/22 FA Amateur Cup were Bishop Auckland – a club that since 1896 had won the trophy five times and been runners-up on four occasions. Fellow north-eastern sides Middlesbrough, Crook Town, West Hartlepool and Stockton all got their hands on the cup. From the south-east, winners included Clapton on three occasions, Bromley, Dulwich Hamlet and South Bank. Armed services teams were allowed to enter and won on two occasions – the Depot Battalion Royal Engineers in 1907/08 and RMLI Gosport two seasons later. Other FA Amateur Cup entrants regularly came from the most curious of places. In 1923, a team from Leavesden Mental Hospital made it as far as the third round before losing out 2-1 to Northampton Nomads.

The 1923 FA Amateur Cup Final was contested between tiny Worcestershire side Evesham Town and London Caledonians at Crystal Palace. Based at Caledonian Park in Holloway, Caledonian were one of the founder members of the Isthmian League in 1905 and their teams were regularly made up of expat amateur Scots footballers who lived in the capital. They soon gained a reputation for playing in the typically Scottish 'passing style' and were one of amateur football's most stylish teams. Before World War One, they won the Isthmian League five times and toured France, Holland and Belgium for regular exhibition matches. But like Evesham, this would be their first time in the FA Amateur Cup Final. Despite the gap in class, it was a tight game. Caledonian took an early lead after 13 minutes through rare non-Scot, Irish international striker Andy Sloane, but Evesham levelled just before half-time. The Worcestershire side defended valiantly against virtual one-way attacking traffic in the second half but finally conceded in the 77th minute, letting in Caledonian's Jack McCubbin for the winner. The Caley team oozed class and included the Gates brothers, Basil and Eric, the former representing Great Britain in the 1920 Olympics in Antwerp.

Thanks to the creation of the north and south regionalisations of the Third Division, England's top amateur leagues had undergone a massive shake-up. Effectively they had lost 44 of their best teams to the Football League and in 1923, everything was in transition, with the leaving teams turning fully or semi-professional. The Southern League particularly experienced an enormous churn of clubs, with many of their new members now being reserve sides from professional teams. Quite simply, not enough lower-tier amateur sides were ready to step up from their much smaller regional leagues into the much bigger, long-established Southern League, which stretched from the shores of Essex right across to Wales and the deep south-west. So for now, professional club reserve teams took up the slack.

The Southern League's English section in 1922/23 contained no fewer than 15 second-string sides from Football League clubs, from Millwall, Watford, Norwich City and Luton Town over in the east to Swindon Town, Plymouth Argyle, Bristol City, Bristol Rovers, Portsmouth and Exeter City in the west. Only five of the Southern League's clubs that season – Boscombe, Torquay United, Guildford United, Bath City and Yeovil & Petters United – were purely amateur. It would be a reserve team – that of Bristol Rovers – who won the English section in 1922/23.

It was a similar story in the north, where the North Eastern League contained reserve teams from Newcastle United, Sunderland, Middlesbrough, South Shields, Hartlepools United and Darlington. In the north-west, the 20-club Cheshire County League included the reserve teams of Crewe Alexandra, Stockport County, Tranmere Rovers and Stalybridge Celtic. In 1922/23, the North Eastern League champions were another second-string side, Newcastle United, who ran away with the title on 68 points from 38 games, 15 ahead of runners-up Blyth Spartans. Around the rest of the country, Bromley won the Athenian League; Sheffield Wednesday Reserves were champions of the Midland League; Eston United won the Northern League; and Ebbw Vale were champions of the Welsh section of the Southern League.

The biggest amateur football stories of 1923, however, all seemed to come from a club who didn't even belong to a league or have their own ground, the legendary Corinthians. Founded in 1882 before the days of professionalism, within 20 years the club had earned a reputation as the most attractive amateur team that football had yet known. Playing only exhibition matches at home and abroad to promote the ideals of fair play in football, the club attracted the country's finest amateur players. They supplied a huge number of players to the England team before professionalism fully set in, and during 1894 and 1895 the entire national side consisted of members of Corinthians – a feat achieved by no other club before or since. The Rolls-Royce of non-professional English football, they toured all over Europe, South Africa, North America and famously, Brazil in 1910, where football aficionados were so taken by the side they founded a Corinthians club of their own in São Paulo. The English club's constitution declared that it should 'not compete for any challenge cup or any prize of any description' and it continually championed the ideals of amateurism in sport around the world until the club's demise in 1939. Along the way, Corinthians inflicted Manchester United's record defeat – 11-3 in a 1904 friendly in Leyton. Real Madrid were so inspired by their idealism they adopted Corinthians' white strip, and the club's former players included a serried hall of fame.

Charles Burgess (C.B.) Fry was arguably this nation's greatest ever sportsman. As well as playing for Corinthians, Fry was a 12-time Blue for Oxford University's football, cricket and athletics teams. Just for good measure, he also played rugby for Blackheath and the Barbarians and went on to captain Sussex and England at cricket, scoring 30,000 first-class runs at an average of 50. He equalled the world record for the long jump and it's said he prepared for his attempt by smoking a cigar. After playing for Corinthians, he turned professional with Southampton and on his sporting retirement he became a highly acclaimed writer and publisher. Corinthian Andrew Watson became the first black player to play at international level, turning out three times for Scotland in 1881 and 1882. The talented full-back also studied Natural Philosophy, Mathematics and Engineering at Glasgow University. Charles Aubrey Smith was a Cambridge graduate who as well as playing for Corinthians became an English Test cricketer, before moving to the USA to become a film star in silent movies and the founder of the expat Hollywood Cricket Club – you can still check out his star on the Hollywood Walk of Fame. Corinthians and many of their players were a true phenomenon, a singular product of their age. But the age would inevitably change.

During World War One, an astonishing 22 Corinthians players died in battle and when football re-started, the heart had been ripped from the club. They played fewer and fewer exhibition games and in an attempt to revitalise the project, Corinthians applied in 1923 to take part in the FA Cup alongside the professional sides.

On 13 January 1923 Corinthians played their first FA Cup first round tie, against the Third Division South's Brighton & Hove Albion, and against all the odds they held the Seagulls to a very creditable 1-1 draw. The replay also ended up 1-1 and the third game was played in front of 45,000 fans at Stamford Bridge – a colossal crowd for a first round replay between a Third Division side and an amateur exhibition team. Once again Corinthians fought like trojans against their professional opponents, this time falling agonisingly short to narrowly lose

1-0. But the battling amateurs had captivated the imagination of the footballing public and beleaguered Corinthians were back in the headlines, even more so when three of their amateur players were selected to play for the full professional England team, all three Cambridge University graduates.

Half-back Basil Patchitt was only 22 years old when he was selected twice for his country in friendlies against Sweden. It may seem surprising that though on debut and then only gaining his second cap, Patchitt was named captain on both occasions. Inside-forward Graham Doggart gained his one and only full international cap against Belgium in a friendly. A Cambridge University Blue and a future Middlesex cricketer, Doggart would become chairman of the FA in 1961. Interestingly, he too was named captain on his debut. Was it just coincidence that all the top professional England players at the time were overlooked as captain? Perhaps not. In 1923, the FA still attempted to portray an image of being proud custodians of the gentlemen's game and were snobbishly classist. When some 'gentlemen' were picked, it was no surprise to anyone at the time that the FA selection panel named the officer class as captains.

Jackie Hegan won four England caps as an amateur in 1923. He played in three friendlies – twice against Belgium and then against France – and then in that year's Home International Championship match against Ireland. Hegan's international career ended with a 100 per cent scoring record – four goals in four games. He also ended the year as England's top scorer. Left-winger Hegan was a remarkable individual. A graduate of the Royal Military College, Sandhurst, he made his debut for Corinthians as an 18-year-old in 1919 in a 7-2 win over the army. It was to be a day of Kismet. Hegan had been picked to play for the forces team, but when Corinthians turned up short of players, he was 'loaned' to the amateur club – and stayed with them for a further 14 years. He continued to serve in the army, and when postings allowed he played many games on Corinthians' foreign tours and in their domestic exhibition matches. In his time with the club he made 167 appearances, scoring 50 goals from the wing, and earned 23 caps for the England amateur team, as well as his four for the professional national side. In an exemplary military career, he finally attained the rank of lieutenant-colonel and won an OBE during World War Two for his valour and service.

The same three Corinthians played too in that year's FA Charity Shield match on 8 October. In its tenth year, the charity game was still trying to find its feet and its best format. Since the war the football authorities had tried league champions versus FA Cup winners, and league winners against Second Division champions. In 1923 they rang the changes again and had two select teams of professional and amateur players. The professionals fielded a particularly strong side that included Bolton Wanderers FA Cup Final goalscorer David Jack, Huddersfield Town goalkeeper Ted Taylor and left-back Sam Wadsworth, Fulham's marauding South African-born centre-forward Frank Osborne, West Ham's cup finalist Sid Bishop, and a man who was regarded as one of the best half-backs in the Football League, Tommy Meehan. Tragically, Manchester-born Meehan would die aged just 28 a year later from the 'sleeping sickness' that was spreading around the world. Known as Encephalitis Lethargica, by 1926, it would kill 500,000.

As well as our fully capped three Corinthians, the amateurs would also field a strong side. Clapton inside-right Stan Earle would go on to play over 250 games for West Ham as a professional and win two full England caps. Dulwich Hamlet goalkeeper Bert Coleman was rated the best stopper outside of professional football and Casual Fred Ewer one of the country's best wing-halves. The amateur XI also included army and Kingstonian player Drummer Frank Macey, who had spent most of World War One as a prisoner of war and then returned home in peacetime to act as an interpreter for German POWs in Britain. The first half was a keenly contested end-to-end affair, but ultimately, superior professional fitness won the day. The amateurs tired badly in the second half and Birmingham City's Joe Bradford and Liverpool stalwart Harry Chambers scored the two winning goals. But the FA were so impressed with the quality of the game – and the 11,000 fans' reactions to it – they continued with the professional XI v amateur XI Charity Shield format for another three seasons.

The mighty Corinthians were indeed reinvigorated in 1923 and throughout the rest of the 1920s they continued to tour the world to proselytise the idea of fair amateur play. To further boost their public profile domestically, the side continued to enter the FA Cup, where their annual forays captured the public's imagination. In 1924 they beat First Division Blackburn Rovers before losing to West Bromwich Albion in the second round, in front of a crowd of 50,000. In 1926, 42,000 watched them go out to Manchester City in the third round, and in 1927 Corinthians got as far as the fourth round, finally losing out to Newcastle United in front of a bumper 56,000 attendance at St James' Park.

Though the England amateur team had a relatively quiet year, playing only four games including their FA Charity Cup against the professionals, their 27 January match against the amateur Wales side was an eight-goal thriller packed with drama and incident. Played in front of 8,000 fans at Middlesbrough's old Ayresome Park, an end-to-end game saw Welsh goalkeeper Williams injured part way through the first half and taken off. Well before the age of substitutions, this meant that Wales defender Frank Blew held his hand up and volunteered to go in goal. Wales were down to ten men but it wasn't long before England joined them when Hegan, their star striker, went down with a bad knock and limped off.

This was back in the day when without replacements, and if it was clear that the wounded hadn't sustained serious injuries, trainers and coaches would work overtime to physio and massage players to try and get them back out on to the pitch. After half-time Williams was back in goal. As Wales went ahead 4-2 with the man advantage, Hegan limped back on again to make up the numbers. In the final 15 minutes England scored twice to level at 4-4. It was a dark, foggy afternoon and amid the confusion of comings and goings on the pitch, there is still to this day total confusion about who scored all the goals.

According to England Football Online, which carries all the official details of the England amateur team's results, Hartley, Minter and Douthwaite with a brace were the men who scored for the home side. The Wales goals came by way of a Davies hat-trick and the fourth added by Nicholls. But at the time, *The Guardian* reported that Davies only scored twice for Wales, with Griffiths scoring the other goal. A local newspaper suggested that it was Jenkins, not Griffiths or Davies. The *Glasgow Herald* went one confusion further, claiming it was in fact Minter who had scored twice for England, not Douthwaite. Back in the day, this was not uncommon. Scrambled goals from close, tapped in among a melee of players, often in poor weather conditions, were sometimes credited to different players depending upon which local, regional or national newspaper you read. Players would often have face-offs and fall-outs with journalists after reading reports of a goal they knew they had scored but had been credited to one of their team-mates. Nothing ever changes. Any true striker worth their salt would probably prefer you steal their watch rather than rob them of a goal. Whatever, it was a thrilling amateur international game.

The England team's other two engagements in 1923 brought mixed results. A trip over the North Sea to Belgium saw them lose 3-0 in front of 20,000 at the Oscar Bossaert Stadium in Brussels, but they would end their year by beating Ireland 3-0.

16

Women's Football

'The kicking is too jerky a movement for women.'

Birmingham Daily Gazette, 7 December 1921

IN 2016, I collaborated with former England player and manager Hope Powell on co-writing a book about her long career, *Hope: My Life in Football*. During our many interview sessions and discussions, we talked a lot about the history of women's football and how it has been treated by the FA in the past. Hope remembered, in her first week as England women's team manager, being on the phone in a shared office when FA coach Derek Fazackerley walked past. 'Oh, is that the new girl?' he said, assuming that all women at the FA were either secretaries or cleaners. Hope put him straight, as she would. Until more recently, the FA's relationship with the women's game has been neither good nor healthy. It all began in the early 1920s and remains one of the greatest scandals in English football.

First we need to backtrack to World War One. After 1915, professional men's football stopped. There would be friendly matches with players home on leave turning out for whichever teams needed a man but these were hardly full-on games. By and large, proper competitive football would not return to the nation's stadiums until the 1919/20 season kicked off. The real football entertainment came from the women's game.

Women were playing organised football well before 1915 but it was during the Great War when the female game really took off. With men away at the front, women were needed in the workplace, and particularly in armaments factories to help feed the war machine. These were dangerous places to work, not just because of accidents and explosions but due to the toxic chemicals that were used in the making of bombs, bullets and missiles. To try and give women workers a healthier workplace, factory bosses encouraged them to get outside during their breaks, so they could exercise and play sports. The game all girls wanted to play was football.

All the major armaments factories around the country had their own teams, and matches began between them to help raise money for war charities. The more they played, the more skilled they became. Professional male footballers invalided out of battle came home to coach and train them. Standards rose, games grew to be ever more competitive and women's football became a big deal. A nationwide tournament, the Munitionettes' Cup, was launched. Matches began to be played at big professional grounds such as Old Trafford, Ewood Park and Highbury, in front of crowds of 20,000 and 30,000. Women's football developed from being a novelty to serious sporting business and commonplace. The *Football Special Magazine* included numerous centre-spread features alongside pieces on men's football with no sign that it seemed unusual or extraordinary. For a good few months, the magazine even included a regular weekly column by 'The Football Girl' who gave insights into the world of women's football at the time.

Then the war ended. The men came home and were given their jobs back in the armaments factories. Most of the women lost work and many of the factory teams folded. But the keenest were determined to play on. One of those clubs became legendary – the Dick, Kerr Ladies team.

The Dick, Kerr factory was originally a tramway rolling stock and electrical works. Set up in 1898, the company soon earned a growing reputation for the high standard of its work and was commissioned to undertake many large and prestigious projects, including the electrification of the Liverpool to Southport railway line. In wartime, the nature of the company's work was soon to change. Desperately short of ammunition, the Admiralty and War Office approached various firms about turning over their production lines to making shells. The Dick, Kerr factory was one of them. By 1917, it was turning out 30,000 shells a week and most of its employees were women.

Towards the end of that year, the Munitionettes were approached by the nearby Moor Park Military Hospital to raise money for the wounded soldiers under its care. It was suggested that they hold some form of charity concert, but the women had other ideas. Already playing organised kickabouts during breaks and after work they'd fallen in love with football, and suggested instead that they play a full 90-minute match against the women employees of the neighbouring Arundel Coulthard Foundry. Arms were twisted and Preston North End let them have full use of their Deepdale ground for the game. It was played on Christmas Day afternoon in 1917, and Dick, Kerr Ladies duly won. But the astonishing takeaway from the day was that 10,000 fans turned up to watch the encounter, raising £600 for the hospital – in today's money, that's roughly £50,000. The team became fully organised, undertook regular training sessions and put together a long fixture list of charity exhibition matches.

Soon, the side were attracting the best women's footballers from around the north-west. Weaver Annie Crozier was recruited from a local cotton mill and four of the well-established Lancaster Ladies side were enrolled: midfielders Molly Walker and Jessie Walmsley, goalkeeper Annie Hastie and an early star of women's football, Jennie Harris. Standing only 4ft 10in tall, she was known as 'Little Jennie' and her prolific goalscoring partnership with fellow striker Florrie Redford earned them the sobriquet, 'Dick, Kerr Box of Tricks'.

The side played, and beat, a French women's national team, their players carried shoulder-high off the pitch. In 1920 they played a match at Goodison Park against St Helens in front of 53,000 paying fans. Their popularity, alongside top women's sides like Stoke Ladies, St Helens and in Scotland, Rutherglen Ladies, continued to pull in big crowds across the country into the early 1920s. There was no actual women's league, but the 60 or so women's teams in England and Scotland regularly played highly attended friendlies to continue to raise money for wartime veterans' charities. They were strictly amateur players and the money from the games they played all went into charity coffers.

In 1921 alone, Dick, Kerr Ladies played 67 matches in aid of charity all over Britain, watched by a total of 900,000 people. Fans turned out in their thousands to watch most women's matches and players such as Lily Parr at Dick, Kerr and the silky-skilled Scotswoman Sadie Smith at Rutherglen Ladies became legends. Parr was renowned for her cannonball shooting and before one game in Chorley she was approached by a professional male goalkeeper who mocked her skills, saying she only had women stoppers to beat. Parr happily picked up the gauntlet and though the keeper just managed to get his hand on her first shot, it broke his arm. Smith was so highly rated as a player, men's team Linfield in Northern Ireland tried to sign her. As an interesting little side note, Smith was also the grandmother of singer songwriter Eddi Reader of Fairground Attraction fame.

Women's football was hugely popular, contained many well-coached and skilful sides and made big pots of money for many good causes. It brought together communities, gave rare and invaluable sporting opportunities to women the length and breadth of the country and entertained an enthusiastic mass audience. It was a win-win all round. Or so you would think. There have been many occasions over the decades when the FA have been castigated for their wrong-headedness, conservatism and an inability to smell the coffee and move with the times. The challenge, however, would be to find another occasion when they acted as loathsomely as the early 1920s in the way they treated the growing emergence of the women's game.

The moment that stung them into action was the Dick, Kerr v St Helens match at Goodison Park, which ended in a 4-0 win for the at the time seemingly unbeatable Dick, Kerr Ladies and produced a hugely entertaining game full of individual skill and great tactical discipline. The fans loved it, but the 53,000 who flooded in to watch the game embarrassed and infuriated the FA. That season the average gate for Everton's home games was 37,189. At Bradford Park Avenue it was 16,000, at Derby just 15,000. Eight other teams in England's top league averaged home gates of below 30,000 that season. OK, so the friendly was only a one-off game. But the attendance dwarfed the best in the First Division that season. The 100 per cent male make-up of the FA found this hard to take. Most of their top brass were, not to put too fine a point on it, old duffers totally against the idea of women even watching football never mind playing it, appalled that 'their version' had become so popular with the general public.

But their major concern was that women's football was drawing fans and potential income away from the men's game. Additionally, the true blue establishment FA had been appalled to discover that some women's teams had been organising games expressly to raise money for striking miners and their families around England's industrial areas, the same communities they came from and lived in and so keenly knew the privations and poverty their own people were struggling through. For all of these reasons, the FA became committed to do everything it possibly could to destroy the women's game.

Relentlessly pursuing any research or information that allowed them to take control of the narrative, misrepresent the women's game and justify and prop up their prejudices, they happened upon the work of Dr Arabella Kenealy and particularly her book, *Feminism and Sex Instinction*. An anti-feminist and eugenicist, Kenealy famously coined the phrase 'feminism is masculism', and it was clear that she spoke the language of the FA of the time. In short, she believed that sport would turn women into men. Her book gravely warned, 'Over-use, in sports and games, of the muscles of shoulder and chest, occasions atrophy of mammary glands ... such sterilisation, where it is not actually producing diseased and degenerate offspring, is producing a pitiful race of pallid and enfeebled babies and children.'

They sought the advice too of Harley Street physician Dr Mary Scharlieb who told them, 'I consider football a most unsuitable game, too much for a woman's frame.'

It was perfectly acceptable, however, for the female frame to step into the breach during wartime and do every job possible in heavy manual industry to keep the country going. Many of these same vulnerable and delicate flowers built tanks, ships and heavy artillery, fully able to match their male counterparts in terms of productivity, making steel, lugging heavy machinery around and working in fire and filth. It was, of course, a nonsense – nothing more than a cheap magician's deflection trick to distract the audience from what was really going on.

With friends in the press on board, the FA began to lobby relentlessly against women's football. In 1921 they were ready to attack and passed swingeing new laws that ultimately put the women's game in this country back 50 years. In a resolution passed by their Consultative Committee the FA top brass

agreed, 'Complaints having been made as to football being played by women, council felt impelled to express the strong opinion that the game of football is quite unsuitable for females and should not be encouraged.'

To add insult to injury, the Consultative Committee effectively accused the women's game of corruption, saying, 'Complaints have also been made as to the conditions under which some of these matches have been arranged and played, and the appropriation of receipts to other than charitable objects … the council are further of the opinion that an excessive proportion of the receipts are absorbed in expenses and an inadequate percentage devoted to charitable objects.'

The FA offered no proof whatsoever to back up these 'opinions' and women's teams were left devastated by the accusations, pointing out that they only received expenses for travel and accommodation and loss of time at work and were never paid to play football as professionals or semi-professionals. But the FA weren't listening. Accordingly, women were banned from playing on any football ground or pitch affiliated to the FA and any referee found to have officiated a women's game would be barred from taking any further part in the men's game. All women's clubs were stripped of FA recognition. Astonishingly, these bans would remain in place for 50 long years.

By 1923, the bans had effectively forced women's football 'underground'. Unable to play on any FA ground or pitch anymore, women's teams were left with no option but to find new 'cuckoo' homes at rugby stadiums, in local parks and even at dog tracks. Sadly, many teams were unable to find new venues locally and were forced to fold. Despite continuing interest from fans, the FA resolutely refused to give women's football any money, resources or material support. Indeed, the FA remained vindictive to the extreme. In 1923, Dick, Kerr and Dumfries Ladies shared a summer tour north and south of the border in a series of friendlies. Their 'resident referee' for the matches was to be Burnley's tough-tackling Scottish defender Davie Taylor, twice an FA Cup winner, with Bradford City in 1911 and then the Clarets in 1914. He was warned by the FA not to take part or he would be banned from football. When Dick, Kerr Ladies went on tour to Canada, the FA wrote to their male Canadian counterparts urging them to ban the team from playing in their country. The men at the Canadian FA agreed, and Dick, Kerr Ladies were forced to travel south to the USA and completely rearrange their tour to play against American teams. Even then, the totally male US football authorities would only let them compete against men's teams. In the six matches, they won two, drew two and lost two.

To help re-organise the game, the English Ladies' Football Association was formed, but they didn't have the money or resources to organise leagues or cup competitions. The order of the day continued to be ad hoc charity match friendlies, but free from any FA control, the new association were able to establish a number of changes to specifically benefit the women's game. The size of the playing field was reduced; a lighter ball was introduced; shoulder charging was outlawed; and the use of hands was allowed to protect the face. The friendly matches continued but crowds and interest dwindled.

Battered and beleaguered by the FA's betrayal of basic sport for all values, the women's game soldiered on. And in 1923, a much anticipated match-up took place – England's Dick, Kerr Ladies versus Scotland's finest, Rutherglen Ladies. It was played at Shawcroft Park in Glasgow and against all the odds, the virtually unbeatable were beaten, with Rutherglen running out 2-0 winners. Henceforward, Rutherglen tried to cash in on the victory by self-proclaiming themselves the 'world champions of women's football'. Dick, Kerr Ladies remained in action from 1917 to 1965 and played 833 games around the world. They won 759, drew 46 and lost only 28. Rutherglen Ladies continued playing until 1939.

17

The New Season

*'There's two times of year for me: football
season, and waiting for football season.'*

Singer-songwriter Darius Rucker

THE 1922/23 season done and spent, the summer began with
an eight-day heatwave in early July. Temperatures around the
south-east of England hit 29°C on 9 July and then spectacular
storms rolled in from the Atlantic. Throughout the night,
6,900 lightning flashes were recorded over Chelsea, on average
one every three seconds. The storm was unrelenting, pouring
82mm of rain on to Seaford in East Sussex over a six-hour
period. A large house in Walton-on-the-Hill in Surrey was
totally destroyed by a rare lightning ball strike, and a tramcar
on London's Victoria Embankment took a direct lightning
hit and was set alight. A *Times* correspondent reporting from
Sydenham Hill described how the thuds, crashes and searingly
threatening shafts of lightning brought back bad memories of
the trenches for ex-soldiers. The rest of July and August were
rather more sedate and allowed for plenty of summer sport.

Football took its usual break and cricket took centre
stage for a few short months, Yorkshire winning the County
Championship. Now playing as an all-rounder, the veteran

slow left-arm bowler Wilfred Rhodes topped the season's bowling averages with a staggering 134 wickets at 11.54. Just for good measure he also scored over 1,000 runs. With the maximum footballer's wage now pinned back to £6 a week in the off-season, several players continued to play county cricket to top up their earnings and to keep fit and competitive over the summer months. Some of them were very good indeed.

Brentford's wing-forward Patsy Hendren was one of the most prolific batsmen of the interwar period, averaging 47.63 in his 51 Tests and 50.80 in all his first-class matches for Middlesex. Trying to maintain both careers was a constant struggle for Hendren and at the start of a few football seasons he missed the opening games. During 1920/21 he only managed two appearances for Brentford due to being in Australia on what would prove to be a disastrous Ashes tour – for the first time in their history, England lost the series 5-0. We would soon get used to it.

Tottenham outside-right Fanny Walden was another all-round sporting phenomenon. He played 214 games for Spurs and won two international caps, making him, at 5ft 2in tall, the smallest player ever to be capped by England. Playing for Northamptonshire in the summers from 1910 right through to 1929, Walden scored over 7,500 runs and took 119 wickets with his slow right-arm bowling in 258 first-class matches. His Tottenham team-mate Arthur Grimsdell regularly played for Minor Counties side Hertfordshire. Brighton's Tommy Cook, the man who would become the club's all-time top scorer with 123 goals, was turning out for Sussex, while Derby County inside-left Harry Storer was a potent all-rounder for Derbyshire. All across the country, dozens of footballers were spending their summers playing first-class cricket.

For those who didn't, it had also been an eventful summer. As well as Nelson's exploits in Spain, many other British teams had travelled to Europe to limber up for the season ahead and test themselves against foreign opposition. They all passed with flying colours. Arsenal enjoyed an unbeaten seven-match tour of Scandinavia, winning six and drawing just one. The big highlight was a 9-2 thrashing of a Norwegian XI in Kristiansand. Huddersfield travelled to Sweden and won six out of their seven games. Birmingham City went to Spain where they beat Barcelona three times and by goals aplenty – 5-3, 4-3 and 8-2. FA Cup holders Bolton toured Switzerland and France, returning home unbeaten with seven wins and a sole draw against Servette. Rangers too travelled to Switzerland and France and during their seven-game winning run beat a French XI 6-1. Dundee travelled abroad for the first time for a seven-match tour of Spain.

Raith Rovers travelled to Spanish soil too, but had a rather more dramatic time of it. Off the back of their best domestic season, Rovers visited the Canary Islands for a short four-match tour. Thirteen players, coaching staff and directors joined a cargo of chilled meat on the Buenos Aires-bound *Highland Loch* at Tilbury Docks, en route to their first stop-off in Vigo to watch a bullfight. The first night aboard was spent playing cards, having sing-songs and enjoying the odd bottle of beer. All went to bed happy and contented on this close-season adventure. But overnight the weather had started to change for the worse, and as the *Highland Loch* made its way across the Bay of Biscay it was caught up in severe storms. Early the following morning, the weather had become more violent and the boat struck rocks off Spain's north Galician coast. The lifeboats were launched but at first the players didn't realise what danger they were in. One of them stayed in his bath, convinced that his team-mates were playing a prank on him. Eventually they understood the gravity of the situation and helped the crew shepherd the women and children on to the waiting lifeboats.

Striker Tom Jennings gave a great short, sharp account of the incident, 'There was a tremendous smash. Being good Scotsmen we first went below to grab our money before getting off the ship. Most of us were still in pyjamas as we scrambled down the rope ladders.'

Spanish fishermen came out to meet them and tow the lifeboats ashore, and on land the travellers were fed and looked after by local villagers. As the storms passed, they were put on a motor launch and taken out to the still-afloat *Highland Loch* to recover their luggage and the hamper containing all the team's equipment. From there, they were taken by tramp steamer to the SS *Darrow*, which took them on the rest of their journey to Gran Canaria, where they played, and won, four games, one against fellow Scots Third Lanark. The close-season excitement didn't seem to do Raith any harm – during the first 15 games of the new league campaign, they won nine and drew three.

Back-to-back league champions Liverpool didn't tour that summer, and once more were very quiet in the transfer market, signing just two players – Billy McDevitt from Belfast United and William Chalmers from Old Aberdeen. This was many decades before transfer windows and clubs were at liberty to sign whoever they wanted, whenever they wanted. During the season, defender McDevitt would manage three first-team appearances and Chalmers not one. What the Reds retained was the greater majority of a tried and tested squad who'd been together for two championship-winning seasons. Would 1923/24 see them win three on the trot? The start of their new campaign seemed to suggest not. On 25 August, they played their opening game, against West Bromwich Albion at The Hawthorns, and lost 2-1. Though they bounced back immediately with a 6-2 thrashing of Birmingham at Anfield, they went on to lose five out of their first ten fixtures. Bolton's FA Cup winner and Wembley scorer David Jack started the season with his shooting boots still firmly on, bagging two against Cardiff City. Unfortunately for Wanderers, Cardiff's Jimmy Gill also scored a brace with team-mate Joe Clennell adding a third to see out the game 3-2 for the Welshmen. Though a side who rose to the occasion in big, one-off matches, no one was really expecting Bolton to be among the serious title contenders, nor the hitherto inconsistent Bluebirds. But five games and five wins later, Cardiff were the First Division's early front runners.

Herbert Chapman's highly rated Huddersfield Town would also be a force to be reckoned with. In two and a half seasons, Chapman had managed them to their first honour, the 1921 FA Cup, and lifted them from 15th in the league to a strong third-placed finish in 1922/23. Chapman was already becoming a different breed of English manager, having been granted full control of the footballing side of things at Leeds Road. He had begun to impose a 'house style' on the first-teamers right down to the reserves and third team, of a strong defence, fast counter-attacking and quick, short passing. Anyone promoted into the first team would know exactly what style to play and Chapman employed an army of scouts to specifically seek out players who would fit into his system. By 1923, he had signed England goalkeeper Ted Taylor and prolific goalscorers Charlie Wilson and George Cook to complete his jigsaw. The Terriers would kick off the season at home in front of 20,000 fans and gain their first win, 2-0 against Middlesbrough. Two victories against Preston home and away, 4-0 and 3-1 respectively, would see them sitting in second place behind Cardiff by the end of September.

With their consistent scorer Charles Buchan once again leading the line up front, the previous year's runners-up, Sunderland, were looking to go one step further. Their opening-day game against newly promoted West Ham in front of 35,000 at Roker Park ended in a frustrating 0-0 draw, which kicked off an indifferent run of three wins, two draws and three losses. The season before, Sunderland had lost only one league game at home. In only their second home match in 1923/24 they went down 3-0 against potential top-of-the-table rivals Cardiff. New boys Notts County made a promising return to the top flight. Their opening game at Meadow Lane on 25 August ended in a 2-1 win against Burnley, which began a ten-match run that contained six wins and just the one defeat.

Manchester City's new season began at their brand spanking new ground Maine Road, in front of a bumper 56,993 crowd against Sheffield United, a new attendance record for the club. There was a glorious, uproarious party feel in the ground and many of the fans got there early to soak up the atmosphere. A band in the centre of the pitch entertained the crowd and when the players ran out, the musicians broke into a jaunty rendition of 'Ours Is A Nice House, Ours Is'. City's captain for the day was the extraordinary Max Woosnam. Dubbed the 'greatest British sportsman', he was the son of the Archdeacon of Macclesfield and in his time at Winchester College Woosnam captained the golf and cricket teams and represented the school at football and squash. At Cambridge University he became a quadruple Blue, representing Trinity College at football, cricket, golf and tennis. Just for good measure, he also scored a maximum 147 break at snooker.

After fighting alongside poet Siegfried Sassoon on the Western Front, Woosnam returned from the war to sign up as an amateur at Manchester City, playing at centre-half. By popular player demand he was soon appointed captain, a rare honour for an amateur player at a professional club in the early 1920s. Alongside his football career, Woosnam won a gold medal in the men's tennis doubles and a silver in the mixed at the 1920 Olympics in Antwerp. The following year, he won the men's doubles final at Wimbledon. For him the great stadium opening was a doubly emotional day. He'd missed the entire 1922/23 season – and the chance to defend his Wimbledon doubles title – after suffering a horror leg break.

Both sides were formally introduced to the lord mayor of Manchester and then to deafening roars, the match got under way. The first half was a tight affair with few realistic chances on goal and it remained 0-0 at the interval. In the second half, and with the huge crowd roaring them on, City began to increasingly threaten and in the 68th minute, the honour of scoring the first goal at Maine Road fell to prolific Blues forward Horace Barnes, who rifled in from a long cross. By Christmas, Barnes would have scored another 14 times.

Johnson made it 2-0 just three minutes later and it could have been 3-0 a few moments after that, when Frank Roberts missed a penalty. The Blades pulled one back in the 88th minute but City hung on for the first win in their new ground and the crowd went mad. What they didn't know at that point was the day's major sadness: Woosnam had limped off towards the end. Desperate to play in City's first game at Maine Road, he'd come back too early from rehab, badly re-injured himself and would not play for the Blues again that season.

In the Second Division, 25 August saw newly promoted Nelson take the field at their Seedhill ground in front of 12,000 – their biggest attendance yet – to play Clapton Orient. They gained a first point in their highest level match in a creditable 1-1 draw. It was an entertaining game but with Nelson mainly on the back foot throughout. Whatever, it was a point on the board. But as August turned into September, the green late-summer leaves of optimism began to turn a depressing brown. Nelson struggled to match the higher standard of play around them. They were solid and determined, but it wasn't Second Division-level football. It would take another eight games before they would get their first win in the Second Division, 2-0 against Stoke City. Their best chance was to strengthen a defence with some new signings and Nelson would start to dig the trenches deeper with some pre-Christmas transfers.

18

La Garra Charrua

'In Uruguay, there is a football pitch every
hundred metres, whether it is made by
grass, small stones or sand. This has been my
football education.'

Edinson Cavani

HALFWAY DOWN South America's long, snaking eastern seaboard is a small parcel of land sandwiched between the two huge nations of Argentina and Brazil. It is the ancestral home of the indigenous Charrua people, but in 1923 it was better known as Uruguay. The Charrua add their name to a phrase that has long been used to describe both the creation of Uruguay and its football, *La Garra Charrua*.

More a concept and a feeling than a phrase, it loosely means achieving the impossible against all the odds through tenacity and determination. It is how the independent nation of Uruguay came into being. Before 1828, the area was known as the *Banda Oriental*, a territory constantly in conflict and fought over and variously occupied by British, Spanish and Portuguese colonial powers from the 18th century onwards. The jewel in the territory's crown and the prize to be controlled was the city of Montevideo, whose port was one of the biggest and most important in all of South America, sitting as it did on the edge of the Atlantic Ocean, a gateway to the world. In among the powerful foreign forces face-offs, constant battles and trade wars, the area's indigenous people continually fought for the right to rule themselves. They took on all-comers, battled to retain their own cultural identity and through sheer bloody-minded determination, finally won out. Through the Treaty of Montevideo in 1828, and against all the odds, their spirit of *La Garra Charrua* won them their independence and the nation state of Uruguay was carved almost intact from the *Banda Oriental* and it first came into being. It was a tiny country, a little nub of a thing squashed between Brazil to its north and east, and Argentina to the south and west. A backwater thousands of miles away from the home of football in England, but by 1923 it would start to teach the custodians and originators of the beautiful game some unexpected and important new lessons. Unfortunately, apart from a small and select band, nobody was listening.

The first recorded football match in Uruguay was in 1881 between Montevideo Cricket Club and Montevideo Rowing Club, and from the very beginning, it was the sporting equivalent of *La Garra Charrua*. The country's early international friendlies were against their neighbours Argentina and Brazil, both nations that dwarfed Uruguay in size and footballing experience. But soon they would overcome.

Uruguayan football found 1923 to be a crucially important year. The country's national team officially joined FIFA, which allowed it the opportunity to play for the first time around the world. This would open a thrilling Pandora's box for the game of football that would help change it forever, because unbeknownst to the rest of the world, the best football was being played in Uruguay. In 1923 they won the Copa América for the fourth time, in their own back yard in Montevideo, cruising past Brazil, Argentina and Paraguay in a four-team mini-league and ended the tournament unbeaten. The side contained four players who would soon become considered to be among the best in the world. Prolific goalscorer and inside-forward Héctor Scarone was nicknamed *El Mago*, the magician. Only 5ft 7in tall, stocky and with a low centre of gravity, Scarone possessed phenomenal close control. His team-mate José Nasazzi said, 'It was like magic. When he approached an opponent, it was as though the ball was glued to his boot.'

Domestically Scarone played for Uruguay's best team, Nacional, and ended up scoring 301 goals in 369 games for them, before travelling abroad to play for Barcelona, Inter Milan and Palermo. Nasazzi was the son of Italian and Spanish immigrants and known as *El Gran Mariscal*, the great marshal. A tall, poised and thoughtful defender, Nasazzi read the game like an open book and was a supremely accurate passer of the ball. He would later become the first captain to lift the Jules Rimet Trophy, and was named by *World Soccer* magazine among its 100 best players of all time.

Goalkeeper Andrés Mazali was nicknamed *El Buzo*, the diver. Ever alert to play in and around his box, Mazali had extraordinarily fast reflexes and reactions and would be Uruguay's number one for the rest of the decade. José Leandro Andrade was known as *Maravilla Negra*, the black marvel. A fast, technically gifted right-half, Andrade was one of the few black footballers playing in world football in 1923. His father, an escaped Brazilian slave, was said to have been 98 years old when José was born.

This quartet would form the core of a gifted, well-coached team that would bring an unprecedented decade of success to Uruguay. In 1924 they would win football gold at the Paris Olympics, the first South American country to do so. Throughout the opening rounds, *La Celeste* (the Sky Blues) showed a short, tidy passing style that shocked their European opponents who still relied more on a highly physical, long-ball game. By the time Uruguay got to the final, people were no longer shocked after they had eased past Switzerland 3-0 with little fuss or problem. As Jonathan Wilson wrote in *Angels With Dirty Faces*, Uruguay 'went to the 1924 Olympics as unknowns; they left having redefined football'. *La Celeste* had begun to show the world that football was not about hard running and muscle, but surprise.

Four years later in Amsterdam, they would retain their title and win a second gold. Two years after that, Uruguay would host the inaugural World Cup and become its very first winners. In between all of these huge tournament successes they would lift the Copa América a further two times and be runners-up once. The obvious question is – and was – how could such a tiny, obscure nation so consistently conquer the world of football?

In 1923, Uruguay had a population of fewer than two million. Nearly two-thirds of its people lived in the metropolitan area of Montevideo and most of its professional teams were based in the capital. Even in 2023, Uruguay's top division of 16 clubs contained 13 from Montevideo. The 12 teams in the Segunda División, the second tier, consist of nine based in the capital. Montevideo is where football has always happened, and if you were a kid playing out in the provinces that's where you would automatically move to. And move in their droves they did because legions of young working-class people around the world were beginning to learn that if you were good at football, it represented a rare opportunity to get out of poverty. From the beginning of the 20th century the future of Uruguayan football was based upon a ball at the feet of every tiny child. It became tradition that the most-valued first birthday present or Christmas gift would be a football. Competitive games began aged four across the country and beyond Catholicism, football became the nation's lay religion. An entire country devoted itself to playing the game. It was utterly focused, concentrated and meticulously well-developed.

There were other sports at the time that were moderately popular, such as volleyball, basketball, cycling and athletics, but Uruguay's utter obsession was with football and that's where the money was. How had this happened and why had Uruguay's footballers become so different and original in their style and focus? As life often does, it all began in the most prosaic and accidental of ways. First, British teachers and railway workers who'd come to work in Uruguay brought the game of football with them. But it was the arrival of a wave of Italian immigrants in the late 19th and early 20th centuries that brought a long-lasting and fundamental change to the game in Uruguay.

The *Azzurri* method was simple – never give up possession of the ball. Coaches in the country began to develop this principle in much greater depth. From a young age onwards, players were coached to retain the pill by working constantly on their ball control skills and awareness of their own position and those around them. They were taught strict tactical organisation, a way of playing always for the team, but crucially within these parameters, to express themselves, to surprise. Every age group through to adulthood played the same style, so that by the time they made it into senior football the Uruguayan 'method' had been drilled into every single player. Because everyone 'knew' how everybody else played and fitted into the jigsaw, the Uruguayans began to pick up a reputation for having a 'sixth sense', almost clairvoyant in their understanding. José Nasazzi summed it up thus, 'We were young, winners, united … we believed we were indestructible.'

What Uruguay, this tiny country towards the bottom of the world, did was to reinvent football. But in 1923, Britain was so far stuck in the mud and still so convinced of its own colonial supremacy and global importance that only the most intelligent and astute of footballing minds had begun to pick up and learn from what 'those foreigners' were doing. British was best! But what they had learned was that it really wasn't. Uruguay was now the standard-bearer for football.

Across Uruguay's southern and western borders in Argentina, football in 1923 was hugely popular but in a state of bitter turmoil. Like Uruguay, the game was first established in the country by British railway company workers sent to create Argentina's new rail system. In the 1860s, and to entertain themselves while working abroad they set up their own sports and social clubs, playing bowls, cricket, golf, rugby union, and of course, football. For the next 20 years, almost all the players and officials were Brits abroad and some of Argentina's oldest clubs, for example Newell's Old Boys, Belgrano AC, Quilmes and Rosario Central, were founded by British expats. Tragically, many of the early clubs excluded the local population, so Argentines took matters into their own hands and established their own clubs, the first, Argentino de Quilmes. By 1907, there were over 300 teams in the country, competing in a national amateur league or in local regionalised tournaments. Professional British teams such as Southampton and Chelsea regularly toured the country, which further popularised the game around Argentina. Internationally, the national team played their first match against neighbours Uruguay in 1901, winning 3-2. Argentina would win their first Copa América in 1921. But domestically, Argentine football was in a virtual state of war.

In 1923, there were two separate leagues – one was the 18-club Argentine Primera Division which already included well-known clubs like Boca Juniors, Huracán and Estudiantes and was officially recognised by the Argentine Football Association. Arraigned alongside and against them, the dissident Asociacion Amateurs de Football. As in the continental Europe of the 1920s, the custodians and fans of football were engaged in a battle over how the game should be played – as an amateur sport or a means of using your talents to earn a living wage. In Argentina, the issue that divided clubs was known as 'brown amateurism'. Though the Argentine Primera Division was meant to be an unpaid, non-professional league and there was a ban on player payments, a good many of its clubs regularly handed out 'ghost' rewards to attract the best players. Most of the time, this would involve pesos in the back pocket, secretly paid after games; sometimes, for the very top players, a car or even a house. Dissident teams such as Independiente, River Plate, Banfield and Vélez Sarsfield – all top clubs today – were strongly opposed to brown amateurism and felt forced to set up their own more purist league. As a result, by 1923 the Asociacion Amateurs de Football had organised an impressive alternate premier league of 21 clubs. The battle between the two competitions would drag on through the 1920s.

It was not a good footballing year further north in Brazil. The national team had won their first Copa América in 1919, beating Uruguay 1-0, then repeated the success in 1922 with a 3-0 victory over Paraguay. But in 1923 they had a dreadful Copa América, losing all three games against Uruguay, Paraguay and Argentina, ending up bottom of the mini-league. Following the wooden spoon, Brazil would go another 27 barren years until they won their next trophy. It was not that they were without talent, containing as they did a player who many rated as the best in the world, Arthur Friedenreich. It was somehow destined that he would become Brazil's first footballing superstar, born as he was, in São Paulo, on the corner of Vitoria (Victory) and Triunfo (Triumph) Streets. The son of a German businessman, Oscar, and a mother, Mathilde, whose family were freed slaves, Friedenreich was the first footballer of Afro-Brazilian origin to play for his country. At the time, Brazil's top clubs were totally dominated by white players and Friedenreich was often the victim of racism on and off the field. Brazil had been one of the last countries on Earth to abolish slavery, in 1888, and racism was still deeply ingrained in Brazilian society.

Friedenreich had scored the winning goal in Brazil's first Copa América triumph and as a result was feted the length and breadth of the country. The boot he scored with was taken on a tour of Rio de Janeiro and then placed in the window of an upmarket jeweller's shop for all to see. Despite his fame, when the 1921 Copa América came around, Friedenreich – by now Brazil's best player – was dropped from the squad. The championship was to take place in Argentina, a predominantly white country. It was announced that only white players would be able to take part. Scandalously, the original 'Black Pearl' was left at home. However, some believe that this outrageous act of racism served as a watershed moment in ending overt discrimination in football. Brazilian fans were appalled that their finest player was not allowed to play, and it opened a lot of eyes.

Though only 5ft 7in and weighing in at 8st, Friedenreich was a tigerish player, almost impossible to shift off the ball. A prodigious dribbler who had pace to burn, he picked up 23 caps for Brazil and scored ten times. Between 1918 and 1929 he is thought to have scored 288 goals for his club Paulistano in just 252 games. He continued to play into his late 30s but tragically died of Alzheimer's disease, unable to even remember that he was once arguably the world's greatest footballer.

Elsewhere, football was taking a little longer to become embedded into national psyches. Bolivia and Peru would not debut in the Copa América until 1926 and 1927 respectively. Venezuela's national league, Liga Venezolana, was still in its infancy having been established in 1921. Venezuela's national team wouldn't take to the pitch until 1938. English railway workers brought the game to Colombia in the early 1900s, but the Colombian Football Federation would not be formed until 1924. Fully organised football came late to Mexico too.

They would play their very first international matches – a series of three friendlies against Guatemala – in December 1923. It would be another four years before they would play their next friendly, a 3-3 draw against Spain. Mexico's official governing body was not founded until 1927 and the following year's Summer Olympics would be Mexico's first international tournament.

The surprising footballing success story of 1923 was how the game was suddenly thriving north of the border in the United States. The American Soccer League, which mainly operated in the north-eastern states, was launched with great razzmatazz in 1921 amid the opulence of Manhattan's Hotel Astoria. In the USA's Roaring Twenties, baseball was king and American football was still trying to establish itself. But with a booming economy and a young population thirsting for sport and entertainment, football – or soccer, as it was known – spent a golden decade in the sun, pulling big crowds, attracting top players from abroad and vying with American football to become the major post-October sport over on the Eastern seaboard. The ASL also annoyed the bejabers out of FIFA by attempting to launch unilateral changes to the laws of the game, including substitutions – four decades before that idea would be embraced by world football. Virtually all the clubs in the ASL were effectively company teams in the steel and heavy industry towns and cities of the north-east. The leading sides were Fall River Marksmen, who won the ASL title seven times, and Bethlehem Steel, who were champions on five occasions. The Marksmen regularly pulled sell-out crowds at their purpose-built, 15,000-capacity Mark's Stadium in the tiny Rhode Island town of North Tiverton. Other top sides included the wonderfully named Bedford Whalers, Paterson Silk Sox and Bridgeport Bears. Big-city teams included New York Field Club, Brooklyn Wanderers and the Boston Wonder Workers.

At the time, the United States had a very welcoming immigration policy and many football-mad Europeans were employed in American heavy industry, keen to watch their favourite game. The wealthy US teams were able to offer much higher wages than their Old World counterparts and by the mid-1920s over 50 top European players, many of them internationals, had been enticed over the water to enjoy lucrative pay days. Among them were Harold Pemberton Brittan, who played for Chelsea before moving to Bethlehem Steel and then Fall River, where he would score 87 goals in 77 games; former Cowdenbeath, Derby County and Coventry City centre-forward Bill Paterson, who would become a prolific scorer for Fall River, New Bedford Whalers, Providence Gold Bugs, Brooklyn Wanderers and Springfield Babes; and Newcastle and Leeds striker Jerry Best, who would score over 100 goals in two spells with New Bedford Whalers before returning home to become one of Darlington's best goalscorers with 68 in 109 games.

But this early golden age of football in the USA would only last for a decade. A mixture of vicious political in-fighting among the ASL and the USA football authorities and the crushing effects upon industry caused by 1929's Wall Street Crash and the resultant Great Depression would see the American Soccer League implode. By 1932 it was no more. Little has been written about the ASL, its records long since lost or destroyed, but one book has managed to piece together much of its story from exhaustive research into local newspapers of the time. If you're a fan of US football, Colin Jose's *The American League: The Golden Years of American Soccer 1921–1931* is a highly recommended read.

19

Europe

'Football is a simple game. Twenty-two men chase a ball for 90 minutes and at the end, the Germans always win.'

Gary Lineker

SIMILAR TO events in South America, one of the hottest issues in European football was amateurism. Some countries were already on the brink of professionalism; others were still putting up strong resistance against passing the rubicon into paying for playing. In 1923, and long before the creation of the renowned national Bundesliga, football in Germany was highly regionalised and almost as a matter of sporting principle, staunchly amateur. Being paid to play football was regarded as the antithesis of sportsmanlike behaviour and represented a cheapening of the game.

Ironically, German football had long been inspired by English team Corinthians, who often toured Germany to spread their message of fair play and good sportsmanship. Many in German football felt that professional English and Scottish footballers were somehow beyond the pale for receiving money to play a sport. This is not to say that all clubs were squeaky clean in their approach to amateurism but certainly, professional football was not introduced in West Germany until 1963.

Like in many other European countries, German football teams were part of a larger local sporting club that competed in everything from athletics and cycling to basketball, handball and gymnastics. During the early 1920s, the championship had become a distinctly arcane and slightly confusing affair. German football was split into seven regional leagues – Baltic, south-eastern, Brandenburg, central, northern, western and southern. At the end of their seasons, the champions came together in a knockout cup competition to contest the German championship quarter-finals. Only there couldn't be four quarter-finals because there were only seven teams, so each year one of the lucky teams was given a bye. In 1923 this was further complicated by the fact that the Western League had decided to extend its local championship to be played over a two-year period, which meant it didn't yet have a champion to qualify for the quarter-finals. Arminia Bielefeld were duly nominated as its unofficial champion representatives, much to the annoyance of other Western League teams. In 1923 the bye would go to VfB Königsberg, which did them few favours. In the semi-finals it meant they played favourites Hamburg, who beat them 3-2. The other semi would see Union Oberschöneweide beat SpVgg Greuther Fürth 2-1. In front of 64,000 at the Deutsches Stadion in Berlin, Hamburg would be crowned German champions after overcoming Union 3-0.

Bizarrely, a season earlier, Hamburg had managed to win, lose, win again and then decline the championship in a matter of days. The final against Nürnberg had ended 2-2. The replay got to 1-1 and was then abandoned because Nürnberg had been reduced to seven men, a player short of the eight required by match regulations. Hamburg were awarded the title but Nürnberg successfully appealed the decision. SV counter-appealed and the German FA gave them the championship cup back – which with studied indifference they declined, no longer wishing to be involved in such a farce. So the 1922 championship would go into the record books as null and void.

Die-hard England fans in particular may be interested to know that in 1923, Germany's national team was, well, pretty rubbish. During the year, they played six friendly internationals and got beaten 2-1 by Sweden and Finland, and 3-1 by Italy. They managed a 0-0 draw against Holland and won only twice, 1-0 against Norway and 2-1 against Switzerland.

Similar to German football, the French game in 1923 was highly regionalised and also supposed to be fully amateur. Only in France, 'amateur' meant something very different. In the 1920s, French football was in the grip of 'shamateurism' – a system that ensured the best players ended up at the most affluent and well-heeled clubs. How it operated was that club directors and officials would 'employ' players in their local mills, factories, car plants and vineyards, give them a bogus job title and then pay them a usually high agreed wage for the 'post'. The footballers concerned would most probably never visit their workplace, let alone put in a minute's work there, but every week a fat pay packet was slipped through their letterboxes. It was, of course, professional in everything but name.

French football in 1923 would also see the emergence of a young player who would first become one of the world's most-admired stars – and then later, the most reviled man in France. Eighteen-year-old half-back Alexandre Villaplane was so good that Victor Gibson, the Scottish manager of his club Sète, decided to fast-track him into the first team during the season. Villaplane was all high energy and hard tackling and his stellar career took off in 1923 at the south-eastern club.

An Algerian immigrant, Villaplane would later become the first Arab to win full international honours for France. For seven or eight years, he was regarded as one of the best players in the world. He played for France in the 1928 Olympics and then became *Les Bleus*' captain at the very first World Cup in Uruguay in 1930. On leading out the team for their first match against Mexico in Montevideo, Villaplane said, 'It was the happiest day of my life.'

He would play for Antibes in the first French professional championship in 1932 and then the slide began. Deeply involved in match-fixing, a series of bribery scandals and sick of the rigours of training, he left football forever to become a petty criminal, jewel thief and fraudster. His first spell in prison came in 1934 for fixing horse races; many more would follow. Early in World War Two, Villaplane was in prison again but this time, he was handed a get-out-of-jail free card which he wholeheartedly accepted. The former international footballer was offered the job of chauffeur to Paris's most notorious traitor and Nazi collaborator, illiterate criminal Henri Lafont, who used his Gestapo connections to get Villaplane released. It was from there that he grew from low-rent hood into murderous evil monster.

Villaplane would be given an officer's commission in the North African Brigade – a propaganda opportunity created by the Nazis to attract native French colonialists towards their cause. SS sub-lieutenant Villaplane and his new boss in the traitorous French Gestapo saw it differently – they were being handed the opportunity to steal, defraud and kill their fellow countrymen and women with total impunity. Villaplane blackmailed French Jewish families into handing over their businesses and their wealth, promising protection – and then handed them over to his German masters, who sent them on to their deaths in the concentration camps. At 32 rue Lauriston, the infamous home of the French Gestapo, he would drink, smoke and trade jokes with his fellow collaborationist thugs as together, they tortured and killed Parisiennes suspected of resistance activities. Villaplane would then spread terror even further.

In 1944, Villaplane and his North African Brigade were despatched to the south of France, their mission to eliminate French Resistance groups who were harrying German forces in the region. On 11 June 1944 Villaplane led his motley band of ex-criminals into the village of Mussidan in the Dordogne, hell-bent on reprisal and revenge. He ordered the villagers out on to the main street and began to demand money and valuables from the inhabitants, his fellow French. Once he had milked the village of its treasures, he ordered and took part in the summary execution of 57 innocent men, women and children. The Massacre of Mussidan constitutes the largest killing of civilians committed in the Dordogne during World War Two.

But time was running out for Villaplane. He would return to Paris shortly before the capital became encircled by the Allied forces and as the city was liberated, Villaplane would find himself back in prison – but this incarceration would be his last. Banged up in the notoriously bleak Montrouge jail, he awaited trial for his long and depressing litany of murderous crimes. In the courtroom, with slicked-back hair and wearing an expensive suit, he looked nothing less than a Pigalle pimp. As the jury listened intently, Villaplane performed a *tour de force* of prevarication. He was a patriot who had tried to help his fellow Frenchmen and was only wearing a Nazi uniform so that he could save French lives. He claimed that he took gold and valuables to keep them in safe keeping and out of the hands of the Bosch; that he put blanks into his revolver in Mussidan. Villaplane took responsibility for nothing. The trial's chief prosecutor called him, 'The greatest con man I have ever met. A pathological liar with no morals. Only ever out for himself.'

Of Villaplane's claim to be a sheep in wolf's clothing, the prosecutor countered, 'They left fire and ruin in their wake. A witness told us how he saw with his own eyes these mercenaries take jewels from the still-twitching and bloodstained bodies of their victims. Villaplane was in the midst of all this, calm and smiling. Cheerful, almost invigorated.'

The jury were unconvinced by his pitiful protestations and inveterate lying; the death sentence was inevitable. On a grey and stormy Boxing Day morning on the outskirts of Paris, Villaplane was walked out in chains alongside his fellow traitors Henri Lafont and disgraced, corrupt local police chief Pierre Bonny into the execution yard of Montrouge jail. As his firing squad lined up, Villaplane nonchalantly asked if he should remove his coat or leave it on. Seconds later, he was put up against a wall and shot dead. The irony was intense. France's first World Cup captain was killed by *balle* – a word which in French means both bullet and ball.

Elsewhere in Europe, several countries were bowing to the inevitability of professional football. Austria and Hungary would become the third and fourth leagues in the world to go pro; Spain and Italy would follow suit in 1926. France would finally stop the nonsense of shamateurism and turn fully professional in 1932. Football was really starting to take off and proof of its increasing popularity came in the number of stadiums being built or expanded. Football crowds had not yet reached the level of England and Scotland's much bigger attendances, but had more than tripled over the previous five years or so. Espanyol, Atlético Madrid and Valencia all built new concrete stadiums to cater for the surge in popularity. Of these, only Valencia's Estadio de Mestalla still exists today. Its original build only held 17,000, but for the time this was a big ground in Spain. Espanyol's new Estadi de Sarrià held just 10,000, while Atlético's Estadio Metropolitano de Madrid was the biggest build of all, holding 25,000 fans. But these were all much bigger upgrades on their previous grounds, which were primitive setups each containing a simple wooden stand and earth banks for terraces. The following year, Real Madrid built their Estadio Chamartín, which had a covered stand that held 4,000 and standing terraces catering for 11,000 fans. The Chamartín would open on 17 May 1924 with a 3-2 friendly win against Newcastle United. Real Madrid would play there for another 24 years before their move to new home, the Santiago Bernabéu Stadium.

The creation of La Liga was still five years away, and in 1923 all clubs competed to win the annual Copa del Rey. The country was broken up into eight regional leagues and the winners of each took part in a knockout competition. In 1923 the eight who made it down to the sudden-death games were Athletic Bilbao, Real Madrid, Real Sociedad, Sevilla, Real Vigo Sporting, Sporting de Gijón, CD Europa and Valencia. Biscay regional league division winners Athletic Bilbao won the championship trophy for the ninth time, with a 1-0 win in the final against CD Europa.

In Italy, football was on the cusp of massive changes and a good number of them extremely sinister. In 1923 the country saw a newly reorganised league system, where groups of regional leagues fed into northern and southern competitions. The winners of those two leagues met up in a national final, and in 1923, northern champions Genoa took on Lazio from the south, with the northern side trouncing the Rome team 6-1.

The re-organised league system showed that change was in the air for Italian football. Behind the scenes, an arch-Machiavellian was determined to turn it into a revolution. In 1922, Benito Mussolini had led the March on Rome, a mass demonstration and *coup d'état*. Terrified that it would lead to armed conflict, King Victor Emmanuel III appointed Mussolini as Italy's prime minister. Mussolini would spend the next few years doing all in his power to bully his country into becoming a one-party dictatorship. At the heart of his brutal and simplistic nationalism was an unquestioning love of country and pride in Italy's greatness. His beady chancer's eye immediately fell upon sport, and football in particular, as a route to spreading his philosophy. For Mussolini, dominance on the pitch underlined Italian supremacy and from 1923 onwards, he poured fortunes into the rapid expansion of football in Italy and the development of its national side. It's also rumoured that he poured many a high-denomination lire note or two into the back pockets of a good few international referees.

The role Mussolini played in the fast-paced change of Italian football could be seen in physical form as grand new fascist-funded football stadiums began to be built all around the country. The Stadio Municipale Benito Mussolini in Turin, Stadio della Vittoria in Bari, Bologna's Stadio Littoriale, the Stadio Edda Ciano Mussolini in Livorno, the Stadio XXVIII Ottobre in L'Aquila and the Stadio Giovanni Berta in Florence were all impressive concrete builds that were meant to emphasise the industrial might of Italy and the artistry of its architectural design. Mussolini shamelessly used football to represent the fascist way. As Bill Murray pointed out in his book *The World's Game; A History of Soccer*, 'Mussolini's Fascist regime was the first to use sports as an integral part of government.'

Further east, Poland's new national league was entering its third season and the country joined FIFA, along with neighbours Czechoslovakia. In the newly emerging Soviet Union, many regions were still torn apart by civil war and as a result, the championship was suspended. Football matches were still played on a local basis in the bigger cities, but Russians had more on their minds than sport. The story in the Hungary of 1923 continued to be all about Jimmy Hogan's ex-club MTK Budapest. Their dominance in the country's football was absolute. Between 1914 and 1925 they won the league title ten times in a row, and in 1923 they achieved a league and cup double, leaving Újpest as the runners-up in both competitions. Third place in the Nemzeti Bajnokság I went to Ferencváros and in the early 1920s, these were by and large the three biggest and most successful clubs in Hungary.

In Holland, RCH won their first Dutch championship. The way the Dutch season was organised was different again. The champions of four regional leagues – east, north, south and west – came together to contest a play-off, each team facing one another home and away. In a close-run contest, RCH won four and lost two, Be Quick 1887 and Go Ahead both won two, drew one and lost three, and Willem II won three and lost three. The Netherlands would finally become professional in 1954.

The Belgian league was far more British-like in its organisation. Its top division consisted of 14 teams, all of whom played one another home and away. The bottom two were relegated to the second tier, whose champions and runners-up would replace them. In 1923 the champions were Royale Union Saint-Gilloise – who won 11 titles between 1904 and 1935, being the most successful Belgian side before World War Two.

All across Europe, the British influence still ran deep. English and Scottish clubs regularly undertook close-season tours around Scandinavia and mainland Europe, including the amateur maestros, Corinthians. Coaches like Jack Hogan, Victor Gibson and Jack Watson weren't the only Brits spreading new footballing ideas across Europe. Former Scottish international Johnny Madden, who played for Celtic, Dundee and Tottenham Hotspur among others, was called the 'Father of Czech Football'. From 1905 to 1930, Madden managed Slavia Prague during an early golden age for the club. Playing the typically Scottish short-passing game, Slavia won the Czech league four times during the 1920s. The European clubs and national teams were fast catching up in terms of tactics, talent and ability and soon, very soon, they would become the football masters.

20

Getting the News

'It's not the world that's got so much worse but that the news coverage has got so much better.'

G.K. Chesterton

TODAY, CONSTANTLY updated and exhaustive news sources both online and off feed us endless football facts about our favourite clubs and players. Much of it is speculation, rumour and often, downright fake news deliberately posted to take us down clickbait rabbit holes of disinformation. But back in 1923 things were a lot simpler and dammit, much more truthful. News was hard to find. BBC Radio was still in its very infancy and didn't yet cover any form of sport; broadcast television was many years away. The football fan of the early 1920s broadly had three sources of news – match programmes, newspapers and, perhaps surprisingly, cigarette cards.

The earliest football programmes were simple one-page affairs that contained little but the most basic of information – the date of the match, the name of the opponents, the two team line-ups and who would referee and run the line. By the early 20th century, advertising had started to get a foothold in the world of football and clubs soon realised that the more ads they could sell in their programmes, the more profitable they would become. Soon they would expand to between eight and 16 pages, generally working on the formula of one page of advertising to one page of editorial and wider content.

In 1923, many local newspapers would carry a whole front page completely made up of advertisements and most football clubs followed suit in their football programme designs. Unsurprisingly, the advert content was totally targeted at men. The front cover of the Hull City v Wolverhampton Wanderers programme from 14 April 1923 gives a perfect example. Apart from bare details of the day's fixture and the names of the teams, the page was thrown over to an illustrated advert for Hull's 'Principal Hatters and Outfitters', Ward and Abercrombie, of 5 Silver Street. Featuring a cartoon of a suave-looking gent in a stylish titfer, the ad read, 'Stetson hats, styled for smart men! Many of the most discerning men of today choose Stetsons. They are appreciative of the Stetson feeling for style, quality and appearance throughout a long and useful life.' Hardly riveting as copywriting goes, but Ward and Abercrombie knew their market. Look at any newsreel or crowd photo from 1923 and the first thing you'll notice is the ubiquity of the hat. From flat cap to trilby and Stetson, headwear was worn by the overwhelming majority of fans.

Another huge advertising market for programmes was beer. Brewers knew that football fans represented a significant section of their customers, so companies went out of their way to place adverts in programmes. The Ireland v Wales British Home Championship match programme from April 1923, for example, threw over its entire front cover to Welsh Ales of Wrexham. Throughout the season, Tranmere Rovers' programme, *The Prentonian*, had on its front page large ads for 'Yates Pale Bitter Ale – Always in Splendid Condition'. Beer was big!

Clubs had fast cottoned on to the fact that another thirst that fans had was for news and information about their teams, and the average programme now contained many more features, editorial notes and short biogs of players. It was all very cheery, uncontroversial and non-threatening fare but pre-radio (though the BBC had set up the year before, the number of radio sets in the country could be counted in the low thousands), and before television and internet, football news was hard to come by. There was a handful of doughty and committed national sports newspapers like *Athletic News*, *Topical Times* and the winningly named *The Sports Budget and Soccer Special* – more of which later – and local newspapers that ran match reports and the odd player or manager interview, but it was a time when information was thin on the ground and hard to come by. As well as creating a connection with their fans, clubs realised that decent matchday programmes added an important revenue stream to their commercial setups. In 1923 the average price of a programme was two old pennies. The cost of producing and printing them was largely covered by the advertising revenue, so sell 12,000 at a match, that's £100 in the club coffers and you're covering three months' wages for a player on the maximum weekly rate.

Outside businesses had already begun to see football and its players as a major money-making opportunity. From well before World War One Great Britain had been massively influenced by new marketing and advertising ideas that swept over the Atlantic from the USA. One in particular would captivate football fans – the cigarette card. In the early 1870s, the American tobacco company Allen and Ginter came up with the very practical idea of inserting pieces of card into their packets to protect the cigarettes from damage. It didn't take the company's advertising department long to realise they were missing a trick – to wit, why not use the 'stiffeners' as an advertising tool? So Allen and Ginter began turning the 'stiffeners' into a series of picture cards that smokers could collect. Initially, these included subjects as diverse as baseball stars and Native American chiefs and soon proved hugely popular with the American cigarette-smoking public. Sales soared and over in Britain, the massive W.O. and W.H. Wills company started to take notice. In 1896 they produced the first set of cards to feature a British sporting theme – 50 cards, each depicting a first-class England cricketer. Later that year, a small Manchester cigarette company, Marcus & Company, published the very first football card set, *Footballers and Colours*, and the ball was set in motion.

Some cigarette companies attempted to educate. In 1923, John Players & Son issued a series of cards depicting and describing characters from Charles Dickens novels, and a second featuring miniatures of famous female paintings containing everyone from Mona Lisa to Lady Hamilton. But it was football that sold the most fags. In his book *Collecting Cigarette and Trade Cards*, Gordon Howson explained the massive popularity of cigarette cards thus, 'At a time when the average family could not afford books, and with the technique of reproducing photographs in newspapers still some years away, these cards could inform and amuse, and bring a little colour into what were all too often very drab lives.'

The cards also encouraged early examples of what we'd now call 'pester power'. Children would nag parents to buy cigarette brands that contained the newest and latest football card series – and encourage them to smoke more, to boot. They were largely kicking into an open goal because the stats on cigarette smoking in the early 1920s are extraordinary. Over 80 per cent of male adults smoked, and over 50 per cent of women. Bolton's ace goalscorer David Jack chain-smoked before and after matches, and sometimes during. Coaching staff would often light one up and pass it over to him for a drag as he trotted along the touchline.

Many of the writers who penned copy for the cards were not only knowledgeable about the game but also highly opinionated, and didn't hold back in their descriptions of individual players.

In 1923, British American Tobacco launched a new 50-card series called *Famous Footballers*; number three in the collection was Cardiff City's James Gill. The card described him as, 'One of the most consistent goal scorers in the Cardiff team, from either inside position, is a Sheffield native and at one time was a serviceable member of the Wednesday team, playing for them as an extreme winger in 1913. When the Hillsborough team lost its place in the First Division at the end of season 1919/20, they allowed Gill to join Cardiff, and his success must have surprised the Wednesday management.'

'Serviceable' is certainly damning with faint praise. It means to fulfil a function adequately, so nothing great by any means. And reading between the lines, the Wednesday management's imagined 'surprise' at how well Gill was performing in Wales suggests they didn't have a clue how to get the best out of a talented player.

Card number 35 in the same series was Sunderland's Charlie Buchan and it's fair to say that the writer of his cigarette card was a fully paid-up fan:

'The star forward of the Sunderland team is a native of Plumstead. He played with Leyton, the old Southern League club, before making Roker Park his headquarters. Buchan is probably the cleverest centre-forward in the country and at the same time, the most unorthodox. A large percentage of his goals are headed though, his long reach and rare judgement enabling him to get many a ball that would elude a man of average height.'

Some cigarette card series were gloriously succinct and contained a broad range of information, expertly expressed in very few words. In 1923, Sunripe Cigarettes ('Which Stand Alone for Size and Tone!) also launched a 50-card football series. Number seven belonged to Charles Alton of Brentford and in just over 60 words it offered the avid reader a veritable wealth of facts:

'5ft 11.5in tall, 12st 10lb, this stalwart back was born at Chesterfield and gained his first experience of league football at Rotherham County, missing two matches only in the campaign following the war. Joining Brentford for season 1921/22, he proved a valuable recruit, his play at right-back creating a very favourable impression. He did not miss a league match in season 1922/23.'

It would not be until 1929 that the first research links were made between cigarette smoking, lung cancer and other serious bronchial diseases, but in 1923 there were already important names in football who were vehemently opposed to smoking. Huddersfield Town's great manager Herbert Chapman totally disapproved of his players indulging in tobacco and alcohol and was never happy to see their faces on cards advertising cigarettes.

Little was written about football in the national newspapers of 1923, aside from fairly brief match reports. Local papers would generally carry fuller, more detailed reports from their local teams' games and perhaps a little general news about life behind the scenes at the clubs. The bigger regional papers in football hotbeds like Manchester, Liverpool, London and the north-east gave much fuller coverage. But the leading sports newspaper of the day was *Athletic News* – a weekly eight-page national publication, published in Manchester, that also covered athletics, boxing, cycling and other sports, but always majored on football. Published every Monday, less than 48 hours after the weekend's games, its match reports covered every First Division game, most from the second tier and many from the two sections of the Third Division.

Originally founded in 1875 as the *Athletic News and Cyclists' Journal*, it later simply became *Athletic News*. Its long-time editor was James Catton – a man many regard to be the godfather of football journalism and one of the first writers to truly understand the importance of the game, what it meant to people, how it drew communities together and how genuinely beautiful the game could be. Catton loved and genuinely cared about football and so it was no surprise that his editorship at *Athletic News* did everything it could to not only popularise the game, but champion its importance in the culture of our country. Because he cared so much about football, the newspaper never shirked from criticising the establishment and the authorities, never shrunk from holding clubs and players to account for their shortcomings, and created an eight-page weekly that would pioneer serious football journalism.

From a reasonably well-to-do family, Catton became disenchanted with the idea of studying to become a doctor and, excited by the ever-expanding world of journalism – from 1856 to 1880, the number of daily newspapers in England exploded from just 15 to nearly 200 – he became an apprentice reporter on the *Preston Herald* in 1875. Working first in general news, he persuaded his editor to let him write regular match reports about Preston North End and cover news of the club in much greater depth. This was in the days when football was regarded as a minority interest, a kickabout game, and such coverage was relatively unheard of. Nearly 40 years later, Catton would recall:

'In days long ago when association footballers wore beards and breeches, instead of being clean-shaven and donning shorts or running pants, newspapers, as a whole, took very little notice of matches.'

The moment that changed everything, both for English football and for Catton's future prospects, happened in 1875 at the Freemasons' Tavern in London's West End; it was there that the FA historically agreed to sanction the beginning of true professional football. It had been a hot potato issue for some years, with the better-off English clubs enticing the best players with regular under-the-counter payments, occasional cash lump sums and bogus jobs in the factories, mills and businesses owned by board members for which they were paid 'ghost wages'. Ranged against them were a legion of clubs who despised such 'shamateurism', determined to uphold the sporting principles of truly amateur football.

At the meeting, and under great pressure from the richer sides, the FA finally decided to give the thumbs-up to full-time paid professional football. Catton was the only journalist present and delivered his first major football scoop for his new newspaper, the Nottingham-based *Daily Guardian*. Not only did he cover the meeting, but also came down fiercely on the side of football adopting professionalism. This made him many fans among a raft of clubs and players, and in 1900, to popular acclaim within the game, he was made editor of *Athletic News*. Under his control, it would soon become the country's most-read newspaper by fans and players alike. And indeed, he would become the first editor to train and employ former players among his editorial staff and harness their knowledge of the game.

The son of a university-educated classics scholar and tutor, Catton's match reports were often peppered with literary references and quotes and allusions to ancient and classical history. Often he went too far and utterly confused his readership. Writing under the pseudonym 'Tityrus' – itself a reference to Greek mythology – his early match reports were sometimes dizzyingly eccentric. Reporting on a Nottingham Forest v Notts County derby match his pen ran deeply purple: 'The fierce partisans of each side rubbed their shoulders together, and as I looked around the parallelogram ... the words of Hecate, in *Macbeth*, were brought vividly to mind: red spirits and grey, mingle, mingle, mingle, you that mingle may! Black spirits and white.'

As the years passed, he learned to become slightly less esoteric to properly serve his audience, but not by much. By 1923, Catton was well into his prime but still reporting every week on matches. Here's 'Tityrus' reporting on Blackburn

Rovers 3 Cardiff City 1 at Ewood Park on 22 January 1923, a week after a round of FA Cup matches:

'Back to the league! That was the order for Saturday. The change seemed too sudden for the Blackburn Rovers, who had been taking ozone at Rhyl. The transition from a tempestuous tie to the hebdomadal amble of league life was evidently appreciated by the Rovers. Rarely did they gallop; they just ambled. But they won. Cardiff ambled even less. The Welshmen sauntered through the game. Generally when I have seen Cardiff City they have been as active as ants. On this occasion they crawled like caterpillars. Please do not take me too literally. As Gulliver in his travels teaches – everything must be judged by comparison. I am comparing the speed and the bustle of a good match, the players keen and fresh, with the measured pace and slow serenity of this game. The first half left me colder than any north wind could do.'

And how about this for a scorching intro? In 1922's Christmas edition, 'Tityrus' reported on Oldham's home 1-1 draw with Burnley:

'Somebody has called darkness "bituminous obscurity". This must have been a politician. It is a phrase worthy of the author of "terminological inexactitude". But whoever invented "bituminous obscurity", there was a lot of it about on the heights above Werneth. At times it seemed to be shadow football.'

Not quite what you might read today in the *Daily Mirror*, *The Times* or *The Sun*. But it was a different game for football reporters in the early 1920s. There was, of course, no TV or radio with pundits summing up the events of a game, adding colour and offering tactical thoughts about what had worked and what hadn't. So *Athletic News*'s correspondents, all writing under pseudonyms, were encouraged by Catton to be analysts as much as straight blow-by-blow match reporters; to be creative, clever and eye-catching with their prose. To make readers think and crucially for newspaper sales, come back again the following week for more. Early in the 1922/23 campaign, 'Impressionist' wrote compellingly about one of his tips for the season ahead. On 4 September he covered Middlesbrough's 2-0 away win at Huddersfield Town and wrote very impressionistically indeed:

'Even the layman can pick out the thoroughbred from a super-annuated equine collection. Even the partisan in football is discerning enough sometimes against inclination to realise the classical amid football mediocrity. The majority of those who followed the scintillating passage of events at Huddersfield no doubt had mixed feelings at the finish; on the one hand, misgivings over the defeat of the Town club, on the other profound admiration for the valour of the conquerors. What the season portends in terms of general innate quality is at present as seen through a glass darkly. Still, I do venture emphatically to say that Middlesbrough will be noted as one of the thoroughbreds.'

Often his correspondents were highly opinionated and pulled no punches when it came to criticism. Unlike football reporters on local and regional newspapers, who were far more partisan and keen to stay onside with their clubs, *Athletic News*'s pseudonymous writers penned their reports without fear or favour. On 4 September 1922, 'Pilgrim' witnessed the 3-3 draw between Manchester City and Sheffield United at their increasingly decrepit old ground on Hyde Road. Despite being an end-to-end six-goal thriller, 'Pilgrim' had little time for either team and let the fans of both teams realise that in no uncertain terms:

'I saw no reason at all to alter the opinion I first formed of the merits of Manchester City and Sheffield United as revealed in the opening game at Bramall Lane. Nor am I yet convinced that either will go far. They are two very ordinary sides indeed.'

In the 2 April 1923 edition, 'Harricus' reported on Blackburn's 1-0 win over Oldham Athletic and left his readers in no doubt about what he thought of the game,

'One feels rather diffident in withholding praise from a winning team because after all they have accomplished what they set out to do, that is the gathering of a couple of points. But I must say that had Blackburn Rovers been playing any other club than the one at the foot of the table – sorry my Oldham friends – I am afraid that the harvest would have been a failure. A late lamented champion supporter of the Blackburn Rovers club, Dr Morley, once stated that his team have played like "old women in clogs". Had he been present at Ewood Park on Saturday I'm afraid that he would have used some similar forcible expression. The team never played like winners until they had actually won! And then there was only 16 minutes left in which to display their talents, for the appreciation of their sorely tried supporters … let me not be misunderstood. The victory was not a lucky one, as we usually understand the term. There was no doubt about the superiority of the winners, but their play was insipid, the forwards terribly weak.'

Athletic News had little competition at a national level apart from *The Sportsman*. First published in 1865, its chief focus was horse racing but a page or so was turned over to regular football reporting. The last edition of *The Sportsman* was published in 1924, when it was absorbed into *Sporting Life*. *Athletic News* would continue to report at the heart of English football until the mid-1930s. Catton would remain as both editor and journalist at *Athletic News* until 1924. According to a splendid piece about Catton by Conor Heffernan on the These Football Times website, on his retirement, players and officials from across England collected several guineas to give him as a leaving present and as the website observed, 'The thought of a modern football journalist receiving a similar token of respect is difficult to imagine.'

But that was not to be the end of Catton's career in football journalism. Still besotted by the game, he continued on for the last 12 years of his life as a freelance reporter. Again as

Conor Heffernan reveals in his These Football Times feature, Sunderland legend Charles Buchan remembered being interviewed by Catton in his final years, and on the day that Buchan was moving home:

'He called at my house for an interview and I was pleased to give it to him. It was an uncomfortable business, though, because he arrived just as our furniture was being carried from a removal van into the house in Mayfield Gardens, Hendon. We sat on two bare packing cases in the bare room and talked. Jimmy was a little tubby fellow, not five feet in height. He was however, the greatest writer of his day, knowledgeable, benevolent and respected by all the authorities.'

Inspired by Catton, who became a mentor, Buchan would go on to become a well-respected football journalist and writer himself, co-founding the Football Writers' Association and launching his highly successful *Charles Buchan's Football Monthly* magazine. These were the days before football agents and many smaller clubs didn't even employ scouts, so teams would literally place small ads in newspaper jobs vacant columns if they needed new players. In *Athletic News*, a close-season small ad read, 'NEWPORT COUNTY AFC LTD – FIRST-CLASS PLAYERS WANTED for the following positions: – CENTRE-FORWARD, LEFT FULL-BACK AND HALF-BACK. Full particulars.' Sometimes adverts gave a strong hint at what a tough close season clubs might have ahead of them in terms of recruitment. Pity poor Third Division North's Tranmere Rovers, who ran an advertisement in *Athletic News* in the summer of 1923 which simply read, 'Tranmere Rovers REQUIRE PLAYERS FOR ALL POSITIONS. Full particulars to Bert Cooke.'

21

Betting and Football Pools

*'Bookies love their regular punters because they
learn nothing but false hope and so come back
again and again and again.'*

Anonymous

IN 1923, Studley Street in Birmingham's Sparkbrook area was
a tight-knit, working-class community in the south-east of the
city. Local families knew one another and everyone knew Alf
Chinn. One of the original Old Contemptibles, he'd joined up
as a soldier before conscription came in and was badly injured
during battle at La Bassée in France in February 1915. He
was invalided home and started a business making parts for
iron fire grates. Working with friends and family members,
Alf's small company was initially successful and earned him
a decent enough living. But as the immediate postwar boom
edged towards economic depression in 1923, profits dropped
dramatically. So Alf became a full-time illegal street bookie.

Following the 1845 Gaming Act, the only gambling
allowed in the United Kingdom was at racecourses. Betting
shops and street operations were strictly unlawful. High-
minded politicians, church leaders and social reformers
regarded betting – and drink – as the scourge of the feckless

working classes and felt it their moral duty to save the masses from themselves. Private casinos and clubs, where the upper classes won and much more regularly lost huge betting fortunes, remained untouched by the legislation. The Gaming Act remained unrepealed for decades. Yet betting on football games and horse races was and would always be an important and hugely popular entertainment and distraction for men who worked long hard hours in factories, mills, shops and shipyards. And so it remained underground.

Alf's street bookie business was typical of the time. His grandson Carl Chinn is a much-noted historian, author and broadcaster who has written over 30 books about the history of Birmingham and the urban working class in Britain. He writes eloquently about his grandad's work. In a piece for the Free Library he described how it all began:

'My great uncle Wal remembered that, "There was Dot Ingram, your grandad and me talking in Studley Street. Nack Carey and Bill Preston was the bookmakers and this kid came round with a tanner bet for them and your Grandad says, 'They've just gone. Where they gone we just don't know.' This kid went to tek this tanner bet to Nack's house. He'd gone out and he was telling your Grandad about it and so he said, 'Gie it me.' That's how he started bookmaking. The bet went down."

'Nack and Billy Preston carried on for a while in Studley Street, whilst Grandad took bets nearby, standing on the corner of Ladypool Avenue, between Ombersley Road and Oldfield Road. He was always on the lookout for the police because cash betting away from racecourses was illegal and conviction entailed a minimum fine of £10.'

Chris spoke of how local police were given roles as 'bookie snatchers', dressing up in plain clothes as coalmen or street singers to catch out men who were paid to act as lookouts for the bookmakers. If the police did manage to best them, the bookies would flee, hiding in local communal toilets and wash houses. In other towns and cities, the police would pose as punters to infiltrate their local illegal bookie worlds, but often with little success. In 1923 most people knew their local bobbies and bookies were highly suspicious of any 'new faces' that came to bet with them. Across the nation, a legion of police officers took bribes, turned a blind eye and often tipped off bookies about potential raids. Illegal betting was so rife across the nation that most local authorities operated a laissez-faire attitude towards it. Secretly, most policemen were laying money on football matches through friends and family members and it was only when senior officers were trying to make a name for themselves that raids occurred.

Some illegal bookies worked out of their own 'shop fronts'. In the Bolton of 1923, husband and wife team Stephen and Bella Thomasson ran a 'tobacconists shop' that contained not one cigarette, cigar or single ounce of pipe tobacco – until it was needed for 'window dressing'. Inside, nothing but empty shelves, a couple of desks, a safe and a ticker tape machine that sent them hot-off-the-press information about football match results and horse race wins. Apart from Bella, women were not allowed inside the shop and certain 'arrangements' they had with local police meant they were seldom raided. On the rare occasion that a police visit was planned, paid-off sources within the local constabulary would warn the Thomassons and instantly, cigarettes and cigars appeared on the shelves and the ticker tape machine was stowed out of sight.

But beyond the local and well-known neighbourhood bookies, there was a darker game at play; more deeply criminal, much more exploitative. A network of illegal bet-makers would descend upon an area, spend a few weeks taking bets and then disappear to another part of the town or city, without paying out the wins. Other gangs would be in charge of collecting debts from punters who'd got behind on their payments. In this totally unregulated world where there was no recourse, no chance to go to the police, debtors were beaten, threatened and intimidated.

Birmingham's betting world was no stranger to hoodlums. The 'Brumagem Boys' were a violent gang of mobsters who throughout the 1920s had a major hold over racecourse bookmakers. Thanks to the ever-expanding railway system, the gang travelled across the country and 'took control' of dozens of racecourses around the Midlands and the north. They demanded a protection money cream-off from on-course bookmakers, sometimes for as much as 50 per cent of their profits, and these Brummie gangsters were brutal men. Bookmakers who pushed against them and employed local hardmen for their own protection soon discovered that the Brumagems stopped at nothing to get their big fat share of what at the time was a massively lucrative betting market. Bookies and the paid henchmen who refused the gang's 'support' were regularly attacked with hammers, blades, flick-knives, bottles and fists.

By 1921, the Brumagems had become so ambitious they decided to take on London's 'Italian Mob', the Sabinis, who controlled the bookmakers at Epsom, Ascot and all points south. It led to vicious fights and ambushes in and around numerous racecourses and even the attempted murder of Brumagem crime boss Billy Kimber, who was shot in the side at a cloak-and-dagger meeting where the Birmingham gang offered a truce to the Sabini family. It was no surprise when you consider that in 1923, on-course betting's annual turnover was £500m.

A more communal and much less threatening illegal market for football betting was inside the nation's workplaces, and bookies ran their own extensive networks of trusted lieutenants to take bets and encourage new punters in and among the local workforce. The modus operandi was to hand out printed coupons containing a series of upcoming football fixtures. Punters bet pennies on any number of matches, win, lose or draw, depending on how much they could afford. Sometimes, for potentially bigger financial gain, on what the precise result may be in a game. Foremen and well-known, well-liked workers would often be targeted as 'actors' by the bookies, who knew the more respected, the more chatty and garrulous were likely to sell on more coupons. Each 'actor' would get a cut of all the coupons they sold. In 1923 it was usually between eight old pennies and a shilling out of a pound, depending how successful they were at drawing more punters into the coupon ring. It was a big deal in factories and mills. No one cared that it was potentially illegal, it was something they did with their mates and drew everyone together. And heck, sometimes you won some money. Rarely a fortune, but for men living week to week on what they earned, enough to make life a little easier for a while. A little bit of unexpected sunshine.

At many factories and larger workplaces, managers also took a cut of the profits in return for turning a blind eye. If it kept the workforce happy and didn't affect output they couldn't give a toss as long as it also made them some serious pocket money. As long as everybody's backs were being scratched, only over-zealous police inspectors looking for increased convictions and promotions really cared about what working men did with their money. Well, them and Whitehall. Governments don't like illegal, unregulated industries that make profits without contributing to the national tax pot. Aware of how much money was being bet on football matches and horse races, the government had tried to put a kibosh on the whole affair in 1920, by passing the Ready Money Football Betting Bill. For hundreds of years the establishment, the aristocracy, and increasingly the newly arisen middle class were well used to regulating, constraining, wagging fingers at and lecturing to the working people of Britain, their peasant class. The buggers might have just got the vote – well, a proportion of them – but they weren't about to get away with depriving the Treasury of cash. By 1920, the government decided to tighten and toughen up existing betting laws.

The Act was passed, 'To prevent the writing, printing, publishing or circulating in the United Kingdom of advertisements, circulars or coupons of any ready money football betting business. Ready money football betting business shall mean any business or agency for the making of ready money bets or wagers, or for the receipt of any money or valuable things as the consideration for a bet or wager in connection with any football game.'

Conviction meant a fine of up to £25, or in default of payment, imprisonment for up to one month. Or in a case of a second or subsequent conviction, a £100 fine or up to three months inside.

During the second reading of the bill, Lord Gainford commented, 'An evil exists in connection with coupon betting and it is detrimental to the great game of football ... it has been found in a great number of factories, mills, workshops and shipyards that a system has been growing up which enables a certain number of firms and bookmakers to reap a great harvest out of the young men by this coupon system. The men in most influence in these works are often induced to become agents, with the result that something like 40 per cent of the money goes in profits to the firms, and those who speculate receive very inadequate terms in connection with this system.'

But screw the system. The Act was passed but made little difference to the reality on the ground. Operations remained clandestine and pretty much tolerated by public and most police alike. The more cautious coupon 'firms' effectively simply dodged around the new regulations by taking payment through postal orders, which by definition were not ready cash. But beyond the one rule for us, one rule for them ruling classes, no one really cared less and all was business as usual. This was a working-class betting culture that had happily existed for years. The demand continued to be huge and there was nothing much new laws could do to stop it. Local illegal bookies continued to make a decent living, but hardly great fortunes. And sometimes they had to take it on the chin when the police were looking for a result.

Then, in 1923, a Liverpool-based Post Office messenger boy spotted a loophole that would truly hit the jackpot. John Moores came from a poor north-west background and was desperate to make money and better himself. He had an entrepreneurial bent, and as a keen young football fan discovered an idea that he was convinced could make him a fortune. A former World War One Coldstream Guard officer, John Jervis Bernard, had started a 'football pool' in Birmingham, in a bid to make a living for himself. The idea was stunningly simple. His family, friends, people he knew and those he could persuade to get involved would pay pennies every week to predict a series of match results for the following Saturday. Those who predicted the most score draws would share the money from that week's 'pool' of money. Bernard would take ten per cent off the top as his operational fee. It would never make him a fortune, as it was so locally based, but it pulled in a moderately decent return. Once Moores got wind of this new scheme, he realised two things: that this new idea was by definition not gambling but a game of skill which Moores believed took it outside of the new 1920 Gambling Act, and that 'scale' was the problem holding Bernard's idea back.

To make real money, it had to be exposed to a much wider market. Moores convinced friends and fellow Post Office workers Colin Askham and Bill Hughes to join him in the venture and together, they invested £50 each into launching their own 'football pools' project. With the cash they rented an office in Liverpool, hired a secretary and bought an old printing press. The plan was to target the people who most wanted to bet on football, the fans. To do that, they would go straight to source – and sell their 'football pools coupons' outside grounds at the biggest games to build their market.

They named their company 'Littlewoods'. Their full-time job contracts at the Post Office prohibited them from taking on any other outside work, so to use their own names would have led to investigations and dismissals. None of the trio could afford to lose their Post Office work, certainly not when they were trying to build this ambitious new project. So they called the firm Littlewoods after Askham's original family name to keep them under the wire. By November 1923, all was ready.

The great launch of their new scheme was a disaster. Printing out 4,000 of their new coupons, the three men travelled to Manchester on 23 November and distributed them to the fans before a Manchester United match. Only 35 coupons were returned, making the three men the princely sum of £4 7s 6d (£4.37½). Their ten per cent cut didn't even cover the train fares back to Liverpool.

Dispirited but undeterred, they persevered and the following week travelled to Boothferry Park in Hull. There they handed out 10,000 coupons before a Hull City game – only one was returned. Throughout the rest of the season, things got little better. Fans were suspicious of unknown out-of-towners hawking their wares at football grounds and as is often the case with human nature, they were fearful of the 'new'. The great new idea was fast going down the tubes. A crisis meeting was called at which Askham and Hughes reluctantly argued they should cut their losses and wind up the company. Moores shocked them both by offering to give each man £200 to buy them out. He was determined to make the idea work and go it alone, convinced that once football pools 'caught on' it would be a surefire winner.

Ever the entrepreneur, Moores gambled once again on scale. He employed 'agents' the length and breadth of the country, made new contacts at grounds large and small and developed an extensive distribution system around Britain, including through the postal service, to get his idea in front of as many would-be punters as possible. Soon, his company was printing tens of thousands of coupons every week – and then hundreds of thousands. More importantly, he was selling most of them. Thanks to the success of the competition, by 1930 Moores had become a millionaire.

Ironically, the year before that, the public prosecutor decided to challenge the Littlewoods 'loophole' that football pools was a game of skill and not gambling, and charged Moores under the 1920 Ready Money Football Betting Act. He was initially convicted but as his company never accepted cash, only postal orders cashed after winning results had been confirmed, his appeal was upheld. He would go on to create Littlewoods catalogues and stores and later become chairman of Everton Football Club. Liverpool John Moores University is named in his honour.

22

The Two Tommys

'We don't even ask for happiness,
just a little less pain.'

Charles Bukowski, US poet and writer

NOVEMBER 1923 was a cold and often icy month. Up and down the leagues, numerous games were called off. Despite a chilly day and an iron-hard Meadow Lane pitch, the Saturday, 10 November game between Notts County and Aston Villa went ahead as planned, which was good news for the visitors. A close-fought battle ended 1-0 in their favour which took Villa to third in the First Division, a place above Notts. It had been a promising few years for the club. They won the FA Cup for the sixth time in 1920 and ended up in a strong fifth place at the end of the 1921/22 season. Talented young players were coming through into the first team and eminent among them was highly promising 23-year-old centre-half Tommy Ball. He shone in the Meadow Lane encounter, but it would be the last game he would ever play. The following day Tommy was shot dead in the garden of his Birmingham home.

Born in Chester-le-Street, Ball was the sixth son of a coalminer – he also had two sisters and a younger brother – and went down the pits himself aged just 13. He shone for a series of colliery teams before being signed up by Newcastle United. By 1923, the Football League was awash with former colliers. The old joke used to be that managers in need of new players in the north-east, Ayrshire, South Yorkshire, the Midlands and south Wales would travel to their nearest mine and shout down the shafts, 'I need a new winger/defender/goalkeeper/whatever. Who have you got down there?'

For years, most collieries had their own teams and most played highly competitive football with tough, super-fit young men in their sides. Before World War One, an army of ex-miners left their jobs underground to play full-time for local sides. In the north-east, league teams like Newcastle, Sunderland, Middlesbrough, Gateshead, Durham and Ashington regularly shouted down the shafts to enlist important new players. In south Wales, Swansea, Cardiff, Aberdare, Merthyr and Newport did the same. Come peacetime, clubs the length and breadth of the country looked increasingly towards former miners to stiffen the backbone of their sides. Because of their sometimes life or death experiences underground, they had a reputation for teak-tough resilience, courage and working as part of a team.

And that described Tommy Ball, who'd signed for Villa on a free transfer from Newcastle United during the 1919/20 season. Standing 6ft tall, he was a great header of the ball, renowned as a hard tackler and positionally astute. He'd never played for the Magpies' first team and found it hard to get into Aston Villa's starting 11, still finding his way in the game. During his first three seasons with the club he managed just 27 games. Talented though he was, keeping him out of the side was one of English football's most controversial characters, Frank Barson. Ball mostly got to play when Barson was suspended, which happened often.

A former blacksmith from Grimesthorpe, near Barnsley, Barson was the club captain and generally acknowledged at the time to be the hardest man in English football. He was violent and bad-tempered, both on and off the pitch. When he signed for Villa from Barnsley, Barson flatly refused to move to Birmingham, saying he had too many 'business interests' in South Yorkshire to leave his home turf. Barson commuted to training and games, and to the constant frustration of Villa officials, often turned up late. His close circle of friends back in South Yorkshire included Lawrence and William Fowler, notorious Sheffield criminal gang leaders, who both ended up being hanged for murder in 1925. Barson regularly exchanged prison letters with the brothers as they awaited their fate. He was the sort of player you'd be overjoyed to have on your side, revolted by him if he was opposing you. Villa put up with his difficult behaviour because he was a fearless leader on the pitch and a ruthless enforcer. His speciality was the 'Barson shoulder charge' which badly injured several players throughout his career. He acted like a thug, constantly intimidating opponents, kidney punching off the ball and legging them over when the ref was looking the other way. A contemporary *Times* column reported, 'On frequent occasions Barson was escorted out of grounds by policemen to protect him from angry opposition fans.' By 1925, opponents had got so tired with his rough play a petition organised by the Chelsea squad was sent to the football authorities demanding that Barson be prevented from 'crocking others'.

Despite this, he was regarded by many as England's best centre-half. He won just one international cap and according to the *Daily Worker* newspaper, 'For years, Barson was without question England's best pivot, yet the selectors consistently passed him over. Boss sport being what it is, it was more than a rumour that it was not only his vigorous play that kept Barson from a heap of caps: that someone behind the scenes in the Football Association had blackballed him.'

By the end of his 400-plus-game career, Barson's suspensions alone totalled well over a year. He even managed to get sent off in his final league game, on Boxing Day 1930, playing for Wigan Borough v Accrington, for stamping on a player and then swearing at the referee as he was given his marching orders. Continually fined and suspended by Aston Villa for his misdemeanours, Barson decided he'd had enough and signed for Manchester United. Villa received £5,000, big money at the time, and Tommy Ball became his young replacement. In the 1922/23 season Ball staked a regular place in the Villa side, played 36 matches and became a more than capable replacement.

'When Barson went he [Tommy Ball] became the Villa's recognised centre-half,' reported the *Daily Mirror*, 'his play improved manifestly, and this season he was regarded by the Villa as a centre-half of quite exceptional ability.'

He was talked of as a future England international and throughout the first few months of the 1923/24 season became Villa's most consistent and popular player. With his good looks and slicked-back, jet-black hair, he was the pin-up of the team, even though he was spoken for. Life was looking good for Tommy. Now a much-lauded Villa regular, he'd met, fallen in love with and married Beatrice, the daughter of a local butcher. They wed in March 1922 and set up home in a rented house in Birmingham's Perry Barr district, near to Villa's ground, and bought a pet dog and some chickens to keep in their back garden. The night after Villa's win at Notts County, the couple went out for a celebratory drink at a nearby pub. They chatted with the Villa-supporting landlord and happy locals about the match and then headed back home on the bus. Tommy took his dog out into the garden and everything started to go horrifically wrong.

Tommy and his wife rented their house from next-door neighbour George Wragg. A former City of Birmingham Police officer, Wragg had joined up during World War One. Badly injured and gassed, he was invalided out disabled, declared unfit to serve in the police or the armed forces. Unable to work, he got by on a pension and spent what money he'd put away on buying up the cottage next door to his home and renting it out to add to his limited income. By all accounts he had become an embittered and angry man but this new tenant brought a new lift to his life. He suddenly became the landlord to a well-known local professional footballer and initially, he enjoyed the kudos. But soon the relationship clearly broke down. Ball's chickens began to escape into Wragg's garden, which incensed him. Regular rows broke out between the two men and their relationship turned toxic. Wragg threatened to poison his chickens, further fall-outs ensued and finally, he served an eviction notice on Ball and his wife.

The day after the Notts County match was Sunday, 11 November, a date that would surely have affected a man whose life had been largely wrecked by his involvement in the war. It was the fifth anniversary of Armistice Day and Wragg had little to celebrate in his own much-diminished life of reduced circumstances and ever-escalating rows with his neighbour. Did the day and the importance of the date help push him over the top a final time? Because as Tommy went out into the garden with his dog, and wife Beatrice set about preparing supper, she heard shouts and a gunshot. She rushed to the back door to witness her husband in a very distressed state staggering towards her. He was covered in blood and sank on to a slab in the garden.

'Oh Bella,' he gasped, 'he has shot me.'

Desperate, she struggled to comfort him and then ran off for help. As she ran, Beatrice heard a second shot whizz past her head. But Tommy was already beyond help. A few short minutes later, he gave an anguished last gasp and died of haemorrhaging and shock. He had a hole in his chest the size of a half crown coin. Wragg was arrested and charged with murder. He owned a weapon because five years on from the end of the war, Britain was still awash with guns. Despite the 1920

Firearms Act which required anyone wanting to purchase or possess a firearm or ammunition to gain a certificate from their local chief constable, literally an army of men had returned from the conflict with service weapons that had never been turned in or recorded. As an ex-serviceman Wragg had been well trained in the use of a gun.

Not surprisingly, his trial attracted lots of attention in the media, the nation's sports fans aghast that a top young footballer had lost his life aged just 23 years old. The court proceedings were widely covered verbatim in the local and national press. Wragg continued to claim Ball's death was the product of an awful and unfortunate accident.

'There was no malice aforethought,' Wragg told the court. 'It was quite an accident. My dog was barking as Ball was going past my garden gate and he was shouting at the dog to stop it. I jumped out of the chair in which I had been dozing. I told my dog to go in and Ball, who was under the influence of drink, shouted to me, "Go in and go to bed or I will bash your brains out." I said, "Now Tom, go in and go to bed. There's a good chap."

'Mrs Wragg was up at the window having gone to bed and shouted from the window, "Go in and don't make a noise to wake the children." Ball shouted, "I will bash your brains out," and went to climb over the garden gate. The gate was latched and bolted. I had the gun in my hand when I went to the gate to see what was the matter because the dog was barking. I told him to get off the gate and go to bed and used the gun to frighten him. He went away and came back again and tried to get over the gate again. I pushed him back with the muzzle of the gun, and he caught hold of the gun and tried to wrench it from me. As I wrenched the gun away I stepped back and the gun went off – a sudden jerk and off it went.'

Wragg claimed that the gun must have caught the top of the gate and gone off. He told the court that he took the gun out because he thought there might be poachers about and claimed, 'I did all I could and when I was lifting him on the sofa with Mrs Ball, she exclaimed, "Mr Wragg, I know you did not mean it. I am sure it was an accident."'

To add to the drama of the evidence that was being given, the judge, Mr Justice Rowlatt, ordered that a 'demonstration' be set up in the courtroom with an identical gate and shotgun. The judge took the gun, cocked it, and banged it multiple times without moving the mechanism.

According to *The Guardian*'s report of the trial, Wragg also claimed that Ball 'used to knock his wife about' and was 'frequently under the influence of drink' – claims that were strongly denied by Beatrice and Aston Villa's trainer, Alfred Miles. Beatrice told the court that they had a happy and contented marriage and her husband had never laid a finger on her. Miles said that Ball was a good footballer and a good-living man – always in the best of condition.

It took the jury just one hour and 40 minutes to find the accused guilty of murder. Unusually, the jury also made a plea for mercy, perhaps taking into consideration Wragg's war service, his injuries and before that, his good reputation as a policeman. Mr Justice Rowlatt waved the plea away and sentenced the father of four to death by hanging. But in a final twist to this already tragic story, Wragg would escape the noose. A Labour government had just been elected and new home secretary Arthur Henderson was a staunch opponent of capital punishment. During his first few weeks in office he saw fit to commute two death sentences into terms of life imprisonment. George Wragg would become the third, but his time in prison was short. Three years after the guilty verdict and a string of mental breakdowns, he was declared insane and sent to Broadmoor. He spent the rest of his life in purgatory, in a string of high-security mental institutions. Wragg finally passed away in Highcroft Hospital in Birmingham 43 long years later.

Tommy Ball was laid to rest on 19 November 1923. The funeral cortege set off from his father-in-law's butcher's shop in Aston and snaked its way slowly through crowds that lined the streets ten deep all the way to St John's Church in Perry Barr. The church was packed, the coffin carried in by Ball's team-mates, past wreaths and flowers sent from football clubs the length and breadth of the country. Aston Villa's own floral tribute came in the form of a yellow and white chrysanthemum football on a moss bed bearing the club's blue and claret colours. Underneath the beautiful 19th-century barrelled roof they carried his coffin past a stained glass mural of the Blessed Virgin and the baby Jesus and laid Tommy's coffin quietly on to the altar. And the packed congregation stayed silent throughout, seeking contemplation.

The service began and Ball's young life was commemorated to a hush. It was just days earlier that he had been so vital and alive. His wife, his family and team-mates were still in shock at a young life stolen. Ball was buried at St John's, just a five-minute drive from Villa Park, in an ornate grave decorated with stone footballs. To this day, it is still a pilgrimage destination for legions of football fans. Thomas Edgar Ball still remains the only active Football League player ever to have been murdered.

Another tragedy was starting to unfold in 1923 at Burnley – another Tommy, club captain and fellow centre-half Tommy Boyle, had a life that was starting to fall apart.

The Yorkshire-born defender played for Barnsley until his transfer to Turf Moor in 1912 for the princely sum of £1,150, at the time a record for Burnley and fair measure of how highly Boyle was rated. A great leader and organiser, he soon became Burnley captain and was the man who would be first to lift the FA Cup for the Lancashire side in 1914. The previous year, Boyle had been picked to play for England against Ireland for what would be his one and only international cap.

And then came the war. Boyle was conscripted as a gunner in the Royal Artillery Corps and was soon promoted to bombardier. In the summer of 1917, he was posted to Ypres on the Western Front and following a heavy attack on the German lines, Boyle and two compatriots were despatched into no-man's land with a field telephone to report on the guns' fall of shot. A German shell burst in the air above their position and Boyle was caught beneath a burning shower of shrapnel. Deaf and with blood trickling down his face, he staggered back with his comrades to home lines. Boyle had also taken a heavy wound to his thigh. He was hospitalised back to Britain where it was touch and go as to whether his leg would be amputated. Fortunately for Boyle, surgeons were able to operate and dug a two-inch piece of shrapnel out of his thigh.

Boyle returned to his day job at Burnley and in the first full season after the war, the Clarets excelled themselves. Under Boyle's captaincy they registered a club record of 30 games unbeaten and went on to lift the league championship for the first time. By 1922, and now in his mid-30s, Boyle knew he needed to start preparing for life after football. He had got married to Annie and together they had a daughter, the gloriously named Decima Betty Boyle. He decided to use his popularity as a footballer to become the licensee of the Pedestrian Pub in Burnley.

As the 1922/23 season began, Burnley gave him a new contract as player-coach of their reserve team, local fans were flocking to his pub and the retirement plan was working out well. He continued to train and coach the youngsters and the professionals coming back from injury and regularly turned out for the reserves as an ever-solid centre-half. Burnley were quite happy to allow Boyle to fit in his coaching alongside his pub duties and everyone was happy. But shit happens and it did to Tommy Boyle in spades. His daughter Decima contracted pneumonia when she was six months old and died. At the end of the 1922/23 season, Burnley let Boyle go and put him on a free transfer.

At 36 years old, Boyle was still convinced he had more playing days left in his legs and signed as a player-coach at Third Division North Wrexham. For the first few weeks all went well, but then Boyle was suspended and finally sacked. Wrexham's board officially said he'd failed to turn up to play for two reserve matches, though the real truth of the matter is probably now buried forever. The rumours were that his behaviour was becoming erratic and unpredictable and he was drinking more. After his Wrexham sacking, he moved with Annie to his sister Margaret's boarding house in Blackpool and without a trade, he could only find work as a labourer and betting on himself in bowls matches. Boyle applied for various managerial and coaching jobs in Britain but with no luck. Eventually a coaching opportunity presented itself at top German side Berliner Tennis Club Borussia and Boyle and his wife relocated to the capital. Annie, however, found life in Germany hard to adapt to and, homesick, she returned to Britain. Boyle remained in Borussia until 1925 and on his return, was to be informed that Annie had left him.

He returned to Blackpool where his behaviour became increasingly troubling and he was arrested for a series of assaults and drunken incidents. Boyle was fined ten shillings for being drunk and disorderly outside the Palatine Hotel, where he got into a fight with a fellow drinker. He was fined £2 plus costs or a month in prison for avoiding payment of a tram fare and assaulting a conductor. Boyle had bought a penny ticket but stayed on the tram for much longer than he'd paid for. The conductor asked him for another penny but Boyle refused to pay, ran down the tram and flung himself on to the road while the vehicle was travelling at full speed. The conductor jumped off the tram and chased after him but Doyle punched him to the floor. The *Blackpool Gazette* reported, 'Boyle, who did not appear, was stated to have appeared at the court on two previous occasions during the past month.'

Boyle was fast becoming a danger to himself and those around him and ultimately, the authorities sent him to a local mental hospital, Primrose Bank in Burnley, for an assessment of his sanity. After exhaustive tests, his psychiatrist told the hospital board that Boyle suffered from grand delusions, 'claiming he owned 27 racehorses, regularly sending them over to Germany to race and that he won a trophy there that took two men to lift'. He struck other patients and staff while in Primrose Bank, refused food and was 'lost to his surroundings'. Boyle was committed to mental health care indefinitely under the 1890 Lunacy Act. From Primrose Bank, he was transferred to Britain's biggest mental institution, Whittingham Asylum, just outside Preston. During his time there it contained over 4,000 patients and was so big in scale that it actually had its own railway station and sports grounds. After nearly a decade spent in mental care, Boyle died aged just 53, on New Year's Day 1940.

He lost his hearing during battle in World War One and almost definitely suffered from shell-shock. As a centre-half, Boyle was well-known for spending countless hours practising his heading and was renowned as a particularly hard header of the ball. Did this all lead to early onset dementia or some other brain injury? It's difficult to know for sure 100 years on, but one thing is clear: the effects of war and his over-dedication to football probably robbed him of his sanity and shortened his life.

We must not forget that Tommy Boyle was one of the greatest players of his day. It's important that these names are never lost to an untold history.

23

The Last Weekend

'Hope
Smiles from the threshold of the year to come,
Whispering "it will be happier"'

Alfred Lord Tennyson

FOR LARGE parts of Britain, it had been the first white
Christmas for years. The heaviest falls were in the north
of England and Scotland – Aberdeen becoming a veritable
winter wonderland with between 60 and 80cm of snow
falling on Christmas Day alone. By the 27th, temperatures
had risen around the country and a great thaw set in. And
then the temperatures abruptly dropped to below freezing
and Britain became dangerously iced over. Trains were
postponed and cancelled; roads closed as motor accidents
soared; bones broken as pedestrians ventured out to go about
their business on pavements and roads that had become iced
sheets of glass.

Come Saturday, freezing fog had also covered much of
the north and Midlands and numerous league matches were
in danger of postponement. Thanks to a mix of ingenuity and
sheer bloody-mindedness, most of the games went ahead.
Darlington were due to play Chesterfield in the Third Division

North but the strong thaw followed by heavy frost and ice had turned their pitch into a frozen pond. The next-door Feethams cricket pitch was in a much better state, so the quick-thinking Darlington board asked for permission to play the match over the road. It would be the first time in 36 years that football was played there, and thanks to an army of volunteers who cleared the turf as best they could, fixed up goalposts and marked out the pitch, the game went ahead. As though in reward for their endeavours, Darlington won 2-1.

In the Second Division, Bradford City's match against Manchester United was saved by ground staff who worked around the clock over three days solid to clear the snow and ice, roll the Valley Parade pitch and then spread a ton of sand on it. The match went ahead and ended up a 0-0 draw, but players from both sides found it difficult to stay on their feet, so poor were the conditions. Reporting on the game, *Athletic News* observed, 'Under the sand, the turf was very hard and very slippery, and some of the men will be very sore this weekend.'

Travelling conditions in the north were so bad that the railway system almost ground to a halt through cancellations and delays. The United players and coaching staff travelled by train from Manchester to Bradford on what should have been a short journey of a little over an hour across the Pennines. It ended up so delayed by the weather that United players were forced to change into their kit on the train and arrived at Valley Parade well after 2pm.

And everywhere there was fog. An *Athletic News* match report on Blackburn's 1-0 Ewood Park win over high-flying Huddersfield Town made clear that the encounter was on a knife-edge throughout: 'The game started with the fear that fog might bring about a postponement at any time, and on a ground that was hard and slippery, skilful play was a matter of great difficulty.'

At Burnden Park, the Bolton staff had been working overtime too, to ensure their First Division fixture against Everton could be played. It was touch and go. They managed to make the beleaguered match surface serviceable but then thick fog began to shroud Bolton. With 23,000 fans already in the stadium, the referee decided to let the game go ahead. For long passages of the match, fans saw only patches of play and players found it difficult to see, let alone pick out, team-mates further up the field. But for Bolton, it was important that the game went ahead because they were on a roll. During the last fortnight of the old year Wanderers had garnered nine points out of ten, scoring 17 goals and conceding just two. Star striker David Jack was on fire. On Boxing Day, Bolton had hammered West Bromwich Albion 5-0 and Jack had scored a hat-trick. All at Burnden Park were eager to keep their momentum rolling. They sat in second place and for the first time in their history, the critics were tipping them as favourites to become league champions.

Athletic News's 'Tityrus' was certainly convinced enough come the festive season, writing, 'The year which is dying has given life for evermore to the Bolton Wanderers who won the association cup in the spring and are now, with grounds in the grip of winter, struggling with more than energy to retain the championship of the league in Lancashire. As the Bolton Wanderers have never been the premier team of the First Division they have a mighty host of well-wishers within the County Palatine now that Liverpool have lost their firm foothold on the peak of eminence.'

The first half was a tense struggle littered with mistakes because of the conditions and ended goalless. The second half was similarly messy, but Bolton's famously pragmatic style saw them playing more speculative long-ball football, launching high balls into forward areas through the fog in the hope that strikers might carve out some unexpected – and largely unseen

– runs. Welsh winger Ted Vizard latched on to a ball eight minutes in on the edge of the Everton penalty box and lashed a ball in. Those fans who were able to see through the fog weren't sure if it was a cross or a shot. Neither was the Everton goalkeeper, who misjudged the ball and allowed it to bend past him into the net. Seven minutes later, the ball was swung over from left to right and David Jack stepped out of the gloom to take one touch and then shoot along the ground.

It was a precious 2-0 win for Bolton, because league leaders Cardiff City were being turned over at Aston Villa. The Villa Park pitch was a mudbath and the first passages of play saw players skidding and slipping, barely able to get a foothold on what was left of the turf. But it would have been a brave referee who'd have called off the match in front of such a vast crowd. Villa Park officially held 60,000 at the time, but local newspapers estimated that the attendance was nearer to 80,000 once the gates had been closed. Villa had been on a good run, sat fourth in the table and were fielding a full-strength side. They were one of the lucky ones. The poor state of pitches in those early 1920s winter months always led to a glut of strains, pulls and injuries in general. Cardiff arrived at Villa Park missing several key players – inspirational captain Fred Keenor was out injured, as was talented inside-forward Billy Hardy and two important first-team regulars out on the left, Joe Clennell and Herbie Evans.

Cardiff and Bolton had been by far the two strongest sides during the season thus far, but these injuries affected the Bluebirds badly. They battled hard but were overwhelmed and finally lost 2-1 to Villa, with *Athletic News* summing up that Villa were 'faster, they were cleverer, they sustained their attacks better, and if there is any criticism to be offered in regard to their play it is that they ought to have obtained more goals even against the wonderful resistance that the Welshmen put up'.

Elsewhere in the First Division, 29 December brought a welcome win for champions Liverpool. By their own high standards, the first half of their season had been a disaster. The Reds hadn't won since 27 October and though still full of top players they were low on confidence. They were fortunate to end their year playing a West Ham team hamstrung with injuries. Key regular performers Tresadern, Bishop, Hufton and Watson were all missing. Liverpool did not play well but they did put away their best two chances to win 2-0. As they moved into the new year, and to everyone's surprise, the Reds still languished sixth from bottom with a meagre 18 points from 23 games, two points off the relegation places. Key players were getting older and the usual reserve team Anfield conveyor belt had not been turning out young footballers good enough to replace them. Despite the loss, newly promoted West Ham stood a very respectable 12th at the halfway point.

Elsewhere in the First Division, a foggy Maine Road saw, or at least saw bits of, an end-to-end 3-3 draw between Manchester City and West Bromwich Albion. Not since 27 August had the Baggies scored even a single goal away from home so this was a late Christmas present. Burnley beat bottom-placed Preston 1-0 and according to *Athletic News*, it was not pretty, 'All was depression, in keeping with the conditions at Burnley – one goal against a weak defence and a generally feeble team takes some gilt off success.'

By the evening of 29 December, the First Division table looked incredibly tight. Sitting mid-table, the Hammers were 12 points from the top and 12 from the relegation places. Down at the bottom, Preston and Chelsea were already looking particularly beleaguered. Chelsea were suffering from a frightening lack of goals – just 14 in 23 matches – and the rest of the winter would be one of eternal struggle.

	P	W	L	D	F	A	Pts
Cardiff City	23	13	8	2	41	21	34
Bolton Wanderers	23	11	10	4	45	19	32
Huddersfield Town	23	13	4	6	38	21	30
Aston Villa	25	9	11	5	29	20	29
Sunderland	23	12	5	6	41	31	29
Blackburn Rovers	23	11	5	7	37	28	27
Newcastle United	24	11	5	8	35	27	27
Sheffield United	23	9	8	6	35	28	26
Tottenham Hotspur	23	9	8	6	25	11	26
Everton	24	10	6	8	34	32	26
Notts County	23	7	10	6	21	25	24
West Ham United	23	7	8	8	19	24	22
Manchester City	22	8	6	8	28	39	22
Burnley	23	6	8	9	31	32	20
West Bromwich Albion	23	6	8	9	30	29	20
Arsenal	23	7	6	10	21	34	20
Liverpool	23	7	4	12	26	30	18
Nottingham Forest	23	6	6	11	27	36	18
Birmingham City	23	4	9	10	18	31	17
Middlesbrough	23	6	4	13	23	30	16
Chelsea	24	4	8	12	14	30	16
Preston North End	23	4	5	14	25	45	13

On 29 December, matches in the Second Division pretty much delivered a series of 'as you are' results with seven draws out of the ten played. The most welcome of those single points went to Nelson, the newly promoted Lancashire minnows who had been finding life extremely hard in the second tier. On Boxing Day they were hammered 6-0 at Derby County and went into their away game at Blackpool looking to restore some pride and get their survival campaign back on track. They picked themselves up admirably and were the better team in a 1-1 draw. Joe Eddleston bagged a deserved equaliser late on, which

made him the first Nelson forward to score a goal for seven matches.

Among the handful of wins in the Second Division that day, one was an unlikely 2-1 Port Vale victory over Bury. After ten minutes, centre-back Connelly was taken off with a bad thigh strain. Well before the days of substitutes, Vale had to play the next 80 minutes with ten men and despite the horrendous muddy conditions, they defended like Trojans and hit Bury twice on the break. At the top of the Second Division, it was all to play for as the season moved into 1924. Derby, Leeds United and Stoke City were all tied on 28 points, with Blackpool just three points behind them. Bottom were Port Vale, but their win against Bury had pulled them level with Bristol City on 16 points. Worryingly for Bristol, after 23 games they'd leaked 44 goals. Nelson sat nervously fourth from bottom on 19 points, having conceded 42 goals.

The prize for the day's most miserable footballing experience for both players and fans alike was played out up in Lancashire at Spotland Park. In the Third Division North second-placed Rochdale took on bottom club Crewe Alexandra and by all accounts, it sounds a miracle that the game took place at all. According to *Athletic News* this was football in the raw: 'The ground was covered with a layer of frozen snow and although sand had been liberally applied it was apparent that the players would have difficulty in keeping on their feet and controlling the ball. In addition, fog hovered low around the ground and it was only with difficulty that the movements of the players on the far side of the field could be discerned.'

Players did indeed find it difficult to trudge through the mire and much of the game was played at almost walking pace. One of the few shots on goal did go in for Rochdale, who wound up 1-0 winners and cemented second place going into the new year. Leaders Wolves also enjoyed a 1-0 win against a battling Ashington side in front of a 16,982 crowd, and stayed top. Crewe remained firmly rooted to the bottom on nine points with just two wins out of their 21 games.

In the Third Division South, leaders Swansea played mid-table Swindon Town and in front of a healthy 16,000 crowd could only manage a 1-1 draw. But they still sat top of the pile, four points ahead of free-scoring Portsmouth who won 2-0 away at Queens Park Rangers to make it 44 goals in 22 games. Reading lost out 1-0 at home to Brighton & Hove Albion, leaving them bottom at the turn of the year, on 13 points with only four wins from of their 22 matches. Worryingly, Aberdare once again struggled to pull in the fans with the day's poorest attendance, just 3,000 against second-bottom Exeter in a dire 0-0 draw. Elsewhere, the London derby between Millwall and Brentford ended in a hefty 4-1 win for the Lions, while Luton and Southend played out a drawn eight-goal thriller.

By the end of 1923, the First Division's mid-season top scorers contained many of the usual suspects. Len Davies of Cardiff City sat on 19 goals, Sunderland's indomitable Charles Buchan on 18, and Bolton's David Jack and Will Chadwick of Everton both on 16. In the Second Division, Blackpool's Harry Bedford carried on his fine goalscoring form from the season before with 17 in 22 matches by the end of the year; in Third Division South, Portsmouth's Willie Haines had scored an impressive 19 from 19, while Percy Cherrett of Plymouth sat on 18. In Third Division North, Wigan Borough's Len Armitage was the top scorer at the halfway stage with 17 goals.

Epilogue

HERBERT CHAPMAN'S Huddersfield Town would become league champions for the first time, in the closest finish in the top league's history. On the same number of points as Cardiff City, they won the 1923/24 title by 0.024 on goal average.

	P	W	D	L	F	A	Pts
Huddersfield Town	42	23	11	8	60	33	57
Cardiff City	42	22	13	7	61	34	57
Sunderland	42	22	9	11	71	54	53
Bolton Wanderers	42	18	14	10	68	34	50

Such are the fine margins of sport. If Cardiff had managed just one more goal during the season it would have been they and not Huddersfield who would have been crowned champions.

As had seemed likely all season long, Chelsea were relegated after finishing second from bottom on 32 points – scoring only 31 goals in 42 games – but it would not be Preston that would join them.

The Deepdale side clawed themselves up to fifth from bottom on 34 points after an impressive late run. Middlesbrough would end up bottom on just 22 points after suffering an atrocious 16-match run-in of 13 losses, two draws and a solitary 1-0 win against Sheffield United.

To replace them, up would come Leeds United for the first time, joined by Gigg Lane's finest, Bury – but only just. Derby County came agonisingly close in third with a virtually identical record, only losing out on the narrowest of goal averages.

	P	W	D	L	F	A	Pts
Leeds United	42	21	12	9	61	35	54
Bury	42	21	9	12	63	35	51
Derby County	42	21	9	12	75	42	51

Nelson's moment in the sun was brief and after a single season in the Second Division they went straight back down, finishing second from bottom. But they had had some fun along the way, beating Manchester United 1-0 at Old Trafford and then on the final day of the season making merry against champions Leeds at Seedhill, winning 3-1. Bristol City ended bottom, managing just one win in their last 14 games. Wolves bounced back into the Second Division as Third Division North champions, and were joined there by Third Division South winners Portsmouth.

Everton's Wilf Chadwick was the First Division's top scorer with 28 goals, but the country's overall top scorer was Second Division Blackpool's Harry Bedford. Darlington's David Brown top-scored in Third Division North with 27 goals, while the Third Division South's premier marksman was Portsmouth's Willie Haines with 28.

Chadwick and Bedford we know about, but Brown and Haines deserve further mention, too. Dundee-born journeyman David Brown was a talented and consistent scorer wherever he travelled. He turned out for nine different Scottish and English clubs and while at Feethams scored 74 goals in 94 games for the Quakers. He would be both Darlington's top scorer the following season with what is still a club record 39 goals and was the Third Division North's leading marksman again, powering Darlo to the championship. At the end of his laudable, largely lower-league career, he had scored 234 goals in 376 matches. To play at so many different clubs, quickly get used to new players and tactics and hit the ground running at so many different homes was testament to his sheer adaptability and professionalism.

The almost poetically named Wyndham William Pretoria Haines became a local Pompey legend, scoring 119 goals in 164 games over six seasons with the club. Nicknamed the 'Farmer's Boy', by reputation he had little pace or industry about his game but he strolled around in a deceptively languid style before pouncing lethally when his instinct spotted threatening positions in front of goal. For adoring Portsmouth fans, who chanted his name to the refrain of the old folk song, 'The Farmer's Boy', he only blotted his copybook when he moved to deadly local rivals Southampton in 1928. It didn't affect his goalscoring skills; in 70 games for the Saints, Haines scored 47 goals.

Successful though these strikers were, goals up and down the league were in increasingly short supply. Newcastle United and Notts County had spent the early 1920s perfecting the offside trap and many other clubs followed suit in a bid to stifle and spoil games against the very top sides. It was not a new practice – many clubs used similar tactics before World War One, but the early '20s saw its employment on a grand scale. At the heart of the problem was an offside law that required there to be three players – usually the goalkeeper and two defenders – to be in front of the opposing attacker for him to be onside, which gave the whip hand to the defending team. But as the offside spoiling tactics continued through 1923, 1924 and into 1925, football became less entertaining, fewer goals were being scored per game and good play was stifled.

For the FA, the final straw was in February 1925 when Newcastle drew 0-0 at Bury's Gigg Lane. It was United's sixth 0-0 draw already in a season where goals scored had hit an astonishingly low average of 2.58 per game. Mindful that attendances were falling and that English football was slowly becoming a dull war of attrition, the FA proposed a rule amendment that would change football and its tactics forever and be adopted around the world. In short, they created the offside rule we all know and love today – just two players between the attacker and the goal line. As Jonathan Wilson so succinctly explained in *Inverting the Pyramid: The History of Football Tactics*, 'Previously a side looking to play the offside trap had been able to retain one full-back as cover as his partner stepped up to try to catch the forward; the new legislation meant that a misjudgement risked leaving the forward through one on one with the goalkeeper.'

As Wilson pointed out, the new legislation appeared to have an immediate effect – in the 1925/26 season the goals per game average immediately rose to 3.69 with more attacking play in the country's matches. But as often happens, changes can lead to unexpected consequences, and in this case, they were brought about by astute tactician Herbert Chapman who developed the notion of the 'third back', otherwise known as the WM formation. Wilson concluded, 'And that, it is widely held, was what precipitated the decline and increasing negativity of English football.' Sometimes there are no happy endings.

Appendix

Final Football League tables for 1922/23

First Division

	P	W	D	L	F	A	Pts
Liverpool	42	26	8	8	70	31	60
Sunderland	42	22	10	10	72	54	54
Huddersfield Town	42	21	11	10	60	32	53
Newcastle United	42	18	12	12	45	37	48
Everton	42	20	7	15	63	59	47
Aston Villa	42	18	10	14	64	51	46
West Bromwich Albion	42	17	11	14	58	49	45
Manchester City	42	17	11	14	50	49	45
Cardiff City	42	18	7	17	73	59	43
Sheffield United	42	16	10	16	68	64	42
Arsenal	42	16	10	16	61	62	42
Tottenham Hotspur	42	17	7	18	50	50	41
Bolton Wanderers	42	14	12	16	50	58	40
Blackburn Rovers	42	14	12	16	47	62	40
Burnley	42	16	6	20	58	59	38
Preston North End	42	13	11	18	60	64	37
Birmingham City	42	13	11	18	41	57	37
Middlesbrough	42	13	10	19	57	63	36
Chelsea	42	9	18	15	45	53	36
Nottingham Forest	42	13	8	21	41	70	34
Stoke City	42	10	10	22	47	67	30
Oldham Athletic	42	10	10	22	35	65	30

Second Division

	P	W	D	L	F	A	Pts
Notts County	42	23	7	12	46	34	53
West Ham United	42	20	11	11	63	38	51
Leicester City	42	21	9	12	65	44	51
Manchester United	42	17	14	11	51	36	48
Blackpool	42	18	11	13	60	43	47
Bury	42	18	11	13	55	46	47
Leeds United	42	18	11	13	43	36	47
The Wednesday	42	17	12	13	54	47	46
Barnsley	42	17	11	14	62	51	45
Fulham	42	16	12	14	43	32	44
Southampton	42	14	14	14	40	40	42
Hull City	42	14	14	14	43	45	42
South Shields	42	15	10	17	35	44	40
Derby County	42	14	11	17	46	50	39
Bradford City	42	12	13	17	41	45	37
Crystal Palace	42	13	11	18	54	62	37
Port Vale	42	14	9	19	39	51	37
Coventry City	42	15	7	20	46	63	37
Clapton Orient	42	12	12	18	40	50	36
Stockport County	42	14	8	20	43	58	36
Rotherham County	42	13	9	20	44	63	35
Wolverhampton Wanderers	42	9	9	24	42	77	27

Third Division North

	P	W	D	L	F	A	Pts
Nelson	38	24	3	11	61	41	51
Bradford Park Avenue	38	19	9	10	67	38	47
Walsall	38	19	8	11	51	44	46
Chesterfield	38	19	7	12	68	52	45
Wigan Borough	38	18	8	12	64	39	44
Crewe Alexandra	38	17	9	12	48	38	43
Halifax Town	38	17	7	14	53	46	41
Accrington Stanley	38	17	7	14	59	65	41
Darlington	38	15	10	13	59	46	40

Wrexham	38	14	10	14	38	48	38
Stalybridge Celtic*	38	15	6	17	42	47	36
Rochdale	38	13	10	15	42	53	36
Lincoln City	38	13	10	15	39	55	36
Grimsby Town	38	14	5	19	55	52	33
Hartlepools United	38	10	12	16	48	54	32
Tranmere Rovers	38	12	8	18	49	59	32
Southport	38	12	7	19	32	46	31
Barrow	38	13	4	21	50	60	30
Ashington	38	11	8	19	51	77	30
Durham City	38	9	10	19	43	59	28

* Stalybridge Celtic withdrew from the league at the end of the season.

Third Division South

	P	W	D	L	F	A	Pts
Bristol City	42	24	11	7	66	40	59
Plymouth Argyle	42	23	7	12	61	29	53
Swansea Town	42	22	9	11	78	45	53
Brighton & Hove Albion	42	20	11	11	52	34	51
Luton Town	42	21	7	14	68	49	49
Millwall	42	14	18	10	45	40	46
Portsmouth	42	19	8	15	58	52	46
Northampton Town	42	17	11	14	54	44	45
Swindon Town	42	17	11	14	62	56	45
Watford	42	17	10	15	57	54	44
Queens Park Rangers	42	16	10	16	54	49	42
Charlton Athletic	42	14	14	14	55	51	42
Bristol Rovers	42	13	16	13	35	36	42
Brentford	42	13	12	17	41	51	38
Southend United	42	12	13	17	49	54	37
Gillingham	42	15	7	20	51	59	37
Merthyr Town	42	11	14	17	39	48	36
Norwich City	42	13	10	19	51	71	36
Reading	42	10	14	18	36	55	34

Exeter City	42	13	7	22	47	84	33
Aberdare Athletic	42	9	11	22	42	70	29
Newport County	42	8	11	23	40	70	27

Final Scottish Football League tables for 1922/23

Division One

	P	W	D	L	F	A	Pts
Rangers	38	23	9	6	67	29	55
Airdrieonians	38	20	10	8	58	38	50
Celtic	38	19	8	11	52	39	46
Falkirk	38	14	17	7	44	32	45
Aberdeen	38	15	12	11	46	34	42
St Mirren	38	15	12	11	54	44	42
Dundee	38	17	7	14	51	45	41
Hibernian	38	17	7	14	45	40	41
Raith Rovers	38	13	13	12	31	43	39
Ayr United	38	13	12	13	43	44	38
Partick Thistle	38	14	9	15	51	48	37
Heart of Midlothian	38	11	15	12	51	50	37
Motherwell	38	13	10	15	59	60	36
Morton	38	12	11	15	44	47	35
Kilmarnock	38	14	7	17	57	66	35
Clyde	38	12	9	17	36	44	33
Third Lanark	38	11	8	19	40	59	30
Hamilton Academical	38	11	7	20	43	59	29
Albion Rovers	38	8	10	20	38	64	26
Alloa Athletic	38	6	11	12	27	52	23

Division Two

	P	W	D	L	F	A	Pts
Queen's Park	38	24	9	5	73	31	57
Clydebank	38	21	10	7	69	29	52
St Johnstone	38	19	12	7	60	39	50
Dumbarton	38	17	8	13	61	40	42

Bathgate	38	16	9	13	67	55	41
Armadale	38	15	11	12	63	52	41
Bo'ness	38	12	17	9	48	46	41
Broxburn United	38	14	12	12	42	45	40
East Fife	38	16	7	15	48	42	39
Cowdenbeath	38	16	6	16	56	52	38
Lochgelly United	38	16	5	17	41	64	37
King's Park	38	14	6	18	46	59	34
Dunfermline	38	11	11	16	46	44	33
Stenhousemuir	38	13	7	18	53	67	33
Forfar Athletic	38	13	7	18	53	73	33
Johnstone	38	13	6	19	41	62	32
St Bernard's	38	8	15	15	39	50	31
Vale of Leven	38	11	8	19	50	59	30
Eat Stirlingshire	38	10	8	20	48	69	28
Arbroath	38	8	12	18	45	71	28

1922/23 British Home Championship

	P	W	D	L	F	A	Pts
Scotland	3	2	1	0	5	2	5
England	3	1	2	0	6	4	4
Ireland	3	1	0	2	3	3	2
Wales	3	0	1	2	2	7	1

21 October 1922: England 2 (Chambers 2) Ireland 0; The Hawthorns, West Bromwich

3 March 1923: Ireland 0 Scotland 1 (Wilson); Windsor Park, Belfast

5 March 1923: Wales 2 (Keenor, Jones) England 2 (Chambers, Watson); Ninian Park, Cardiff

17 March 1923: Scotland 2 (Wilson 2) Wales 0; Love Street, Paisley

14 April 1923: Scotland 2 (Cunningham, Wilson) England 2 (Kelly, Watson); Hampden Park, Glasgow

14 April 1923: Wales 0 Ireland 3 (Irvine 2, Gillespie); Racecourse Ground, Wrexham

Final league tables for top amateur leagues in 1922/23

Isthmian League

	P	W	D	L	F	A	Pts
Clapton	26	15	7	4	51	37	37
Nunhead	26	15	5	6	52	32	35
London Caledonians	26	13	7	6	43	26	33
Ilford	26	11	7	8	57	38	29
Casuals	26	12	5	9	68	51	29
Civil Service	26	9	10	7	39	36	28
Wycombe Wanderers	26	11	4	11	61	61	26
Dulwich Hamlet	26	9	7	10	60	44	25
Leytonstone	26	9	7	10	45	56	25
Tufnell Park	26	9	5	12	41	45	23
Wimbledon	26	10	2	14	49	50	22
Woking	26	7	6	13	42	67	20
Oxford City	26	6	5	15	45	68	17
West Norwood	26	5	5	16	25	71	15

Northern League

	P	W	D	L	F	A	Pts
Eston United	26	17	3	6	60	41	37
Bishop Auckland	26	16	4	6	54	35	36
Cockfield	26	13	4	9	56	40	30
Crook Town	26	10	8	8	41	43	28
Esh Winning	26	12	3	11	48	47	27
Loftus Albion	26	10	7	9	41	41	27
Stockton	26	11	3	12	49	35	25
Tow Law Town	26	8	8	10	36	39	24
Darlington Railway Athletic	26	10	3	13	35	40	23
Stanley United	26	8	7	11	44	57	23
Langley Park	26	11	0	15	45	60	22
Scarborough	26	10	1	15	51	52	21
Willington	26	9	3	14	37	47	21
South Bank	26	9	2	15	36	56	20

Athenian League

	P	W	D	L	F	A	Pts
Bromley	24	18	4	2	64	25	40
St Albans City	24	15	4	5	69	31	34
Southall	24	13	6	5	48	31	32
Kingstonian	24	13	3	8	60	42	29
Enfield	24	12	5	7	38	35	29
Barnet	24	11	5	8	43	40	27
Sutton United	24	10	6	8	46	39	26
Hampstead Town	24	9	2	13	48	53	20
Summerstown	24	7	5	12	37	43	19
Windsor & Eton	24	6	6	12	36	53	18
Luton Clarence	24	6	4	14	37	68	16
Cheshunt	24	4	4	16	37	64	12
Guildford	24	4	2	18	32	71	10

Midland League

	P	W	D	L	F	A	Pts
The Wednesday Reserves	42	28	7	7	88	37	63
Doncaster Rovers	42	26	9	7	72	28	61
Worksop Town	42	26	5	11	86	45	57
Denaby United	42	24	9	9	76	48	57
Grimsby Town Reserves	42	21	9	12	77	58	51
Scunthorpe & Lindsey United	42	18	13	11	65	68	49
Wath Athletic	42	18	10	14	59	38	46
Notts County Reserves	42	16	12	14	76	55	44
Boston Town	42	18	8	16	61	46	44
Nottingham Forest Reserves	42	16	11	15	74	60	43
Rotherham County Reserves	42	18	6	18	56	52	42
Hull City Reserves	42	14	13	15	63	63	41
Mansfield	42	17	6	19	79	64	40
Barnsley Reserves	42	14	12	16	67	65	40
Wombwell	42	12	14	16	50	63	38
Castleford Town	42	15	6	21	61	70	36
Chesterfield Reserves	42	14	8	20	56	79	36
Mexborough	42	11	13	18	44	63	35

	P	W	D	L	F	A	Pts
York City	42	11	12	19	56	70	34
Gainsborough Trinity	42	8	8	26	42	111	24
Rotherham Town	42	8	6	28	45	105	22
Lincoln City Reserves	42	7	7	28	39	114	21

Northern Alliance

	P	W	D	L	F	A	Pts
Ashfield Plain	34	21	7	6	66	32	49
Ashington Reserves	34	21	6	7	64	24	48
Newburn	34	21	5	8	75	38	47
Craghead United	34	15	11	8	59	41	41
Durham City Reserves	34	16	9	9	60	42	41
Walker Celtic	34	18	4	12	64	56	40
Mickley	34	15	9	10	54	40	39
Hebburn Colliery	34	14	9	11	63	48	37
Felling Colliery	34	13	8	13	49	41	34
Gateshead Town	34	12	7	15	40	46	31
Hexham	34	10	10	14	54	67	30
Lintz Institute	34	11	8	15	35	52	30
Chopwell Institute	34	12	5	17	53	49	29
Prudhoe Castle	34	11	8	15	47	63	28
Birtley	34	10	7	17	45	65	27
Backworth United	34	10	7	17	49	81	27
Spen Black & White	34	7	6	21	38	59	20
Consett	34	3	6	25	28	99	12

Southern League English Section

	P	W	D	L	F	A	Pts
Bristol City Reserves	38	24	5	9	84	39	53
Boscombe	38	22	7	9	67	34	51
Portsmouth Reserves	38	23	3	12	93	51	49
Bristol Rovers Reserves	38	20	8	10	59	41	48
Plymouth Argyle Reserves	38	20	7	11	74	41	47
Torquay United	38	18	8	12	63	38	44
Brighton & Hove Reserves	38	20	3	15	95	60	43
Luton Town Reserves	38	16	11	11	67	56	43

Southend United Reserves	38	18	6	14	69	68	42
Southampton Reserves	38	18	5	15	65	54	41
Millwall Athletic Reserves	38	15	10	13	61	55	40
Coventry City Reserves	38	15	8	15	56	61	38
Guildford United	38	15	7	16	65	59	37
Swindon Town Reserves	38	13	6	19	54	73	32
Bath City	38	10	8	20	44	71	28
Watford Reserves	38	11	6	21	34	79	28
Yeovil & Petters United	38	10	6	22	56	104	26
Norwich City Reserves	38	9	7	22	42	68	25
Exeter City Reserves	38	10	5	23	43	81	25
Reading Reserves	38	7	6	25	37	95	20

Southern League Welsh Section

	P	W	D	L	F	A	Pts
Ebbw Vale	12	6	5	1	22	15	17
Aberaman Athletic	12	7	2	3	30	19	16
Swansea Town Reserves	12	6	2	4	25	14	14
Pontypridd	12	6	2	4	18	18	14
Barry	12	4	3	5	15	11	11
Bridgend Town	12	4	2	6	15	21	10
Porth Athletic	12	0	2	10	8	35	2

North Eastern League

	P	W	D	L	F	A	Pts
Newcastle United Reserves	38	30	8	0	109	24	68
Blyth Spartans	38	23	7	8	78	43	53
Sunderland Reserves	38	23	3	12	74	35	49
Middlesbrough Reserves	38	20	8	10	76	45	48
South Shields Reserves	38	21	5	12	74	44	47
Carlisle United	38	19	8	11	56	43	46
Workington	38	20	4	14	85	57	44
Shildon Athletic	38	17	10	11	74	55	44
Jarrow	38	17	6	15	56	63	40
Preston Colliery	38	16	7	15	48	47	39
Hartlepools United Reserves	38	14	9	15	64	56	37

Bedlington Town	38	14	5	19	50	61	33
West Stanley	38	10	12	16	43	60	32
Darlington Reserves	38	13	5	20	46	57	31
Chester-le-Street	38	12	6	20	47	71	30
Seaton Delaval	38	10	7	21	40	68	27
Wallsend	38	8	9	21	43	89	25
Leadgate Park	38	8	8	22	38	82	24
Scotswood	38	6	10	22	40	91	22
Spennymoor United	38	6	9	23	42	92	21

Yorkshire League

	P	W	D	L	F	A	Pts
Bradford PA Reserves	30	24	2	4	119	43	50
Halifax Town Reserves	30	22	3	5	90	37	47
Frickley Colliery	30	18	3	9	58	35	39
Castleford & Allerton United	30	17	4	9	58	40	38
Doncaster Rovers Reserves	30	14	8	8	52	38	36
Wakefield City	30	11	11	8	53	39	33
Selby Town	30	14	5	11	56	52	33
Wombwell Reserves	30	11	9	10	55	44	31
Brodsworth Main	30	11	9	10	51	56	31
Bentley Colliery	30	12	5	13	57	52	29
Fryston Colliery Welfare	30	9	6	15	45	48	24
Yorkshire Amateur	30	8	7	15	49	78	23
Harrogate	30	8	6	16	30	50	22
Rothwell Athletic	30	6	5	19	27	81	17
Houghton Main	30	5	5	20	36	76	15
Acomb	30	4	4	22	42	108	12

Lancashire Combination

	P	W	D	L	F	A	Pts
Chorley	34	19	9	6	78	38	47
Lancaster Town	34	17	10	7	55	30	44
Darwen	34	17	9	8	77	60	43
New Brighton	34	16	9	9	69	32	41
Rossendale United	34	19	3	12	85	55	41

Fleetwood	34	17	6	11	67	54	40
New Cross	34	16	7	11	66	51	39
Leyland	34	14	7	13	55	47	35
Atherton	34	12	9	13	62	58	33
Eccles United	34	14	5	15	59	56	33
Rochdale Reserves	34	13	7	14	50	64	33
Hurst	34	12	7	15	58	63	31
Bacup Borough	34	13	5	16	44	59	31
Skelmersdale United	34	12	4	18	54	84	28
Morecambe	34	9	8	17	41	60	26
Dick, Kerr	34	6	13	15	38	68	25
Horwich RMI	34	7	10	17	54	76	24
Great Harwood	34	5	8	21	32	89	18

Cheshire County League

	P	W	D	L	F	A	Pts
Crewe Alexandra Reserves	38	27	6	5	102	42	60
Stockport County Reserves	38	20	8	10	89	58	48
Altrincham	38	19	10	9	86	60	48
Macclesfield	38	18	10	10	84	52	46
Ellesmere Port Cement	38	18	7	13	69	48	43
Saltney Athletic	38	20	3	15	75	83	43
Winsford United	38	17	7	14	51	52	41
Tranmere Rovers Reserves	38	16	9	13	69	71	41
Mossley	38	15	10	13	76	62	40
Stalybridge Celtic Reserves	38	15	9	14	56	49	39
Ashton National	38	14	10	14	75	57	38
Whitchurch	38	14	9	15	66	78	37
Congleton Town	38	14	8	16	64	71	36
Nantwich	38	15	5	18	61	84	35
Chester	38	13	8	17	59	60	34
Sandbach Ramblers	38	10	10	18	53	81	30
Runcorn	38	11	5	22	56	85	27
Northwich Victoria	38	8	10	20	47	75	26
Witton Albion	38	9	7	22	43	83	25
Middlewich	38	8	7	23	40	70	23

APPENDIX

Birmingham and District League

	P	W	D	L	F	A	Pts
Shrewsbury Town	34	23	4	7	82	41	50
Bilston United	34	22	3	9	100	46	47
Nuneaton Town	34	20	5	9	77	45	45
Worcester City	34	18	7	9	64	50	43
Willenhall	34	16	9	9	76	44	41
Stourbridge	34	18	5	11	66	46	41
Wellington Town	34	18	2	14	63	47	38
Darlaston	34	16	6	12	61	50	38
Cradley Heath	34	12	13	9	60	52	37
Burton All Saints	34	13	8	13	58	50	34
Redditch	34	15	3	16	59	65	33
Hednesford	34	11	9	14	55	63	31
Stafford Rangers	34	10	8	16	65	72	28
Brierly Hill Alliance	34	11	3	20	46	80	25
Cannock Town	34	7	9	18	42	79	23
Kidderminster Harriers	34	8	6	20	37	71	22
Wednesbury Old Athletic	34	7	6	21	41	94	20
Tamworth Castle	34	5	6	23	41	98	16

Birmingham Combination

	P	W	D	L	F	A	Pts
Oakengates Town	28	15	7	6	85	42	37
Bloxwich Strollers	28	16	5	7	61	48	37
Hinckley United	28	16	4	8	76	56	36
Halesowen	28	15	6	7	73	54	36
Birmingham Trams	28	15	4	9	66	55	34
Wellington St George's	28	14	3	11	66	45	31
Bromsgrove Rovers	28	11	7	10	55	52	29
Round Oak Steelworks	28	10	8	10	63	58	28
Foleshill Great Heath	28	11	5	12	55	49	27
Rugby Town	28	11	5	12	56	53	27
Wolesley Athletic	28	10	4	14	35	68	24
Leamington Town	28	7	7	14	52	67	21
Bourneville Athletic	28	5	10	13	41	68	20
Atherstone Town	28	6	5	17	55	68	17
Newhall Swifts	28	7	2	19	34	90	16

Bibliography

Books

Bolchover, David, *The Greatest Comeback: From Genocide to Football Glory* (Biteback Publishing, 2017)

Brighouse, Harold, *The Game* (play script, 1920); adapted into the film, *The Winning Goal*, directed by G.B. Samuelson

Buchan, Charles, *A Lifetime in Football* (Phoenix House, 1955)

Chapman, Herbert, *Herbert Chapman On Football* (Garrick, 1934)

Goldblatt, David, *The Ball Is Round: A Global History of Football* (Viking Press, 2006)

Graves, Robert, and Hodge, Alan, *The Long Weekend: A Social History of Great Britain 1918–1939* (Faber and Faber, 1940)

Holt, Richard, *Sport and the British: A Modern History* (Oxford Studies In Social History, 1989)

Howesden, Gordon, *Collecting Cigarette and Trade Cards* (Pincushion Press, 1995)

Inglis, Simon, *Football Grounds of England and Wales* (Willow Books, William Collins Sons & Co. Ltd, 1983)

Jose, Colin, *The American Soccer League: The Golden Years of American Soccer 1921–1931* (American Sports History Series, 1998)

Korr, Chuck, *West Ham United: The Making Of A Football Club* (University of Illinois Press, 1987)

Marr, Andrew, *The Making of Modern Britain* (Macmillan, 2009)

Meisl, Willy, *Soccer Revolution* (Sportsman Book Club, 1956)

Mowatt, Charles Loch, *Britain Between The Wars* (Heinemann, 1955)

Murray, Bill, *The World's Game: A History of Soccer* (Chicago: University of Illinois Press, 1996)

Newsham, Gail, *In A League Of Their Own! The Dick, Kerr Ladies 1917–1965 (Paragon Publishing, 2014)*

Palme Dutt, R., *World Politics 1918–36* (Gollancz, 1936)

Pawson, Tony, *100 Years of the FA Cup* (Heinemann, 1972)

Powell, Hope (with Marvin Close) *Hope: My Life in Football* (Bloomsbury Press, 2016)

Rafferty, John, *One Hundred Years of Scottish Football* (Pan, 1973)

Sanders, Richard, *Beastly Fury: The Strange Birth of British Football* (Transworld Books, 2009)

Seed, Jimmy, *The Story of Jimmy Seed* (Phoenix Sport, 1957)

Smith, Mike, *Tommy Boyle – Broken Hero* (Grosvenor House, 2011)

Taylor, A.J.P., *English History 1914–45* (OUP Oxford, 1965)

Taylor, D.J., *On The Corinthian Spirit: The Decline of Amateurism in Sport* (Yellow Jersey Press, 2006)

Taylor, Matthew, *The Leaguers: The Making of Professional Football in England 1900–1939* (Liverpool University Press, 2005)

Wall, Sir Frederick, *Fifty Years of Football* (Cassell, 1935)

Williams, Jean, *A Game For Rough Girls: A History of Women's Football in England* (Routledge, 2003)

Walvin, James, *The People's Game, A Social History of British Football* (London, 1975)

Wilson, Jonathan, *Inverting The Pyramid: The History of Football Tactics* (Orion, 2013; new edition)

Wilson, Jonathan, *Angels With Dirty Faces: The Footballing History of Argentina* (Orion, 2016)

Wrack, Suzanne, *A Woman's Game: The Rise, Fall and Rise Again of Women's Football* (Guardian Faber Publishing, 2022)

Collections, archives and Acts of Parliament
The National Museum of Football Archives
Scottish National Football Museum Archives
The British Newspaper Archives
National Museum Archives
Hansard
1845 Gaming Act
1920 Ready Money Football Betting Act
1920 Firearms Act
1921 Census

Magazines, periodicals and newspapers
Athletic News
Birmingham Gazette
Blackpool Gazette
Daily Express
Daily Mail
Daily Telegraph
Daily Worker
East Ham Echo
The Engineer
Football Special
Four Four Two
The Gem
Glasgow Herald
The Guardian
The Herald
Huddersfield Examiner
The Independent
Liverpool Echo
Lancashire Evening Post
London Evening News
Manchester Evening News
Nelson Leader

Northern Echo
Nottingham Evening Post
Sheffield Independent
Sheffield Telegraph and Star
Sports Budget and Soccer Special
The Sportsman
The Times
Topical Times
These Football Times
Yorkshire Post and Leeds Intelligencer
Western Daily News
Western Daily Press

Television and video
Kicking and Screaming (BBC, 2005)
Metroland (BBC, 1973)
Pathe News
BBC Sounds

Online
anfieldwrap.co.uk
avfchistory.co.uk
bleacherreport.com
englandfootballonline.co.uk
englishfootballstats.co.uk
footballrates.com
footballsite.co.uk
Football-Stadiums.co.uk
groundhopperguides.com
liverpoolfc.com
Stats.football.co.uk
theanfieldwrap.com

Index